Rethinking Durkheim and His Tradition

This book offers a major reassessment of the work of Émile Durkheim in the context of a French philosophical tradition that had seriously misinterpreted Kant by interpreting his theory of the categories as about psychological faculties. Durkheim's sociological theory of the categories, as revealed by Warren Schmaus, is an attempt to provide an alternative way of understanding Kant. For Durkheim the categories are necessary conditions for human society. The concepts of causality, space, and time underpin the moral rules and obligations that make society possible.

A particularly original feature of this book is its transcendence of the distinction between intellectual and social history by placing Durkheim's work in the context of the French educational establishment of the Third Republic. It does this by subjecting student notes and philosophy textbooks to the same sort of critical analysis typically applied only to the classics of philosophy.

This will be an important book for historians of philosophy, historians of ideas, sociologists, and anthropologists.

Warren Schmaus is Professor of Philosophy at the Illinois Institute of Technology.

Rethinking Durkheim and His Tradition

WARREN SCHMAUS

Illinois Institute of Technology

CAMBRIDGE
UNIVERSITY PRESS

PUBLISHED BY THE PRESS SYNDICATE OF THE UNIVERSITY OF CAMBRIDGE
The Pitt Building, Trumpington Street, Cambridge, United Kingdom

CAMBRIDGE UNIVERSITY PRESS
The Edinburgh Building, Cambridge CB2 2RU, UK
40 West 20th Street, New York, NY 10011-4211, USA
477 Williamstown Road, Port Melbourne, VIC 3207, Australia
Ruiz de Alarcón 13, 28014 Madrid, Spain
Dock House, The Waterfront, Cape Town 8001, South Africa

http://www.cambridge.org

First published 2004

Printed in the United States of America

Typeface ITC New Baskerville 10/13 pt.   *System* LaTeX 2$_\varepsilon$ [TB]

A catalog record for this book is available from the British Library.

Library of Congress Cataloging in Publication Data

Schmaus, Warren, 1952–
Rethinking Durkheim and his tradition / Warren Schmaus.
p.   cm.
Includes bibliographical references and index.
ISBN 0-521-83816-9
1. Durkheim, Emile, 1858–1917.   2. Durkheimian school of sociology.
3. Sociology – History.   4. Sociology – France – History.   I. Title.
HM465.S36   2004
301′.0944–dc22   2003061523

ISBN 0 521 83816 9 hardback

In memory of Walter F. Schmaus (1922–1994)
and Richard J. Thome (1928–2002)

Contents

Preface and Acknowledgments   *page* ix

1   Durkheim and the Social Character of the Categories   1
    The Durkheimian Tradition   2
    Durkheim and the Cultural Construction of Reality   7
    Durkheim's Argument for the Social Character of the Categories   12
    Durkheim and the Philosophical Tradition   18
    Drawing Lessons from Durkheim for Today   21
    Overview   24

2   Historical Background: Aristotle and Kant   27
    Aristotle   28
    Kant's Theory of the Categories   30
    Problems of Interpretation   49

3   The Categories in Early-Nineteenth-Century
    French Philosophy   57
    The Introduction of Kantian Philosophy into France   57
    Victor Cousin's Eclectic Spiritualism   60
    Maine de Biran   68

4   The Later Eclectic Spiritualism of Paul Janet   76
    Janet on Method   78
    Janet on Meaning   80
    The Categories   82
    The Origin or Source of the Categories   84
    Janet on Kant   89
    Janet's Derivation of the Categories   91
    Conclusion   94

5   The Early Development of Durkheim's Thought   96
     Eclectic Spiritualism in the Sens Lectures   101
     The Method of Hypothesis in the Sens Lectures   104
     Durkheim's Conception of Philosophy and Psychology
     in the Sens Lectures   107
     The Categories in the Sens Lectures   112
     The Sens Lectures on Kant   117

6   Durkheim's Sociological Theory of the Categories   120
     Causality in The Elementary Forms of Religious Life   123
     Conclusion   136

7   Prospects for the Sociological Theory of the Categories   137
     The Relation between Sociology of Knowledge and Psychology   140
     Evolutionary Perspectives and the Sociology of Knowledge   143
     Causal Cognition   147
     Conclusion   151

Notes   153
Bibliography   167
Index   183

Preface and Acknowledgments

This project owes its inception to an invitation from the British Centre for Durkheimian Studies in Oxford to participate in a conference on Durkheim's *The Elementary Forms of Religious Life* in 1995. It was the paper that I presented there that first got me thinking about the social functions of the categories. I am especially grateful to Bill Pickering for his encouragement and continued interest in my work, as well as to Nick Allen and Willie Watts Miller, his coeditors for the proceedings volume that resulted from that conference. Throughout this and three other book projects with Bill in which I have been involved as either an author or a coeditor, I have had the opportunity to try out some of the ideas in this volume. Bill is one of the kindest, most generous people in academics with whom I have ever worked.

I am also deeply indebted to the Pittsburgh Center for Philosophy of Science, which hosted me during my sabbatical year in 1996–7, as well as to my family for allowing me to take them away from their comfortable home in Oak Park, Illinois, to live in Pittsburgh for a year. I would also like to thank the Illinois Institute of Technology for granting me this sabbatical year. I was able to conduct much of the research for this book and some of the initial writing during my stay in Pittsburgh. But most important, Pittsburgh provided a philosophical community where I felt that people valued what I was doing and gave me useful criticism. I would like to thank Ted McGuire and Peter Machamer for inviting me to come back to Pittsburgh for a year and to present the annual alumni lecture during my time there. They, along with Nicholas Rescher and Jim Lennox, also gave me some useful advice at the beginning stages of this project. I would especially like to thank Merrilee Salmon for her comments on an

early draft of Chapter 1 that I would be too embarrassed to show anyone today. And I would like to thank Gerry Massey for all he did as director of the Center to keep things running smoothly and make everyone's stay as pleasant as possible.

There are two scholars who deserve special thanks, for without their help this would have been a very different book. First, I would like to thank John Brooks for sharing chapters of his book *The Eclectic Legacy* with me while they were still in draft form. Although he sent them to me for help and comments, I was learning at least as much from him as he was from me. It was John who convinced me that the eclectic spiritualist philosophical tradition was the source for much of Durkheim's thinking. Without John, I would never have been persuaded to read Victor Cousin, Paul Janet, or Elie Rabier. John's interpretation of the philosophical origins of Durkheimian social science then received independent corroboration when Neil Gross discovered André Lalande's notes from Durkheim's philosophy class at the Lycée de Sens. Lalande's notes reveal the young Durkheim teaching eclectic spiritualism, drawing on thinkers like Cousin and Maine de Biran for his account of the categories. The entire scholarly community owes a debt of gratitude to Neil for making these notes available to us. Bob Jones is to be thanked for making these notes even more widely available by putting them on his Durkheim web pages at the University of Illinois. Neil and Bob, as well as Daniela Barberis, also deserve thanks for their participation in a session devoted to the discovery of these notes that I organized for the History of Science Society meetings in 1997.

There are several other forums besides those provided by the Pittsburgh Center where I have received helpful criticism and advice concerning the ideas presented in this book. Sharon Crasnow, Jim Maffie, Jean Pedersen, and Stephen Turner provided helpful comments, for which I am very grateful, on the papers concerning the social functions of the categories that I presented at the 1995 meetings of the History of Science Society and the Society for the Social Studies of Science. I would like to thank Cassandra Pinnick for organizing these sessions. I also presented some of my early thoughts on this topic to a philosophy of social science interest group that met at the Philosophy of Science Association meetings in 1996. I no longer remember everyone who was there, but I do recall Alison Wylie giving me some helpful bibliographic advice, for which I thank her. Some of these people also attended my paper on functionalism at the 1998 meetings of the Philosophy of Science Association, where I was subjected to some very serious criticisms by Paul Roth and

Jim Bohman. Doug Jesseph rallied to my defense, and the four of us had a good argument. Mark Risjord was also there and supported my reading of Ruth Millikan. I thank them all for a great session. I am also very grateful to the philosophy department at Michigan State for allowing me the luxury of presenting what amounted to a précis of this entire book in 1999. I would like to thank Fred Gifford for inviting me to participate in their colloquium series and for being a gracious host. I would also like to thank Fred Rauscher for his friendly suggestions both during and after the talk.

Some of the historical material on Durkheim was presented at the 1998 meetings of the History of Philosophy of Science Working Group (HOPOS) at the University of Notre Dame. I would like to thank Lanier Anderson for organizing the session in which I presented my paper. I learned much from him and from Gary Hatfield, the other participant in that session, as well as from a question from the floor by Don Howard. I would also like to thank Gary for some help he gave me on a previous occasion. Before I had ever met Gary, I was intrigued by a paper he wrote concerning Kant and psychology (Hatfield 1992) and sent him an early draft of Chapter 2 of this book, thinking he might be sympathetic to my interest in how Kant came to be read psychologically in France. Gary sent my chapter back with detailed comments and criticisms, which was extremely generous of him considering that I was a total stranger to him at the time and a mere novice at Kant scholarship. Terry Godlove, whom I had met at the Oxford conference in 1995, also gave me valuable comments on this draft of Chapter 2, for which I am very grateful.

I presented some additional historical material concerning Kant's reception in France at the HOPOS meeting at Concordia University in Montreal on June 21, 2002. The discussion was very constructive. I would especially like to thank Alan Richardson for asking whether Paul Guyer's claims about Kant transforming philosophy, which I was challenging in this paper, should be understood in a descriptive or normative sense. I am pleased to say that my paper was selected for publication in a special issue of *Perspectives on Science* devoted to this conference. Alan Richardson and Don Howard gave me much useful feedback on the published version of this paper, which was also helpful in revising some of the middle chapters of this book. HOPOS, especially through its e-mail discussion list, at times has been a nearly daily preoccupation for me. I am very grateful for the time that some people on this list, especially Lanier Anderson, Peter Apostoli, Gary Hatfield, Michael Kremer, John Ongley, and

Richard Smyth, have devoted to helping me straighten out my thoughts about Kant and his interpreters.

The St. Louis Philosophy of the Social Sciences Roundtable at their meeting on March 15, 2002, provided me with the opportunity to try out some of my ideas in the concluding chapter. I would especially like to thank Steven Lukes and David Rubinstein for their comments on Durkheim, Bill Wimsatt for his comments on evolutionary psychology, and Paul Roth and Alison Wylie (once again) for their comments on a written draft of my paper, which was chosen for publication in *Philosophy of the Social Sciences*.

My colleagues in the Lewis Department of Humanities at Illinois Institute of Technology also deserve thanks for their comments on various papers I have presented in our own departmental colloquium series. The philosophers in the department, including Jack Snapper, Michael Davis, Bob Ladenson, and Vivian Weil, have proved to be especially helpful. Of course, I take full responsibility for all the opinions and interpretations expressed in this book.

Finally, I would like to thank my family one more time. My son, Alexander, has still not entirely forgiven me for dragging him off to Pittsburgh for a year. On the other hand, my daughter, Tekla, thoroughly enjoyed herself and wants to know when we can visit Pittsburgh again. I thank them both, but I want to give special thanks to my wife, Constance, for making possible the kind of support that only a loving, peaceful, happy home and family can provide.

Durkheim and the Social Character
of the Categories

Around the turn of the twentieth century, Émile Durkheim (1858–1917) and Marcel Mauss (1872–1950) proposed that the most basic categories of thought, including space, time, class, and causality, are social in character. Their thesis – that language and experience are structured by categories that are social in character – had a profound impact on twentieth-century thought, especially in the social sciences. Among sociologists and anthropologists in particular, it was a major source of inspiration for the popular and heady doctrine that people construct culturally specific perceptual realities through the use of culturally variable sets of categories. For these social scientists, the term "category" took on a very different signification than the original meanings we find in either Aristotle or Immanuel Kant (1724–1804). They treated the categories as belonging to some sort of conceptual scheme or framework through which we perceive the world, rather than as Aristotle's highest predicables or Kant's concepts that are logically presupposed by experience. To understand how this change in the conception of a category came about, we have to consider how Kant was interpreted in the nineteenth-century philosophical tradition from which Durkheim's sociological theory of the categories emerged. That is the purpose of this book.

In arguing for the social causes and origins of the categories, Durkheim was responding to the way in which Kant's philosophy was understood in the Third Republic. Academic philosophy in nineteenth-century France had been shaped by the eclectic spiritualist tradition of Victor Cousin (1792–1867) and Pierre Maine de Biran (1766–1824), who had bequeathed to Durkheim the legacy of interpreting Kant's theory of the categories as part of a philosophical psychology of the individual human

mind. In this tradition, it was thought that the universality and necessity of the categories could be epistemologically grounded in a Cartesian introspection of the self as active being. Durkheim, in proposing that the categories were instead derived from our experience of the patterns, rhythms, and forces of collective life, thought that he was offering a superior explanation of these characteristics of the categories.

Durkheim hoped to show that a person's ways of thinking and communicating about such things as space, time, and causality owed a lot more to his or her culture than had previously been thought, and that these concepts played an important role in helping to hold society together, for instance through making moral rules possible. His sociological project is distinct from Kant's philosophical project of determining the concepts that are presupposed by and necessarily found in experience. Durkheim's project is worthy of pursuit in its own right, provided that it is not only kept separate from the Kantian project but also freed of the encumbering mentalistic assumptions about meaning that Durkheim inherited from his philosophical tradition. Although beginning with Cousin the eclectics had endorsed Thomas Reid's (1710–96) common-sense rejection of the philosophy of representative ideas, Paul Janet (1823–99) subsequently brought back this concept in his account of the meanings of general terms. Durkheim adopted and expanded this philosophy, dividing these representative ideas into two sorts, individual representations and collective or shared representations, identifying the meanings of the categories with the latter. Of course, the meaning of a concept can no more be identified with a kind of mental representation than with a kind of physical representation. However, there is an alternative account of the meanings of the categories implicit in Durkheim's sociology of knowledge, according to which the categories take at least part of their meaning from their role in organizing social life as well as individual experience. If we link the meanings of the Durkheimian categories with their social functional roles rather than with their collective representations, it becomes easier to see how different cultures can have different ways of representing the same set of categories. Understanding what concepts different cultures may have in common is then the first step to sorting out the relative contributions of culture and individual psychology to our mental and social lives.

The Durkheimian Tradition

In a 1903 paper titled "On Some Primitive Forms of Classification," Durkheim and Mauss drew on ethnographic studies from Australia, North

America, and elsewhere to argue that classificatory concepts such as genus and species were originally constructed on the model of human social groupings. According to Durkheim and Mauss, the Australian native considers everything in the universe to belong to his or her tribe. The entire tribe thus provided the archetype for the category of totality, the class that includes all other classes. Just as the members of the tribe are divided into phratries that are subdivided into clans, each thing in nature has its place in this nested hierarchy of phratries and clans. That is, all living and non-living objects, including the sun, the moon, the stars, the seasons, and even weather phenomena, belong to a particular clan as well as to a more inclusive phratry. This system of social organization thus serves as the origin and the prototype of the concept of classifying things by genera and species (Durkheim 1912a: 201, 205–6, 630, t. 1995: 141–2, 145–6, 443). What has come to be known as the Durkheim–Mauss thesis thus states, "the classification of things reproduces the classification of men" ([1903a(i)] 1969c: 402, t. 1963b: 11).[1]

Although Durkheim and Mauss's 1903 paper was concerned largely with classification, the authors suggested that similar sociological accounts could be provided for space, time, cause, substance, and the other categories ([1903a(i)] 1969c: 461, t. 1963b: 88). Their collaborators on the journal *L'Année sociologique* soon followed with works that attempted to do just that. These included Henri Hubert's essay on magical and religious conceptions of time (1905), the essay by Mauss and Henri Beuchat on conceptions of time among the Eskimos (1906), Célestin Bouglé's account of classification in the caste system of India (1908), and Robert Hertz's account of the role of right- and left-handedness in classificatory systems (1909). At around this time, Lucien Lévy-Bruhl (1857–1939), who was loosely associated with this group, produced the first of his many works on what he called "primitive mentality" (1910).

Durkheim drew on works such as these in formulating his sociological theory of the categories in *The Elementary Forms of Religious Life* (1912a). According to this theory, the categories of time, space, number, cause, substance, class or genus, totality, personality, and so on are all social in origin. The category of causality derived from our experience of social forces and moral obligation. The category of time was formed from the seasonal and daily rhythms of social life, and the category of space was patterned after the spatial distribution of social groups. The Zuñi, for example, conceive space as having seven directions, each named for the clan that occupies the corresponding section of the circular campsite when the entire tribe gathers (1912a: 16, t. 1995: 11; Durkheim and Mauss [1903a(i)] 1969c: 425ff., t. 1963b: 42ff.). For Durkheim in *The Elementary*

Forms, such categories as causality, space, and time were necessary for our ability to form judgments about objects:

> There are, at the root of our judgments, a certain number of essential notions that dominate our entire intellectual life; they are those that philosophers, since Aristotle, have called the categories of the understanding: notions of time, space, genus, number, cause, substance, personality, etc. They correspond to the most universal properties of things. They are like the solid framework that encloses thought; it appears that it cannot free itself from them without destroying itself, because it seems we cannot think of objects that are not in time or space, which are not numerable, etc. Other notions are contingent and changeable; we conceive that they may be lacking to a person, a society, an epoch; the former appear to be nearly inseparable from the normal functioning of the mind. (1912a: 12–13; cf. t. 1995: 8–9)

In spite of the Kantian-sounding language about the categories of the understanding being at the root of our judgments, what Durkheim meant by the categories is not exactly what Kant meant. First of all, Kant did not include space, time, or personality among the categories. Also, Durkheim identified the categories with culturally variable collective representations that make it possible for the members of a society to think and communicate about spatial, temporal, or causal relations and thus permit important social functions to be carried out. Social life as we know it, he thought, would not be possible if people did not share certain conceptions of time, space, causality, and classification. Convocations to feasts, hunts, and battles require that a system be established for fixing dates and times so that everyone conceives time in the same way. For people to cooperate with the same end in view, they must agree upon a causal relationship between that end and the means to achieve it. In addition, individuals must be classified into groups that are then classified in relation to each other. To avoid conflict, space must be divided among these groups according to a system of directions recognized by everyone (1912a: 629–32, t. 1995: 441–4).

Durkheim also distinguished his usage of the term "category" from what he took to be its acceptance among the philosophers of his day. As he explained elsewhere, for "the recent disciples of Kant . . . the categories preform the real, whereas for us, they recapitulate it. According to them, they are the natural law of thought; for us, they are a product of human art" (1909d: 757 and n. 1, t. 1982: 239–40 and n. 1). Of course, neither of these senses is what Kant meant by the categories. To say that the categories "preform" the real is to suggest that they are part of a psychological account of the formation of experience, which is not what

Kant intended for his theory of the categories, as I will explain in the following chapter. Durkheim's categories actually depend upon whatever psychological capacities he thought were responsible for "preforming" reality. For instance, he said that even the most primitive systems of classification presuppose the ability to recognize resemblances among the particular things the mind perceives (1912a: 206, t. 1995: 146). In the conclusion to *The Elementary Forms*, he distinguished the categories of space, time, causality, and class from the individual's sense of space, duration, regular succession, and resemblance. According to Durkheim, an individual human being has no more need than an animal does of the category of space in order to orient herself. Nor does an individual human being need the category of time in order to satisfy her needs. Similarly, a human being does not need the category of genus and species to recognize that one thing resembles another or the category of causality in order to seek her prey and avoid her enemies. Purely empirical regularities of succession among our representations will suffice to guide our actions (1912a: 632, t. 1995: 444). According to Durkheim, "the relations that the categories express exist, in an implicit manner, in individual consciousnesses" (1912a: 628, t. 1995: 441).

If Durkheim's categories were not involved in what he regards as the psychological processes of preforming reality, there would then seem to be a sense for him in which the mind could function without these categories. This would explain the reason that, in the passage quoted earlier, he qualified his remarks by saying that it only "appears" or "seems" that the mind cannot function without the categories. The reason he added the qualification that the categories are "nearly inseparable from the normal functioning of the mind" is perhaps that he also thought that one could not be psychologically normal if one had not acquired certain ways of thinking about the categories from one's society.

If, as Durkheim argues, categories such as space, time, causality, and class are necessary for certain social functions to be carried out, it would seem that they would be found in all cultures. However, as I will discuss in Chapter 6, Durkheim appears to have reversed his position on the cultural universality of the categories in his lectures on pragmatism given in the year following the publication of *The Elementary Forms*. After this work, research on the sociological theory of the categories tended to emphasize their differences. Works in this tradition included Marcel Granet's analysis of Chinese categories (1934), Mauss's essay on the category of a person (1938), Maurice Halbwachs's account of the category of time in *The Collective Memory* (1950), and Lévy-Bruhl's numerous books

on primitive mentality (1922, 1927, 1931, 1935, 1938, 1949). Mauss, especially, defended the view that the categories were culturally and historically variable and that the list of categories was open-ended: "Above all it is essential to draw up the largest possible catalogue of categories; it is essential to start with all those which it is possible to know man has used. It will be clear that there have been and still are dead or pale or obscure moons in the firmament of reason" (Mauss 1924, t. 1979: 32). Among the concepts that were formerly but are no longer categories Mauss included big and small, animate and inanimate, and right and left. He also suggested that the category of substance derived from the concept of food (ibid.). Claude Lévi-Strauss endorsed this passage from Mauss as a statement of the goals of ethnology (1950: 66). He added to the catalogue of categories such concepts as cooked and raw, fresh and rotten, and moist and dry (1964: 41).

Already with Mauss we find an ambiguity with regard to what is meant by a category. In one sense, a category is simply a classificatory concept, like plant or animal. In the philosophical sense of category that goes back to Aristotle, however, a category is only the highest classification into which a thing may fall. Hence, for Aristotle, "plant" and "animal" are not categories since both belong to the category of "substance." Space and time, however, are categories since they are not kinds of substances, or kinds of anything else, for that matter. For Kant, it was only the categories in this highest sense that structured human judgment and perception. When categories are not carefully distinguished from classificatory and other concepts, serious confusions may arise about purported cultural differences in the categories and the effects of these differences on perception and understanding.[2] Systems of natural classification and ways of dividing and measuring space and time may be culturally variable, while the categories themselves are not. For there to be cultural variability in the categories, there would have to be cultures that had no conception whatsoever of, say, space, time, causality, or classification.

Although Lévi-Strauss (1945) thought very highly of Mauss's work, unlike Mauss he emphasized what cultures held in common and thought that the analysis of social structures would reveal the universal structure of human thought. Also, unlike both Durkheim and Mauss, Lévi-Strauss (1966: 214) carefully avoided characterizing the relationship between social structure and the categories as a causal one. Subsequent thinkers were not always so careful or so clear. Influential philosophers like Michel Foucault and Jean-François Lyotard held that social structures external to individual consciousnesses shape our experience of the world. These

poststructuralist thinkers emphasized the historical and cultural variability of these structures and thus of the categories (May 1997: 26). Foucault (1966) and Jacques Derrida (Lilla 1998), for instance, share with Mauss (1938) the belief that the category of an individual human person is a product of history, culture, and language.

Durkheim and the Cultural Construction of Reality

Among British social anthropologists such as Max Gluckman (1949–50), Edmund Leach (1964), and Mary Douglas (1970), Durkheimian sociology of knowledge was a major stimulus for the intoxicating belief in the cultural construction of reality. According to this doctrine, the way we perceive the world is shaped by culturally variable categories that are transmitted from one generation to the next through language and other cultural systems of representation.[3] Douglas (1970: 20) sees an affinity between Durkheim's sociological theory of the categories and the linguistic determinism of Edward Sapir,[4] which, through the work of Sapir's student Benjamin Lee Whorf, may have been more directly influential in encouraging cultural constructionism in the United States.[5] However, Durkheimian sociology of knowledge may have actually contributed to the creation of an intellectual climate in anthropology in which the hypothesis of linguistic determinism would be seriously entertained.

Today, one tends to hear about the "social construction" more often than the "cultural construction" of reality. The phrase "social construction of reality" was introduced in 1967 by Peter Berger and Thomas Luckmann. They conceived their work as a purely phenomenological analysis of the form or structure of our intersubjective experience of everyday life. The phenomenological method, they said, refrains from offering any causal hypotheses. Hence, they claimed that such concepts as space and time merely have a "social dimension" (Berger and Luckmann 1967: 20, 26). They never argued that these categories depend on social causes. Nevertheless, the word "construct" has definite causal overtones. After all, the literal meaning of "to construct" is to build or make something by combining parts. By the conclusion of the book, the authors themselves lapse into causal talk: "Man is biologically predestined to construct and to habit a world with others. This world becomes for him the dominant and definitive reality. Its limits are set by nature, but once constructed, this world acts back upon nature. In the dialectic between nature and the socially constructed world the human organism is transformed. In

this same dialectic man produces reality and thereby produces himself" (Berger and Luckmann 1967: 183). It should then come as no surprise that subsequent writers have adopted Berger and Luckmann's terminology of "social construction" to express what appears to be a causal thesis with roots in Durkheim rather than a claim about the structure of human thought with roots in phenomenology.

In Germany, Max Horkheimer and Theodor Adorno (1997: 21) interpreted the Durkheim–Mauss thesis as indicating the dominating power that society has over our thought, with even the deductive structure of science yielding evidence of coercion and hierarchy. For these critical theorists, human emancipation necessitates an alternative to this logic. The connection between their thesis and the Durkheim–Mauss thesis may not be immediately clear. Although Durkheim did suggest that the very notion of logical contradiction depends on social causes (1912a: 17–18, t. 1995: 12), he did not subscribe to the view that different cultures have different systems of logic. On the contrary, he argued that the logic of modern scientific thought evolved from that of primitive religious thought. It was actually Lévy-Bruhl who advanced the hypothesis that so-called primitives have an alternative to our logic and thus do not recognize what we take to be contradictions. For Durkheim, on the other hand, evidence that primitives group human beings, animals, colors, and celestial objects together in the same totemic classes did not suffice to support this hypothesis. He argued that to identify kangaroos with human beings is no more a contradiction than to identify heat with the motion of molecules or light with electromagnetic vibration (1912a: 339–42, t. 1995: 239–41; cf. 1913a(ii)6&7, t. 1978: 145–9).[6] For Durkheim, totemic systems of classification function like scientific theories in the sense that what counts as a contradiction depends on what else one thinks. Today, the primitive mentality thesis is perhaps best known through Edward Evan Evans-Pritchard's account of the Azande's apparently inconsistent beliefs about the heritability of the power of witchcraft (1937). More recent sociologists of knowledge such as David Bloor (1991: 138–46) and Bruno Latour (1987: 186–94) cite this account as evidence that logic is a variable social and cultural construction.[7] For the contemporary cognitive relativist, no culture's logic is superior to any other's (Littleton 1985: vi). However, there is no clear evidence that different cultures actually have different logics. Toward the end of his career, Lévy-Bruhl decided that all cultures use the same logic and that what appeared to be cultural differences in recognizing contradictions were actually due to cultural differences in the categories.[8]

If logic, the categories, and even perceptual reality were culturally variable constructions, intercultural communication would not be possible, for who could make sense of the words and actions of people who lived in a different reality? We would be faced with an incommensurability of cultures much like the incommensurability of paradigms by which Thomas Kuhn characterized the history of the sciences. Kuhn proposed that the categories that shape perception or "world view" vary even among scientific communities. As these perceptual categories take their meanings from paradigms that are incommensurable with one another, "The proponents of competing paradigms practice their trades in different worlds. . . . Practicing in different worlds, the two groups of scientists see different things when they look from the same point in the same direction" (Kuhn 1970: 150).

At the time of *The Structure of Scientific Revolutions*, Kuhn (1970: vi) acknowledged an intellectual debt to Whorf's hypotheses about the relation between language and world view. In more recent writings, he described his position as "a sort of post-Darwinian Kantianism" (Kuhn 1991: 12; 2000: 104). He saw his position as Kantian insofar as he regarded taxonomies of kind concepts, like Kantian categories, as preconditions of possible experience. For Kuhn (1991, 1993, 2000: passim), these taxonomies include natural kinds, artifactual kinds, social kinds, kinds of personality, and so on. His position is post-Darwinian insofar as it allows for variability in these categories: "But lexical categories, unlike their Kantian forebears, can and do change, both with time and with the passage from one community to another" (Kuhn 1991: 12; 2000: 104). Although he denied that the world is merely constructed (1991: 10; 2000: 101), it is not clear how he could reconcile his post-Darwinian Kantianism with this disavowal of constructionism. Kuhn (1993: 337–8; 2000: 251) even asked us to set aside the notion of a "fully external world" that is independent of the practices of the scientists who investigate it. Gürol Irzik and Teo Grünberg (1998) suggest the somewhat charitable reading that for Kuhn only the phenomenal and not the noumenal world is constructed. However, as they point out, on their reading of Kuhn the relationship between the phenomenal and the noumenal worlds is once again as mysterious and unintelligible as it was for Kant (ibid., 219–20).

Other philosophers, psychologists, anthropologists, and linguists have come to question the claim that people in different cultures perceive the world through incommensurable sets of categories. Donald Davidson (1974), for example, argued that the assertion that there are fundamentally different conceptual systems amounts to the statement that there are

languages that are not intertranslatable, which he found to be inconsistent with the notion that languages can be used to make true claims about the world. Dan Slobin (1971: 12off.) found the claim that linguistic categories shape our thought to be ambiguous between the lexical sense of category and grammatical categories such as parts of speech. The ethnographic evidence for cultural differences in the structure of language and thought has also been questioned. Rodney Needham (1963: xi–xxix) has objected that Durkheim and Mauss's evidence does not support their thesis that classification systems vary with social structure. Similarly, Eric Lenneberg (1953: 464–5) and Roger Brown (1958: 231ff.) have argued that Whorf's evidence for fundamental conceptual differences between Hopi and English speakers turns on literal, unsympathetic translations from the Hopi (cf. Devitt and Sterelny 1987: 177 and Pinker 1994: 6off.). According to Maurice Bloch (1977: 290), Ladislav Holy, Milan Stuchlik (Holy and Stuchlik 1983: 100ff.), and Pascal Boyer (1994a: 112), the ethnographic evidence adduced for cultural differences in thought reflects a misplaced emphasis on religious beliefs and ritual discourse. The case is quite different when one turns to more practical matters. Ethnographers continue to find increasing evidence of a high degree of consensus across languages and cultures regarding color terms (Berlin and Kay 1969), biological taxa (Atran 1987, 1990, 1994, 1995; Berlin 1992; Berlin, Breedlove, and Raven 1973), and even patterns of legal reasoning in land disputes (Hutchins 1980). The psychologists Michael Cole and Sylvia Scribner (1974) have questioned whether anything about human cognition can be inferred from ethnographic evidence for cultural differences in beliefs and language. Boyer (1994a: 22, 27; 1994b: 396), Christopher Hallpike (1979: 70–1), John Tooby, Leda Cosmides (Tooby and Cosmides 1989: 41–3; 1992; Cosmides and Tooby 1994), and Steven Pinker (2002) criticize the cultural constructionist position for assuming that the human mind is a blank slate that passively acquires a set of ready-made categories from a culture. This assumption, they argue, runs counter to current research on learning, perception, and other psychological processes. Tooby and Cosmides (1989: 44) also find this assumption suspect from an evolutionary point of view.

With the wealth of conceptual and empirical criticisms of the cultural constructionist thesis that have already been offered, one might be tempted to think that it has been put to rest and that we can move on to other topics. However, the thesis that reality is socially and culturally constructed continues to be supported by countless scholars in the humanities and social sciences. The very popularity of social constructionist

doctrines suggests that it is incumbent upon philosophers to try to make clear the social character of human thought and perception. Like academic buzzwords generally, the phrase "social construction of reality" means different things to different people. What it means to say that reality is socially constructed depends not only on what one includes under "reality," but also on one's views on the social and cultural practices through which this reality is supposed to be constructed. Few would object to the thesis that social and political reality is the product of human social interaction, although academics may disagree about how to characterize this interaction. Even the claim that physical reality is socially constructed is relatively innocuous if one includes as part of this reality only such things as the built environment, technological devices, and other human artifacts. It is hardly surprising that there are economic, political, and social reasons for the fact that we now have electric instead of gas refrigerators, or gasoline instead of electric cars, or bicycles with wheels of equal size (Bijker 1995). The fact that social and economic factors enter into scientists' choices of research problems is also generally accepted today. As Ian Hacking (1999) argues, sometimes the claim that something is socially or culturally constructed is made simply for the rhetorical purpose of suggesting that things need not be the way that they are. For example, to say that gender is socially constructed is to imply that we need not accept the status quo with respect to gender relations in our society and that they can and even should be changed.

Constructionism begins to challenge commonsense and scientific realism only when it is applied to scientists' descriptions of the nonhuman physical world. For example, in the science studies disciplines it is sometimes claimed that unobservable entities such as quarks (Pickering 1984), pulsars (Woolgar 1988, chap. 4), or the hormone thyrotropin releasing factor (Latour and Woolgar 1986) are socially constructed. Woolgar (1988), for example, denies any reality to these entities independent of the theories that characterize them or the laboratory techniques used to detect them. How radical such claims actually are depends on one's conception of the social practices that are involved in the construction of scientific theories. Scientists may draw on cultural resources as a source of metaphors, models, and analogies in proposing new theories, but the important issue here is about which theories the scientific community ultimately accepts. If the constructionists claimed merely that which theories we come to accept reflect a consensus among scientists about which theories best account for the evidence, they would be saying nothing new. Their philosophy would then entail that the entities postulated in these

theories are simply useful fictions agreed upon by scientists to explain the experimental evidence. But this claim is only what skeptics, radical empiricists, pragmatists, positivists, instrumentalists, and indeed idealists have been arguing for a very long time. Constructionism differs from these older philosophies only to the extent that it suggests that either the observational evidence or logic itself is a culturally variable construction. Of course, observations are ambiguous and open to differing interpretations. It is also true that people with the right sorts of skills and training can make perceptual distinctions that the rest of us cannot. However, these facts alone do not imply that people from different cultures or paradigms live in different perceptual realities. Cultural and social practices could radically alter our vision only through constructing the categories that organize perception. Even the social or cultural construction of logic would not affect the way people see things, but only what they say about them.

Hence, the doctrine that reality is socially constructed has no real bite without the additional claim that reality is culturally constructed, that is, that our perceptions are shaped by culturally transmitted categories. The most daring claims made by the constructionists depend on the thesis of the cultural construction of the categories. This thesis derives from the tradition that began with Durkheim and Mauss and continued through French structuralism and poststructuralism. However, as I will show, what Durkheim originally meant was simply that our collective representations of the categories were social products. These collective representations do not preform reality for Durkheim. To defend the more radical claim that the categories that shape perception are themselves culturally constructed, one might try to argue that if the collective representations of space, time, and class are cultural products, then the categories must be as well, as these are abstracted from their representations. This defense, however, would be unacceptably circular, for how could the categories be formed by abstraction from experience if they are needed to make experience possible in the first place?

Durkheim's Argument for the Social Character of the Categories

In the introduction to *The Elementary Forms*, Durkheim defended his theory of the social causes of the categories by arguing that it provides the best explanation of their most important characteristics. Specifically, he argued that his sociology of knowledge gives a better account than do any of the philosophical alternatives, whether empiricist or a priori, of the generality, universality, necessity, and variability of the categories.

According to Durkheim, the a priori philosophy regards the categories not as derived from experience but as "logically antecedent" conditions of it. He seems to have regarded logically antecedent as equivalent to psychologically antecedent or innate conditions, attributing to the a priori philosophy the view that the categories are "so many simple givens, irreducible, immanent to the human mind in virtue of its native constitution" (1912a: 18, t. 1995: 12). The empiricist, on the other hand, holds that the categories are constructed by the individual from bits and pieces (ibid.). That is, Durkheim treated both the a priori and the empiricist philosophy as concerned with the causes and origins of the categories. Unlike contemporary philosophers, Durkheim did not separate questions about origins from questions about the epistemological warrant for the application of the categories to experience.

Durkheim rejected empiricism for its failure to account for the universality, necessity, and generality of the categories. The generality of the categories is a question of the range of things to which they apply. Just as the generality of the categories has to do with their being independent of particular objects, their universality has to do with their being independent of individual subjects: According to Durkheim, the categories are "the common ground where all minds meet" (1912a: 19, t. 1995: 13). The universality of a concept is its property of being communicable at least in principle to all minds (1912a: 619 n. 1, t. 1995: 435 n. 9). The necessity of the categories has to do with the fact that we cannot escape from them. Empiricism cannot account for the categories because the sensations from which it attempts to construct them have exactly the opposite characteristics: sensations are particular and private as opposed to general and universal. Nor can empiricism account for the necessity of the categories, given the freedom we enjoy with respect to our sensations. That is, although sensations may impose themselves on us, we can conceive them as we wish, even representing them as taking place in a different order. On the empiricist philosophy, the universality and necessity of the categories is but an illusory appearance that corresponds to nothing in the things themselves. Empiricism "thus denies all objective reality to the use of logic in life [*la vie logique*] that the function of the categories is to regulate and organize" (1912a: 20, t. 1995: 13).

Unlike empiricism, according to Durkheim, the a priori philosophy at least leaves intact the generality, universality, and necessity of the categories. However, the a priori philosophy does not *explain* these characteristics. Specifically, it cannot explain or justify the mind's ability to go beyond experience and to perceive relations in things that are not

revealed by mere sight. For Durkheim, it is no explanation to say that this power is inherent in the nature of human intelligence, for then it is still necessary to explain the mind's "surprising prerogative" to give form to our experience. Nor was he satisfied with the transcendental argument that the categories make experience possible. He responded that this argument only raises the question of why experience depends on conditions that are external and antecedent to it and how these conditions are met at the appropriate time and in the appropriate way. He then added that in order to answer these questions, it has been suggested that the human mind is an emanation of the divine intellect. Durkheim rejected this suggestion for not being experimentally testable. At the same time, however, he implied that it is false, arguing that the immutability of God's mind cannot account for the way in which the forms of the categories vary with time and place (1912a: 20–1, t. 1995: 13–14). Assuredly, it is hardly consistent or fair for Durkheim to criticize a hypothesis for being untestable and then to offer evidence against it. Perhaps what he meant to say is that the hypothesis of divine immutability cannot account for the variability of the categories and that there is no independent evidence to test the hypothesis of divine immutability.

If one accepts that the categories have social origins, Durkheim argued, all the difficulties faced by empiricism and the a priori philosophy can be explained. He believed that his hypothesis preserves the insight of the a priori philosophy that our knowledge is composed of two distinct types of elements, empirical and conceptual, that come from distinct sources and are irreducible to one another. Unlike the a priori philosophy, however, his sociology of knowledge identifies the categories with collective representations. Durkheim and Mauss had in fact subtitled their 1903 paper on primitive classification "Contribution to the Study of Collective Representations." For Durkheim, all general ideas and concepts, including the categories, are collective representations. He conceived collective and individual representations as two types of mental entities, providing the subject matter of sociology and psychology, respectively. Individual representations are particular ideas derived from sensations. Collective representations originate from the "fusion" of individual representations during periods of "collective effervescence." These original collective representations may then recombine to form new ones. As mental representations or ideas, collective representations have contents that provide the meanings of general terms. As mental entities, collective representations have a force, power, or "vivacity" that far surpasses that of the individual representations from which they are formed, which he believed gives

them a kind of moral authority that allows them to control individual thought (1912a: 296–8, 339, t. 1995: 209–10, 238; cf. 1898b). Thus, according to Durkheim, the social character of the categories explains the necessity with which they impose themselves on our thought. This necessity is a kind of moral necessity, analogous to moral obligation. That the categories are produced collectively, he thought, also explains the fact that their extension is more general than the experience of any individual. Collective representations may reflect the accumulated experience of many generations. That these concepts are held collectively explains their universality, that is, the fact that they are communicable from one individual to another. Finally, he argued that the social character of the categories accounts for their variability with place and time (1912a: 21–5, 619–20, t. 1995: 14–17, 435–6).

As Terry Godlove (1989: 40) argues, Durkheim appears to have placed conflicting demands on a theory of the categories, criticizing the empiricists for failing to explain their necessity and universality while criticizing the a priori philosophy for failing to explain their cultural variability. To the extent that his own theory succeeded in explaining this inconsistent set of properties, the theory would appear to be inconsistent or ambiguous. One might try to defend Durkheim by saying that he simply meant that a set of categories is universal only within a given culture, within which they are perceived to be necessary. But if that is all that he meant, his argument against the empiricists could not be sustained. Furthermore, as we saw earlier, Durkheim had also argued that the categories made social life possible, which would imply that they actually are necessary and not merely felt to be so, and that they must be found in every culture as well. This apparent conflict could be resolved if we interpret him as meaning that the same set of categories is represented in every culture and that it is only the ways in which they are represented that is culturally variable. That is, when Durkheim said that the categories are culturally variable, he was not necessarily making the radical claim that there are cultures that are wholly without the concepts of space, time, or causality. The necessary conditions of social life, are the same everywhere. What differ are merely the collective representations of the categories, which each culture draws from its own collective experience. Briefly, each culture has its own particular conceptions of the same universal set of concepts.[9]

However, as I mentioned earlier, Durkheim seems to have changed his mind on the question of whether every culture had the same set of categories. Part of his equivocation is due to the fact that he identified the categories with their culturally variable collective representations.

The relationships between categories and mental representations, both collective and individual, need to be made clear. A culture's classificatory concepts, systems of measurement, and other such concepts may be thought of as its collective or cultural representations of categories such as substance, space, and time. As there can be more than one way of classifying or measuring, it is possible that it is only these representations that vary with social groups. The Zuñi provided Durkheim with ethnographic evidence for the cultural variability only of ways of representing space, not of the category of space itself. Durkheim also recognized that "The principle of causality has been understood differently in different times and countries; in the same society, it varies with the social milieus and with the reigns of nature to which it is applied" (1912a: 527, t. 1995: 373). He brought forth ethnographic examples of collective representations of causal powers in nature, such as the Sioux notion of *wakan*, the Iroquois notion of *orenda*, and the Melanesian notion of *mana* (1912a: 290–2, t. 1995: 205–6). But one need not travel to exotic cultures to find alternative collective representations of causality. Ways of representing the categories could vary even among social groups within a larger society. As Durkheim pointed out, the idea of causality is not only different for the ordinary person than it is for the scientist, but it is different even in different branches of science, such as physics and biology (1912a: 527 n. 1, t. 1995: 373 n. 30). He left the investigation of the historical and cultural development of all these conceptions of causality as an open question for further research. I would suggest that not only do lay people and scientists in the same society have different conceptions of causality, but also that even a single individual may use different conceptions of causality on different occasions.

In order to get clear about the question of the universality of the categories, Durkheim needed to distinguish these from a culture's collective representations of them or ways of conceiving them. But as I will explain in Chapters 5 and 6, given his theory of meaning, it is not clear that he would have been able to make this distinction. He had no ready way of identifying what different conceptions of the same concept have in common that makes them conceptions of one and the same concept. For instance, although he recognized that different people even in the same society might have different conceptions of causality, he never explained what it is about all of these conceptions that makes them conceptions of causality.

The distinction between the categories and their collective representations is also needed to remove the celebrated circularity objection according to which Durkheim was wrong to say that the categories are

derived from our experience of social life because these categories are presupposed by such experience in the first place. Some of Durkheim's earliest critics outside of France, including Charles Elmer Gehlke (1915: 52), Edward L. Schaub (1920: 337), and William Ray Dennes (1924: 32–9), regarded Durkheim's sociological theory of the categories either as question-begging or as confusing Kantian categories with something like David Hume's ideas. In more recent years, Godlove (1986: 392–3; 1989: 32) and Steven Lukes (1973: 447) have argued that the entire Durkheimian program of seeking social causes for the categories is ill conceived, question-begging, or circular. That is, they contend, Kant's categories could not have social or any other sort of causes in the realm of experience, since the categories are logically necessary for experience in the first place. Without presupposing the categories, one could not have the experiences needed to acquire the categories from one's culture. The categories are not part of some sort of culturally variable framework or conceptual scheme through which we experience the world. Nor should they be thought of as belonging to some sort of psychological mechanism for processing sensations into conscious experience. Kant's logically necessary conditions should not be confused with the psychologically necessary conditions for experience. When Kant said, for example, that the category of quantity is necessary for experience, he meant only that one could not experience objects without their having some quantity or other, since the very concept of an object logically presupposes that of quantity. Furthermore, to assign social causes to the categories would be to make them contingent upon these causes and thus to deprive them of the very necessity and universality that Durkheim sought to explain, unless of course he were prepared to argue that these social causes themselves existed necessarily.[10]

This circularity objection is not entirely just, since what Durkheim meant by the term "category" was not what Kant meant or even what Durkheim believed other Kantian philosophers of his day meant. For Durkheim, the categories were neither the logically nor the psychologically necessary conditions of experience. As we saw earlier, Durkheim said that his categories do not preform our experience of the real world but merely recapitulate it. He was proffering an empirical derivation of the collective representations of the categories that he believed made it possible for the members of a society to think and communicate about its plans, its rules, and other socially important matters. Furthermore, we have recently learned that Durkheim, in his philosophy course in 1884, had raised this very same circularity objection against Herbert Spencer's

attempt to derive the Kantian categories and forms of intuition from experience (1884a: 135–6).[11] It is unlikely that Durkheim could have been aware of this difficulty as early as 1884 and yet overlooked it in 1912.

However, we cannot let Durkheim entirely off the hook by appealing to his idiosyncratic notion of a category, for it is not entirely clear how even these collective representations could be drawn from the experience of social life. This is perhaps best illustrated by the collective representation of causality. For Durkheim, as we shall see in Chapter 6, collective representations of causal power have their origins in our collective experience of social forces. Hume, however, had famously argued that we receive no idea of power, force, energy, or necessary connection from experience in both *A Treatise of Human Nature* (1739: 155ff., 632ff.) and *An Enquiry Concerning Human Understanding* (1748: 63ff.). We can understand how Durkheim could have overlooked Hume's arguments, however, if we consider him as having proposed his theory of the social origin of the categories as an alternative to the eclectic spiritualist tradition of Cousin and Maine de Biran. According to this philosophy, the category of causality derives from our inner experience of willed effort. Because Durkheim and much of his philosophical audience were schooled in this philosophical tradition, the question of whether we are in fact able to experience any sort of force or power other than through its effects went unexamined.

Durkheim and the Philosophical Tradition

Despite his assertion that empiricism and the a priori philosophy are the two conceptions of the categories that have competed for centuries (1912a: 21, t. 1995: 14), Durkheim said little to enlighten us about just who the philosophers are who held these conceptions, other than to name Spencer among the empiricists (1912a: 18 n. 1, t. 1995: 12 n. 15). Generally, one does not think of the empiricists as even having had theories about the categories. Although John Locke, George Berkeley, and Hume may have discussed general ideas, it was Kant who initiated modern discussions of Aristotle's concept of a category. The very idea of an empiricist theory of the categories strikes the contemporary reader as puzzling, as Kant is now generally understood as having said that the categories of the understanding are not derived from experience but are what make experience possible in the first place. Also, Kant did not include space and time among the categories. Furthermore, he explicitly denied that the categories were simply ways of thinking placed in us by the creator, as this

would deprive them of their necessity and render them merely subjective and illusory (Kant 1781/1787 B 167–8).[12] Finally, it is not even clear that Kant would have accepted Durkheim's ready identification of the categories with representations.

Durkheim was clearly responding not simply to Kant but to post-Kantian philosophers in addition to Spencer. But which philosophers did he have in mind? Who among the a priori philosophers, for instance, was arguing that the human mind with its categories represented an emanation of the divine intellect? The secondary literature on Durkheim contains little illumination on this topic.[13] This is somewhat surprising, as it would seem that to give a fair assessment of Durkheim's argument, one would have to know something about the alternative theories he was rejecting. This is not just because we need to determine whether Durkheim misrepresented his philosophical adversaries. We also need to examine the philosophical tradition against which he was reacting in order to get some sense of which positions he felt he needed to defend and which he felt he could take for granted given the intellectual community to which his arguments were addressed. It may very well be that it is precisely those positions that he was able to take for granted that we need to examine most carefully today. We should also look at this tradition in order to find out the generally accepted meanings of the philosophical terms he used, which may be very different from the meanings we give them today. Another reason to look more carefully into the theories that he was rejecting is that they may provide some insight into Durkheim's own intellectual development. The theories a thinker attacks will be those that are important in his intellectual environment. Thus, they would have played a role in shaping his own thinking, initially by accepting them as part of his education and then subsequently by reacting against them as he forms his own mature system of thought.

At the turn of the twentieth century in France, sociology was only beginning to be recognized as an academic discipline, and the Durkheimians held some of the very first chairs in this field (Besnard, ed., 1983). Durkheim, Mauss, and many other early French sociologists received their doctorates in philosophy, began their careers teaching philosophy in lycées, and competed with philosophers for university positions. Lévy-Bruhl in fact later became the editor of the *Revue philosophique*. During much of the nineteenth century, French academic philosophy was dominated by the eclectic spiritualist tradition initiated by Cousin.[14] Cousin was appointed to the Royal Council of Public Education in 1830, a post he held until his retirement in 1852. As this council was in charge of

what was taught in the lycées and university and as Cousin was the only philosopher on the council, he had an enormous influence over the philosophical curriculum. From 1835 to 1840, he was also director of the École Normale Supérieure, which was the leading institution in France for the training of academics, and he was briefly the minister of public education.[15] His conception of philosophy is reflected in the official philosophy syllabus of 1832, which laid out the philosophical topics that all lycée students needed to cover in order to prepare for the baccalaureate examination. It specified that the program of philosophical study for all the lycées in France was to begin with a foundational philosophical psychology. Contrary to the claims of Ulrich Schneider (1998), the reign of Cousin's eclectic spiritualism did not end with his retirement. His posthumous influence on the philosophical curriculum is reflected in the syllabi published by the Ministry of Public Instruction in 1874, 1880, and 1902, which more or less follow the order of topics in the syllabus of 1832.[16]

The 1880 syllabus was drafted by a committee that included Paul Janet (1823–99), a member of Durkheim's dissertation examination committee who was considered Cousin's successor as the leading eclectic spiritualist.[17] Janet was also the author of a standard philosophy text used in the lycées, the *Traité élémentaire de philosophie à l'usage des classes*, first published in 1879 and reissued in a new edition in 1883 that reflects the syllabus of 1880. Durkheim closely followed the syllabus of 1880 when he taught philosophy in the lycées. In a set of notes taken in Durkheim's class at the Lycée de Sens in 1883–4, André Lalande wrote that Durkheim said that Cousin's division of philosophy was the simplest and the best, "and we will adopt it" (1884a: 25–6). It also appears that Durkheim used Janet's text in this course.

Cousin followed the Cartesian tradition of grounding philosophy in an introspective inquiry into the human mind. This philosophical psychology was then supposed to provide a foundation for logic, ethics, and metaphysics. As a young man, Cousin had taught the first course in France on Kant, and the categories were central to his concerns in his foundational philosophical psychology. In Cousin's psychology, questions about the epistemological warrant for the application of the categories to experience were closely tied to questions about the psychological causes and origins of these concepts. In order to avoid what he took to be the skeptical implications of Kant's theory of the categories, Cousin proposed that the categories were divine in origin. Because of Cousin's legacy in the French academy, when Durkheim criticized the theory of the divine origin of the categories, his audience would have easily recognized whose

theory Durkheim was talking about without his having to mention Cousin by name.

Although in Durkheim's day French academic philosophers were still expected to follow Cousin's order of presentation of philosophical topics in their teaching, they enjoyed an increasing degree of freedom with respect to their positions on these topics. Some defended an empiricist interpretation of the categories. Indeed, Cousin himself had promoted the works of an earlier philosopher, Maine de Biran, who, in answer to Hume's skeptical challenge to our knowledge of causes, had attempted to derive the categories from the individual's internal experience of willed effort. Lycée philosophy texts that Durkheim knew continued to defend a position much like Maine de Biran's.[18] Although Durkheim claimed to reject empiricist theories of the categories, in effect he differed from other empiricists only with regard to the kind of experience from which the categories could be derived. Where the spiritualists appealed to our internal experience of the power of the will, Durkheim appealed to our experience of the power of society over us. This difference comes out most clearly with regard to the category of causality, as I will show in Chapters 3 through 6.

By arguing that the categories are social in character, Durkheim was proposing nothing less than to reestablish philosophy on a new socio-logical foundation. Indeed, he explicitly sought to place ethics as well as epistemology on a sociological foundation (e.g., 1920a). One could also regard his sociology of religion, in which he accounted for religious experience in terms of underlying social forces, as his replacement for metaphysics or the philosophy of religion. In sum, Durkheim was offer-ing a sociological alternative not simply to Kant's theory of the categories but also to the way in which this theory was understood by thinkers in the eclectic spiritualist tradition and to the alternatives to Kant that were proposed within this tradition. In this tradition, philosophers did not sep-arate logical and epistemological questions from psychological questions. When Durkheim's sociological theory of the categories is understood in this context, it begins to appear to be far more reasonable than it is made to look by Durkheim's critics, who would fault him for attempting to give empirical answers to Kant's philosophical questions.

Drawing Lessons from Durkheim for Today

Another legacy of the Durkheimian tradition is the assumption that, once one accepts that the contents of the individual human mind are

cultural constructions, one can safely ignore subsequent developments in psychological research. In *The Rules of Sociological Method,* Durkheim (1895a: 135, t. 1982: 134) had said that the causes of social facts should be sought among other social facts and not among states of individual consciousness. Alfred Reginald Radcliffe-Brown and his followers read this passage as advocating the complete exclusion of psychology from anthropology (Gluckman 1963: 2–3; Jahoda 1982: 33). Assuming that ideas and concepts, including the categories, are cultural products, anthropologists regarded them as falling within their domain, not that of psychology (Jahoda 1982: 40). However, Durkheim's sharp distinction between sociology and psychology needs to be understood in context. As I mentioned earlier, when Durkheim began his academic career, psychology was still a branch of philosophy, at least in France. Separating sociology from psychology was thus part of his strategy for making sociology an empirical discipline. His former classmate Pierre Janet (1859–1947), the nephew of Paul Janet, was in fact engaged in trying to introduce the methods of the natural sciences into psychology at about the same time that Durkheim was trying to make sociology an empirical science (Brooks 1998, chap. 5). For social scientists today to continue to snub psychology is for them to risk the inadvertent retention of assumptions about the human mind that subsequent psychological research has called into question. To disregard psychology now is thus to weaken rather than strengthen the empirical status of sociology, which is not at all what Durkheim intended.

It is also necessary to make a clear separation between Durkheim's causal and functional accounts of the categories and to clarify the distinction between social and psychological functions. As I mentioned earlier, according to Durkheim the categories make possible the performance of certain necessary human social functions. What Durkheim in fact provided is a theory of the social functions of the categories and a theory of the social causes of their various representations. If we separate this functional hypothesis from the claim that the categories have variable social causes, his theory of the categories suggests a program of cooperative research between the sociology of knowledge and the cognitive neurosciences. As I will explain in Chapter 7, this research program would attempt to gain some insight into the cognitive or conceptual requirements for human social life. It would begin by comparing the collective representations of the categories of different cultures in order to determine which categories exist in all cultures and which are culturally variable. It may then investigate the extent to which the common features of different cultures' representations of the categories can

be explained by convergent cultural development. Commonalities that cannot be explained in this way may be due to the very structure of the human mind. The degree to which conceptual commonalities can be explained by our innate psychological mechanisms is then a question for the cognitive neurosciences.

Maintaining this distinction between Durkheim's functional account of the categories and his causal account of their collective representations will also help us get clear about the question of how and to what degree intercultural interpretation and communication are possible. Implicit in Durkheim's sociological theory of the categories is the suggestion that the categories take at least part of their meanings from the social functions they serve, which are necessary for social life and thus are found in all societies. In order for the categories to play these social roles, however, they need to be represented in some public way that permits their use in communication among the individual members of a social group. However, not all social groups need to represent these categories in the same way in order for these functions to be carried out within each group. That is, cultural representations of the categories need not resemble each other or have the same causes or origins in order to perform the same functions. It is also possible for the individual members of a social group to have private mental representations of the categories that do not resemble these cultural representations or have the same causes or origins.

Once it is understood that the categories take their meanings from their functional roles rather than from the causes of their individual or collective representations, it becomes easier to explain how it is possible to interpret people in other cultures and to communicate with them. If the meanings of the categories depended on the social causes of their representations, then people from different social groups who had been exposed to different social causes would mean different things by the categories and would face something like Kuhn's problem of meaning incommensurability. On the other hand, this obstacle to communication among people of different cultures is removed if the meanings of the categories have to do instead with their social functions, which are found in all societies and cultures. A person may recognize that a representation is being used in another culture in a way that is similar to that in which a different representation is used in his or her own culture and thus assume that these two are representations of the same category. For instance, we may interpret a certain cultural representation as representing the category of causality if it is used in ascribing moral responsibility, as I will explain later. Similarly, we understand that the traditional Chinese

periods of yin and yang, like the four seasons of the Europeans and Americans, are cultural representations of the category of time by the fact that they perform similar social functions, such as organizing agricultural work. We may also recognize the seven directions of the Zuñi as well as the points of the compass of Western societies as ways of indicating parts of space. These Chinese and Zuñi concepts may have other meanings as well, but these will be understood through the additional functions they serve. Thus, our understanding of our own culture provides at least a starting point for the interpretation of other cultures.[19]

Overview

In the next chapter, I shall begin with a brief history of theories of the categories, including their origin in the philosophy of Aristotle and their development in Kant's critical philosophy. Kant offered the critical philosophy at least in part as an answer to Hume's skeptical doubts regarding our ability to infer the existence of causal relationships from past experience. Kant then generalized Hume's doubts into an epistemological problem about all of the categories. Of course, one could write an entire book on just Kant's theory of the categories and whether it succeeds in answering Hume's doubts. For my purposes, however, it will suffice to say just enough about Kant to reveal the ambiguities in his thought that made it possible for subsequent philosophers to read him as if he were offering a psychological account of human perception, consciousness, and thought.

In Chapter 3 I will provide a brief account of the introduction of Kantian philosophy into France. I will show that Cousin, like some of Kant's early German critics with whom he was familiar, understood Kant as having said that space, time, and the categories were limited in their application to our subjective experience. In Cousin's mind, Kant had thus failed to provide a sufficient epistemological justification of the categories. For Cousin, the false premise in Kant's philosophy is that we are aware of only our own mental representations. He adopted instead Reid's common-sense philosophy according to which perception is not mediated by any sort of representative idea. For Cousin, this was as true of internal as of external perception. He also assimilated Kant's transcendental apperception of the unity of consciousness, which plays a key role in the transcendental deduction of the categories, to the Cartesian cogito. Drawing on the philosophy of Maine de Biran, Cousin held that this apperception revealed the self as substance or cause and thus provided

the source of the categories. Thus an empirical deduction of the categories was substituted for Kant's transcendental deduction. In order to justify the application of these concepts to the external world, Cousin appealed to their source in divine reason.

Cousin had retired before Durkheim was born and thus had no direct effect on Durkheim's schooling. To understand the character of eclectic spiritualism at the time Durkheim was a student, I shall turn in Chapter 4 to an examination of the views of Janet as expressed in his textbook, the *Traité élémentaire de philosophie à l'usage des classes*. Janet broke with his mentor, Cousin, by defending the concept of representative ideas, arguing that the common-sense philosophers had shown merely that such entities do not mediate external perception. For Janet, the concept of representative ideas was still useful for explaining memory and the meanings of concepts. Durkheim appears to have accepted from Janet the identification of meanings with representative ideas. Furthermore, he seems to have adopted Janet's methodological stance and regarded it as licensing the postulation of collective in addition to individual representations.

In Chapter 5, I will turn to Durkheim's early views on the categories, as revealed in his early philosophy lectures at the Lycée de Sens. These lectures, which are still relatively unknown, are important because they reveal that Durkheim began his career teaching in the eclectic spiritualist tradition. I will explain how although he accepted from Cousin the notion that a psychology of mental states is the foundational philosophical discipline, Durkheim defended the use of the hypothetico-deductive method in philosophy and psychology as an alternative to Cousin's introspective method. In fact, in these early lectures Durkheim maintained an even more thoroughgoing empirical scientific methodology than did Janet. Like Cousin, Janet continued to seek a foundation for philosophy, including the theory of the categories, in the introspective study of the faculties of the human mind. The young Durkheim broke with Janet in regarding the study of the categories as part of empirical psychology. Also, I will not only show how he shared with Janet the notion that representative ideas could be used to explain where words get their meaning, but also propose that this theory of meaning may have been the source of his later notion of collective representations.

In Chapter 6, I will provide a more detailed analysis of Durkheim's mature sociological theory of the categories, paying particular attention to his account of the category of causality. Of course, his account of the origin of the concept of causal power in our collective experience of social forces fares no better than the psychological accounts of his predecessors.

However, in addition to this account of the causal origins of the concept of causality, he provided an account that is worth preserving of the social function of causal concepts in making moral rules possible. Furthermore, causality was not a univocal concept for Durkheim, as it appears to have been for his eclectic spiritualist predecessors. As I mentioned earlier, he suggested that there might be different conceptions of causality even in different social groups within the same society, presumably serving different social functions in each.

In Chapter 7, the last chapter, I will address the issue of the relevance of Durkheim's sociological theory of the categories for today and the ways in which it may be extended and developed, once we get rid of the philosophical assumptions he inherited from the eclectic spiritualist tradition. I will argue that if we define the categories at least in part in terms of their social functions, instead of simply identifying the meanings of the categories with their collective representations, the cultural incommensurabilist implications of his sociology of knowledge can be avoided. Also, once we stop thinking of sociology as concerned with collective representations understood as a kind of mental entity distinct from the individual representations studied by psychology, sociology and psychology can work together instead of at cross-purposes in understanding the conceptual requirements for social life.

2

Historical Background

Aristotle and Kant

The history of philosophical theories of the categories is nearly coextensive with the history of philosophy itself.[1] Even if I were able to, I would not want to tell all of this history, but only those parts of it that are relevant to making sense of the sociological theories of the categories that arose in France at the turn of the twentieth century. As I mentioned in Chapter 1 and will explain more fully in the following chapters, Durkheim's theory of the categories was proposed in response to a French academic philosophical tradition in which theories of the origins and causes of the categories played a fundamental role. To appreciate Durkheim's arguments for reestablishing philosophy on the basis of a sociological theory of the categories, we need to understand this tradition. But to understand the tradition that Durkheim was rejecting, it would help first to survey briefly the prior history of philosophical accounts of the categories.

Our history should start with Aristotle. Not only did Aristotle dominate philosophical thinking about the categories until Kant, but Durkheim and Mauss themselves suggested that this is where we ought to begin. As we saw in Chapter 1, Durkheim in *The Elementary Forms of Religious Life* traced the concept of the categories back to Aristotle: "There exist, at the root of our judgments, a certain number of essential notions that dominate all of our intellectual life; these are those that the philosophers, since Aristotle, call the categories of the understanding" (1912a: 12–13, t. 1995: 8). Mauss also claimed that the Durkheimian school was attempting to provide sociological accounts of Aristotle's categories. He reported that they regarded even Aristotle's list of ten categories as nothing more than a starting point and sought to draw up "the largest possible catalogue of categories" (Mauss 1924, t. 1979: 32; cf. 1938, t. 1979: 59; 1985: 1).

Kant chose the term "category" for his concepts of the understanding because, as he somewhat cryptically said, his aims were fundamentally the same as Aristotle's (A80/B105).[2] In this chapter, my purpose is simply to lay out just enough of Kant's views on the categories so that the reader can appreciate the historical relationship between Durkheim's project and Kant's. I wish to show how certain ambiguities in Kant's theory of the categories made it possible for nineteenth-century philosophers to have given it a psychological reading. It is not my goal to make this interpretation convincing to a modern reader. Of course, there may still be better and worse psychological readings of Kant's theory of the categories. For example, the ambiguities we find in Kant may allow one to interpret his theory of the categories as a psychological theory but not as an *empirical* psychological theory. We would then need to seek some explanation other than Kant's ambiguity for the fact that such theories of the categories were being proposed. Clarifying this historical situation will help us to appreciate how Durkheim's attempt to provide an empirical, sociological theory of the categories was not a result of his simply having misunderstood Kant but was a response to subsequent developments in philosophy.

Aristotle

Aristotle's categories are substance, quantity, quality, relation, place, time, being-in-a-position (position or posture), having (state or condition), doing (action), and being-affected (affection, passivity) (*Categories* 1b25–7).[3] These categories are the highest genera: they cannot be regarded as species of any higher genera. One may think of them as the kinds of concepts needed to answer the most basic questions we can ask about things: what, where, when, how many, and so on.[4] They are not mutually exclusive (1b20–4): something could be both a quality and a relation.

Consistent with Mauss's interpretation, there is nothing in Aristotle that would rule out the possibility of there being more than ten categories.[5] However, there are some important differences between Durkheim's and Aristotle's notions of the categories. First of all, when Durkheim spoke of the categories as being at the "root of our judgments," he seems to have been following Kant rather than Aristotle. For Kant, as we shall see, each of the categories reflected one of the forms that judgments could take. The same concepts that organized perceptual experience, in other words, gave structure to our judgments about it. Aristotle, however, treated the categories and judgments separately, discussing the categories in a book by that name and forms of judgment

in *On Interpretation*. Aristotle's categories are a classification of words or terms and the things to which they refer considered in isolation from the judgments, propositions, or sentences in which they may be used. As he put it, all "things said without any combination" signify (or denote or refer to) things that fall under one or more of the categories (1b25). By "things said without any combination," he meant expressions considered apart from their joining with one another to produce an "affirmation" (2a4–10) or judgment. A second difference between Aristotle's and Durkheim's notions of the categories is reflected in the fact that Durkheim calls them "categories of the understanding." Durkheim takes this term from Kantian philosophy. Unlike Aristotle's account of the categories, Kant's belongs to a part of philosophy that he called "transcendental logic," a theory of the understanding that purports to explain how it is possible to have knowledge of objects. To be sure, in both the *Posterior Analytics* II.19 and *Metaphysics* A (I).1, Aristotle did write about how our knowledge of universals derives from experience. However, he did not explicitly tie these discussions of universals back to his account of the categories.

Durkheim, Aristotle, and Kant differ with respect to which concepts they consider to be categories. All three regard substance as a category. However, Aristotle and Kant include "quantity" in their lists of categories rather than Durkheim's "number." Also, while Durkheim and Kant take cause to be a single category, Aristotle has two categories, doing or acting and being-acted-upon. For Kant, as I will explain, space and time are forms of intuition, not categories, as they are for Durkheim and Aristotle. Aristotle included "place" instead of "space" among the categories, as he conceived the space that something occupies in relation to the things that surrounded it. Also, for Aristotle, genus is not a distinct category from substance but is subsumed under "secondary substances." The "primary substances" are individual substances, such as individual men or horses, while the "secondary substances" are the species and genera under which these individuals are classified (2a11–18). Substance is a category, while genera and species are merely kinds of substances. That is, "horse" and "human being" would be kinds of substances for Aristotle but kinds of species or genera for Durkheim.

Some of the things regarded by ethnologists as categories, such as Mauss's animate and inanimate or Leach's bush and tree,[6] would be secondary substances rather than categories for Aristotle. Other concepts that have been proposed as categories would be subsumed under Aristotle's category of quality: Mauss and Hertz's categories of left- and

right-handedness, Lévi-Strauss's cooked and raw, and Gluckman's shapes (10a11) and colors (1b30).[7] Mauss's categories of big and small would fall under either relation or quantity. Finally, Durkheim and Mauss's category of personality is on neither Aristotle's nor Kant's list. This complex concept appears to combine at least three notions: Aristotle's primary substance, or the notion of an individual; a secondary substance, specifically that of a human being; and particular, perhaps culturally variable, moral qualities that are assigned to human beings. Durkheim and Mauss's inclusion of personality probably reflects their reading of Charles Renouvier (1815–1903). Renouvier listed nine categories in order from simplest and most abstract to most complex and concrete: relation, number, position, succession, quality, becoming, causality, finality, and personality (1875: vol. I, 120ff.). Roughly speaking, much as Aristotle's categories are those concepts needed to answer the most basic questions about things, Renouvier believed that the category of personality was needed to answer the question of in what or in whom a representation takes place (ibid., 122–3).

In sum, it is not at all clear that Durkheim and Mauss had initiated a tradition of cross-cultural studies of specifically Aristotelian categories. I suggested in the previous chapter that they were not investigating specifically Kantian categories, either. To underscore this claim, it would be helpful to take a more detailed look at Kant's theory of the categories.

Kant's Theory of the Categories

As I mentioned in Chapter 1, Durkheim was providing a sociological alternative to a philosophical tradition of writing about the categories that was initiated by Kant. However, from the perspective of today's prevailing philosophical interpretations of Kant, if one assumes that Durkheim meant the same thing by the categories that Kant did, Durkheim's project looks simply confused. Durkheim sought the causes of the categories in the social and hence the empirical realm. But it is not difficult to find passages in Kant where he clearly distinguished his theory of the categories from empirical psychology and thus, presumably, from any other empirical science. In the *Prolegomena to Any Future Metaphysics* (1783), for instance, he said that he was not offering his theory of the categories as an empirical, psychological account of the origin of experience. The categories are the concepts that are found in experience rather than those that generate it. To say, for instance, that the category of quantity is necessary for experience would then be to say only that one

could not experience objects without their having some quantity or other. According to Kant, "The discussion here is not about the genesis of experience, but about that which lies in experience. The former belongs to empirical psychology and could never be properly developed even there without the latter, which belongs to the critique of cognition and especially of the understanding" (1783 4: 304).[8]

In this passage, Kant said merely that his theory of the categories does not belong to an *empirical* psychology. That leaves open the possibility that it belongs to some other sort of nonempirical, philosophical psychology.[9] By a philosophical psychology, I do not mean what the Germans called a "rational psychology," which concerned the existence and characteristics of the soul. Kant criticized this rational psychology as based on a "paralogism" or misuse of reason (B421). Although Kant distinguished the critical philosophy from both empirical and rational psychology, words like "cognition" and "understanding" could easily be taken to be psychological terms. In fact the whole argument of the *Critique of Pure Reason* seems to be expressed in terms of mental states, mental capacities, and mental processes of one kind or another. Kant was perhaps one of the first philosophers even to try to draw a clear distinction between psychology and philosophy, and hence it should come as no surprise that he did not entirely succeed.

The categories of the understanding themselves are a species of mental representation for Kant. His taxonomy of terms for mental representations is presented in Figure 1. Where other philosophers have used the term "idea" as the most general term for mental states of all kinds, Kant preferred the term "representation" or *Vorstellung*.[10] A *conscious* representation is a "perception." Considered simply as a subjective mental state, that is, as a state belonging to a perceiving subject, a perception is called a "sensation." However, when a perception is considered as the representation of an object, it is called a "cognition" (*Erkenntnis*). A cognition can be either an "intuition" or a "concept." An intuition is a single representation that relates directly to an object considered by itself. A concept refers only indirectly to objects, by means of something that that object has in common with other things. In what follows, I shall refer to this as Kant's generic sense of concept. Concepts for Kant can be either empirical or pure, that is, they are either drawn from experience or prior to it. Pure concepts have their origin in the understanding and are also called the categories. For Kant, an idea is a concept that results from the reason extending the use of the categories beyond the realm of anything one could possibly experience (A320/B376–7). The idea of

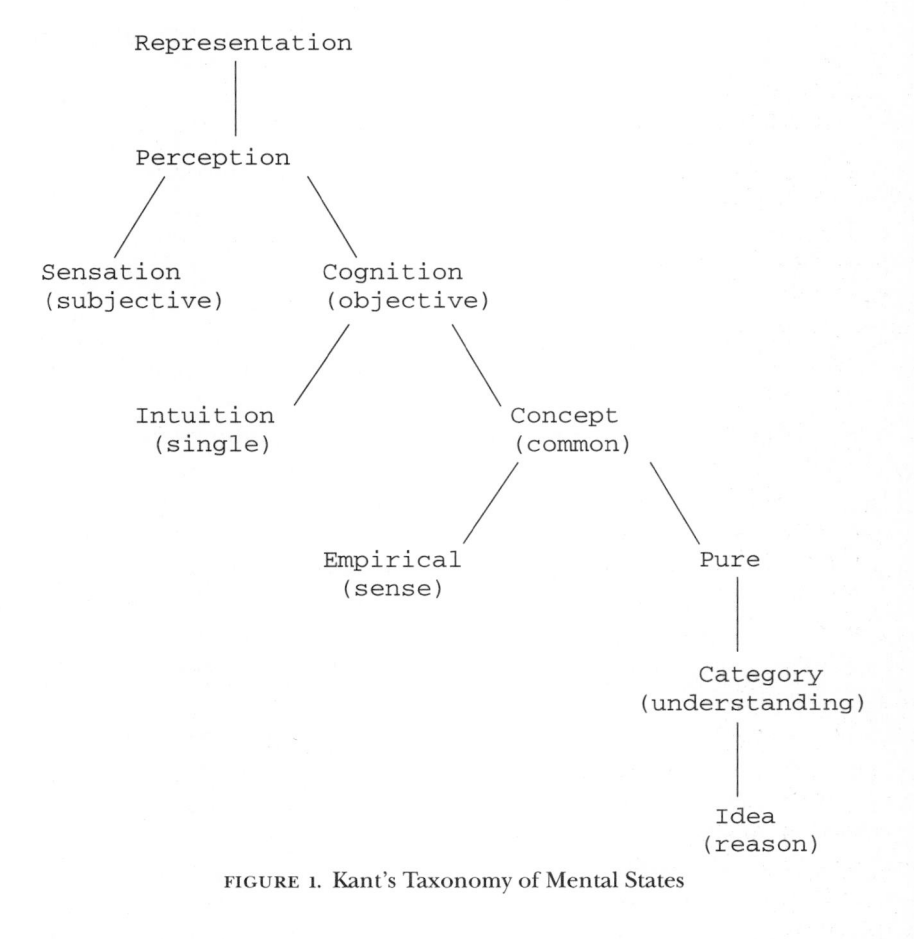

FIGURE 1. Kant's Taxonomy of Mental States

the soul, for instance, is constructed in this way from the category of substance.

Kant conceived his theory of the categories as belonging to a part of philosophy that he called "transcendental logic," which he distinguished from "general logic." General logic for Kant includes the necessary rules of thought, without which the understanding could not be used at all (A52/B76). *Pure* general logic is close to what philosophers today mean by logic. It abstracts from all content of our knowledge and deals with only the formal principles of reasoning. Also, in contrast with *applied* general logic, pure general logic abstracts from all considerations of empirical psychology and is completely a priori (A53–4/B77–8). *Transcendental* logic, on the other hand, does not abstract from all content but only from

empirical content. It concerns the rules governing our pure thoughts of objects (A55/B80). That is, it concerns that aspect of the content of our thoughts that has to do with the pure concepts of the understanding or categories. As Kant defined it, transcendental logic is "a science of pure understanding and rational cognition" that determines the "origin, range, and objective validity of rational cognitions" (A57/B81). General logic, on the other hand, is not concerned with the origins of our cognitions (A56/B80). Also, while general logic applies to both the empirical and the pure content of our knowledge, transcendental logic deals with the laws of understanding and reason only insofar as these relate to the a priori aspects of our knowledge of objects (A57/B81–2). Transcendental logic includes two parts, a transcendental analytic and a transcendental dialectic. The transcendental analytic consists in a "dissection" into its elements of the part of our cognition of objects that we owe to the understanding. There are two sorts of these elements, the pure concepts of the understanding and the principles that are necessary to the very thought of an object (A62/B87, A64/B89). The transcendental analytic thus includes Kant's theory of the categories as well as these principles of the understanding. His transcendental dialectic consists in a critique of the illusory use of reason and understanding (A63/B88).

In sum, logic for Kant includes more than just a purely formal study of syllogistic and other patterns of inference; it also includes an a priori investigation of the conditions that make cognition possible. It deals with epistemological questions in a way that brings in considerations having to do with the philosophy of mind. Patricia Kitcher (1990) argues that Kant's transcendental logic is in effect a transcendental psychology.

Kant and Hume

Given that our objective is one of historical understanding, a reasonable way to begin an account of Kant's theory of the categories is to consider it as a response to Hume. Insofar as Kant's philosophical project was to initiate a science of the limitations of human knowledge that would undermine traditional metaphysics, it resembled Hume's. In both the *Prolegomena* and the introduction to the second edition of the *Critique*, Kant described his theory of the categories as a response to Hume's problem of causality. As Kant told us, it was Hume's analysis of causality that awoke him from his "dogmatic slumber" and gave his philosophical investigations a new direction (1783 4: 260). Kant's dogmatic slumber is generally understood to be that induced by his study of Wolffian and Leibnizian

metaphysics. Hume's analysis of causal inferences raised doubts for Kant about the concept of causality. These doubts led him to formulate an answer to Hume that he then generalized to what he regarded as the rest of the categories.

Hume distinguished between two sorts of knowledge: relations among ideas, which can be demonstrated through the use of the principle of non-contradiction, and matters of fact, which cannot be demonstrated in the same way since each of their opposites implies no contradiction. Matters of fact seem to be based on perceptual experience. Hume then inquired into the sort of evidence that we can have for knowledge of matters of fact regarding things that are beyond our present or past perceptions. Since any attempt to reason about such facts appears to rely upon the relation between cause and effect, he thought it necessary to inquire into how we arrive at knowledge of causal relations (1748: 25–7; cf. 1739: 73–4).

Knowledge of causal relations cannot be attained by a priori reasoning but only from the experience of the constant conjunction of one object with another, according to Hume. Providing the example that Adam would not at first have known that water could drown or fire burn him, he argued that reason does not allow one to determine the causes or effects of an object from its observable qualities alone. Hume anticipated the objection that this conclusion held only for unusual events and not for such ordinary events as one billiard ball hitting another. In reply, he insisted that the motion of the first ball is an entirely distinct event from that of the second and that, without past experience to guide him, he could imagine one hundred different things that could result from the impact (1748: 27–9; cf. 1739: 86–7).

For Hume, the result that knowledge of causal relations is based on experience only raised the question of how in fact we gain knowledge from experience and whether such knowledge is justified. To illustrate this problem, he analyzed his reasons for thinking that the next piece of bread would nourish him much as the previous one did. As he explained, he could perceive only the observable properties of the bread and not those hidden properties by which it nourished him. He merely presumed that since the observable properties of the next piece of bread are the same, they resulted from the same "secret powers," which will then also have the same nourishing effects. There is no basis for this assumption, he said, as perception can provide us with knowledge only of the past and present and not of the future (1748: 32–3).

Generalizing from the bread example, Hume then argued that we cannot infer the second proposition from the first: "[1] I have found that

such an object has always been attended with such an effect, and [2] I foresee, that other objects, which are, in appearance, similar, will be attended with similar effects" (1748: 34). The connection between these two propositions is not immediate: one is about the past and the other is about the future. Hence, Hume reasoned, there is a need for a middle term to derive the second from the first. He then enumerated the branches of knowledge once again to show that none of them could supply this middle term. As I mentioned earlier, knowledge of the relations among ideas depends upon the principle of noncontradiction. The missing middle term could not come from this source, Hume explained, as there is no contradiction in there being a change in the future course of nature, such that an object could have different and even contrary effects. However, the other sort of knowledge, matters of fact, could not supply this middle term either. Our knowledge of matters of fact depends upon experience. Since all of our conclusions drawn from experience presuppose that the future will be like the past, to try to prove this supposition on the basis of experience would be to argue in a circle (1748: 34–6; cf. 1739: 89–90).

It would not answer Hume's philosophical worry to say that we infer future effects from causes after repeated experiences of observing similar effects resulting from similar causes: if this inference were based on reason, he argued, it would be just as valid for the first instance as after a long course of experience. Nor will the appeal to hidden causes or "secret powers" help us. Even if we could observe these hidden powers, there is no way to prove that the same observable qualities must always result from the same secret powers. Hume concluded that it is not by a process of reasoning that we suppose that the future resembles the past or expect that similar effects will result from similar causes (1748: 36–9; cf. 1739: 88–91). In contemporary philosophical parlance, Hume showed that inductive generalization is not a valid form of inference.

Hume's conclusion is purely philosophical and not intended to undermine everyday practical reasoning about causes and their effects. He said that if practical reasoning is "not supported by any argument or process of the understanding," then the mind must simply follow some other principle (1748: 41). Inquiring into what that principle might be, he imagined an intelligent person brought into our world all of a sudden. Such a person would not at first arrive at the idea of cause and effect but would merely observe a continual succession of one event following another. The powers of nature would be hidden from her view. Hume then suggested that as this individual acquired further experience and

observed the constant conjunction of similar objects or events, she would then be able to infer the existence of one from the appearance of the other, even though she still had no idea of any secret powers. Nor would this person draw this inference by any process of reasoning. Therefore, she must use some other principle: "This principle is Custom or Habit," Hume proposed (1748: 42–3). That is, from repeated experience of the conjunction of two objects, we form the habit of expecting one upon the appearance of the other.

True to his empiricist avoidance of causal explanations, Hume simply postulated a human tendency to form habits through repetition and did not attempt to account for this propensity. He defended this hypothesis on the grounds that it can explain how we are able to make causal inferences after repeated experiences but not after the first. This fact cannot be explained by the alternative hypothesis that causal inference is based on reason. Hence, all inferences drawn from experience are based on habit and not on reason. Our practical activity thus depends on habit. He concluded that all belief in matters of fact beyond our current perceptions or memories is based upon a present perception or memory of some object and a habitual relationship of that to some other object (1748: 43–6).

Kant formulated Hume's question as follows: how can I go beyond a concept that is given me and connect it with another that is not contained in it and yet connect it in a necessary way? Hume thought that such connections could be furnished only by experience as the result of habit, leading us to mistake subjective necessity or mere association for objective necessity (1783 4: 277; cf. 1787: B5). As Kant described it, Hume challenged reason, which "pretends" to have given rise to this concept, as to its right to infer the existence of one thing from another, which is how Hume defined cause. Hume showed that reason could not arrive at such necessary connections a priori. Reason mistook this concept for one of its children, Kant said, when in fact it is a "bastard of imagination, impregnated by experience," which connected ideas by association (1783 4: 257–8). Kant then generalized Hume's objection, applying it to concepts other than cause and effect (1783 4: 260; cf. 1787: B19ff.). Although we cannot comprehend the concept of causality through reason alone, Kant argued, we just as little comprehend the concept of substance, that is, the concept that in order for things to exist there must be a subject that is not the predicate of any other thing (1783 4: 310). Metaphysics is full of concepts by which it tries to connect things a priori (1783 4: 260). These are what he called the pure concepts of the understanding or the

categories. He did not believe that these concepts are derived from experience or that the necessity in them is an illusion resulting from habit, as it was for Hume (1783 4: 310–11). They are a priori, deriving from the pure understanding (1783 4: 260).

In the preface to the second edition of the *Critique*, Kant proposed that we undertake a Copernican experiment in philosophy. Up to that time, he said, it had been assumed that our cognition must conform to objects. On this assumption, it is not clear how we can have any a priori knowledge of objects. Kant thought we might have more success in metaphysics if we were to suppose that objects must conform to our cognition, that is, to our intuition and concepts (B xvi–xvii; xix, footnote a). On this supposition, "we cognize a priori of things only what we ourselves put into them" (B xviii). Hence, his answer to Hume is that the principle of causality is not derived from experience, but is one of the principles that make experience possible in the first place (1783 4: 313). For Kant, such principles are "synthetic a priori." They are a priori because they are not derived from experience. However, for Kant there are two kinds of a priori judgments: analytic and synthetic. Analytic judgments contain nothing in the predicate that is not already implicit in the subject, while the predicate of a synthetic judgment does go beyond what is in the subject. The question of the *Critique* is precisely whether and how synthetic a priori knowledge is possible (B19; 1783 4: 276).

However, even if Kant had shown that synthetic a priori knowledge of the principle of causality were possible, would that really answer Hume's skepticism? That is, even if Kant had shown that the principle of causality was necessary for experience rather than derived from it, would that answer Hume's specific question about receiving nourishment from the next piece of bread? In other words, does Kant's philosophy justify the particular causal laws concerning the properties of bread? As with most questions about Kant, there is a considerable literature on these issues, also. Michael Friedman suggests that in order to answer this question, we need to consult the *Metaphysical Foundations of Natural Science* (1786) as well as the *Critique*. According to Friedman's interpretation of Kant, particular empirical laws are grounded in the principle of causality not in the sense of being deduced from it, but by being instances of it (1992: 185–6). In the *Metaphysical Foundations*, however, Kant showed this only for the laws of physics, specifically, for Newton's first and third laws of mechanics (1786 4: 543ff.).[11] He was not able to show this for the laws of chemistry, which presumably would be needed for an account of the nourishing properties of bread. Kant regarded the laws of chemistry of

his day as no more than empirical generalizations and not as necessary truths. Necessary truths are expressed in the language of mathematics, and physics is able to arrive at such truths only by representing its concepts in pure intuitions. In order for chemistry to achieve the same scientific status as physics, he thought, there would have to be some concept that could be represented in a pure intuition and that governs the interactions of the parts of matter. Lacking such a concept, chemistry is more of an experimental art than a science (1786 4: 468, 470–1). Whether or not the laws of chemistry were necessary truths, Kant nevertheless believed that there were such truths in the sciences. What makes such truths possible, according to Kant, are the a priori forms of intuition and the pure concepts of the understanding or the categories.

Kant's Categories and Forms of Intuition

As I mentioned earlier, Kant generalized Hume's problem with causal inference to include all the concepts by which metaphysics tries to draw connections among things without the benefit of evidence drawn from experience. These concepts are included in the list of categories or pure concepts of the understanding (1783 4: 303; 1781/1787 A80/B106) in Table 1.

Although, as I mentioned earlier, Kant said that he called these the categories because his goals were the same as Aristotle's (A80/B105), there are some important differences between Kant's list of twelve and

TABLE 1. *Kant's Categories*

1. Quantity
   a. Unity
   b. Plurality
   c. Totality
2. Quality
   a. Reality
   b. Negation
   c. Limitation
3. Relation
   a. Substance (inherence and subsistence)
   b. Cause (and effect)
   c. Community (reciprocity between agent and patient)
4. Modality
   a. Possibility (vs. impossibility)
   b. Existence (vs. nonexistence)
   c. Necessity (vs. contingency)

Aristotle's list of ten categories. Unlike Aristotle's, Kant's are grouped in triads. The headings for the first three of these triads are three of Aristotle's categories, at least in name, which would seem to indicate that Kant's categories were not Aristotle's highest genera. Also, there is nothing in Kant's list to correspond to Aristotle's place and time. For Kant, space and time were not categories or even concepts, but "forms of intuition." Space is the form of outer sense and time of inner sense (A22–3/B37–8). This is not to suggest that we cannot have concepts of space and time. In order to make geometrical knowledge possible, obviously it must be possible for us to have a concept of space that can serve as "a constituent of judgments concerning space" (Parsons 1992: 69). Kant meant to argue only that our "original representation of space is an a priori intuition and not a concept" (B40).

Like many philosophers in his intellectual milieu, Durkheim rejected Kant's distinction between the forms of intuition and the categories and included space and time among the categories. The French philosophers Durkheim knew were probably at least indirectly influenced by Kant's earliest critics in German. According to Frederick Beiser, the first person to deny Kant's distinction between the forms of intuition and the categories was Johann Georg Hamann (1730–88) in his *Metakritik über den Purismum der reinen Vernunft* (1784). Hamann had understood Kant as relegating the forms of intuition and the categories to two separate mental faculties, the sensibility and the understanding, respectively, and criticized Kant for failing to explain how they interact. In particular, Kant could not explain how the pure concepts of the understanding applied to sensible intuitions. According to Hamann, it was better not to separate these faculties in the first place but rather to consider all the intellectual functions of human beings as forming an indivisible whole (Beiser 1987: 41–2). This criticism of Kant could have entered France by way of Cousin, as he spent a month in 1818 in Munich visiting Friedrich Heinrich Jacobi (1743–1819), who had read and greatly admired Hamann's *Metakritik*, and Friedrich Wilhelm Joseph von Schelling (1775–1854).[12] At least we know that Cousin, like Jacobi, rejected the distinction between the forms of intuition and the categories and influenced his eclectic spiritualist followers in this regard. Hamann's critique of Kant's distinction survived for at least a century in France and is reflected in Durkheim's argument, which we saw in the previous chapter, that the Kantian philosophy could not explain the mind's "surprising prerogative" to impose the categories on experience. But before we go into this history in more detail, it would be helpful to explain Kant's reasons for drawing this

distinction. A discussion of these arguments could promote our understanding of his notions of space, time, and category and how they relate to experience.

In the section called the Transcendental Aesthetic, Kant provided four arguments that space is not a concept and five that time is not a concept. In presenting these arguments, I am less concerned with their validity than with the assumptions that underlie them, specifically his assumptions regarding the notion of a concept. First, Kant argued that space and time are not empirical concepts. The representation of space cannot be obtained from experience, because it is presupposed by our ability to represent objects as outside ourselves and as occupying different places (A23/B38). Similarly, the representation of time is presupposed by our ability to represent things as existing either simultaneously or in succession (A30/B46). He then argued that space is not only an a priori representation but also a necessary one. Although we can think of the absence of objects in space, we cannot represent to ourselves the absence of space (A24/B38–9). He added that if the representation of space were an empirical concept, geometry would consist of nothing but contingent truths and not necessary and universal truths. For example, if space were an empirical concept, at best we would be able to say only that all the space we have observed so far is three-dimensional and not that space must be three-dimensional (A24; cf. B40–1). Time is also necessary: although we can think of time as void of appearances, we cannot represent the absence of time itself. If time were an empirical concept, we could not say with certainty that time is one-dimensional or that different times were successive and not simultaneous (A31/B46).

Having argued that space and time are not empirical concepts, Kant then provided two reasons for believing that they are not concepts at all. First, he argued that there is only one space: "If one speaks of many spaces, one understands by that only parts of one and the same unique space. Also, these parts cannot precede the one all-embracing space, as though they were its constituents (out of which its composition would be possible); rather, they can only be thought in it" (A25/B39). He similarly insisted on the unity of time (A31–2/B47). The significance of these arguments is that they assume his definition of a concept in terms of its being what many representations have in common, that is, what I am calling his generic sense of concept. Space and time are not concepts for him because the relationship between the many spaces or times in particular representations and the one space or time is that of part to whole, not species to genus (cf. Godlove 1996: 443).

There appears to be a contradiction in Kant regarding the unity of space and time. In the Aesthetic, he appealed to the unity of space and time as an argument for their not being concepts. Yet in the metaphysical deduction,[13] as we shall see, he spoke of the pure concepts of the understanding as bringing unity to our representations (A68/B93), which would suggest that the unity of space and time depends on concepts. However, there is no real contradiction here: as he explained in the second edition's version of the transcendental deduction, space and time are not only *forms* of intuition, but can also be represented themselves as the objects of intuition (B160). Considered as objects of intuition, the unity of space and time depends on pure concepts of the understanding:

> In the Aesthetic I had merely included this unity in the sensibility, in order only to note that it precedes all concepts, although it presupposes a synthesis that does not belong to the senses but through which all concepts of space and time first become possible. For since by its means (in that the understanding determines the sensibility) space or time are first *given* as intuitions, thus the unity of this a priori intuition belongs to space and time, and not to the concept of the understanding. (B160–1, note a)

What Kant was saying is that although our cognition of space and time and thus of their unity may require concepts, we nevertheless represent space and time each as one whole or a unity. I shall try to explain the role of the concepts of understanding in providing unity to our objects of representation later in my account of the transcendental deduction.

My interpretation of the assumptions underlying the argument regarding the unity of space and time coheres with Kant's final argument that space and time are not concepts because they are infinite. The argument regarding space is perhaps more clear. Here he said that a concept should be thought of as a representation that is contained in an infinite number of possible representations that fall under that concept. However, no concept can be thought of as containing an infinite number of representations within itself, which is precisely the relation of the parts of space to the whole of it. That is, our representation of space is not something that all our representations of the parts of space have in common: Rather, space, which is infinite, contains all these parts (A25/B39–40). Similarly, the parts of time can be represented only through limitations of one infinite time. Hence, just as in the case of space, the representation of the whole of time is not that of what all the parts of time have in common; that is, it is not a concept (A32/B47–8).

In sum, Kant did not include space and time among the categories because he did not even consider them generic concepts. Hence, at least one thing he appears to have meant by the pure concepts of the understanding is that they are categories in the classificatory sense, as the categories were for Aristotle. Kant still held on to this generic notion of a category in the schematism chapter, which opens with a discussion of how the objects of intuition can be subsumed under the categories (A137/B176). However, when Kant considered the role in cognition of the categories or pure concepts of the understanding, they acquired an additional meaning. As I will explain, in the metaphysical deduction of the categories he introduced the notion that the categories rest on functions that give unity to both our representations and our judgments.

Categories and Forms of Judgment

In order for our intuitions to yield cognitions, for Kant, it is not sufficient for them to be subject to the forms of space and time. They must also be connected or unified by the pure concepts of the understanding. Kant introduced the notion of a function in explaining his sense of a concept: "All intuitions as sensible rest on affections; concepts however rest on functions. By 'function' I mean the unity of the act of ordering various representations under one common representation" (A68/B93). He characterized the function referred to in this passage as a higher-order representation of the unity among several representations that have been brought together by the understanding. For the understanding to unify our representations in this way is for it to make judgments: "All judgments are functions of unity among our representations" (A69/B94). That is, concepts are representations of what several intuitions have in common, and it takes an act of judgment to recognize what these intuitions have in common and bring them under concepts. However, there is more than one way in which a group of representations could be judged as having something in common. For Kant, each of the ways in which a group of representations could be brought under a concept by an act of judgment is called a "function."[14]

Hence, Kant thought that by analyzing the different forms that judgments could take, he could discover the different functions that underlie the concepts of the understanding and thus arrive at a complete list of the categories:

Now we can reduce all acts of the understanding to judgments, and the understanding may therefore be represented as a faculty [*Vermögen*] of judgment. For,

as stated above, the understanding is a faculty of thought. Thought is cognition through concepts. . . . The functions of the understanding can, therefore, be discovered all together if we can give a complete description of the functions of unity in judgments. (A69/B94)

It is not at all difficult to see how such passages could have been read as making psychological claims. Even in the twentieth century, the metaphysical deduction was read as relying on some sort of faculty psychology, one that Kant merely assumed and for which he gave no evidence (Horstmann 1981: 34; Meerbote 1990: 161; Wilkerson 1976: 45). Indeed, sometimes he also used the term "function" in the apparently psychological sense of a power, faculty, or characteristic activity, as, for example, when he characterized the imagination as a "blind but indispensable function of the soul" (A78/B103). However, it is not clear that he meant the term "functions of the understanding" in this psychological sense. Rather, these functions of the understanding seem to be those functions that are presupposed by our concepts of the understanding. Elsewhere, in the chapter on phenomena and noumena, he characterized these as "logical functions" or "logical forms": "Every concept requires first, the logical form of a concept (of thought) in general, and secondly, the possibility of giving it an object to which it may refer. In the absence of such object, it has no meaning and is completely lacking in content, though it may still contain the logical function which is required for making a concept out of whatever data there may be" (A239/B298). If the understanding has a psychological function for Kant, perhaps we could characterize it as one of bringing our representations of objects under one or another of these logical functions.

To return to the metaphysical deduction, Kant argued that these logical functions and hence the categories could be discovered by giving a complete analysis of the "functions of unity in judgments," that is, of the different logical forms that judgment could take. These forms of judgment are presented in Table 2 (A70/B95). For Kant, every judgment includes one concept from each of these four groups. For example, the statement that "All whales are mammals" is universal, affirmative, categorical, and assertoric.

The categories for Kant are simply the twelve logical functions underlying these forms of judgment in their application to the synthesis of intuitions (B143; B159). His definition of synthesis suggests that it is the act referred to in his definition of function (at A68/B93) quoted earlier: "I understand by synthesis, in its most general sense, the act of putting different representations together and of grasping their manifoldness in

TABLE 2. *Kant's Forms of Judgment*

1. Quantity
a. Universal
b. Particular
c. Singular
2. Quality
a. Affirmative
b. Negative
c. Infinite
3. Relation
a. Categorical
b. Hypothetical
c. Disjunctive
4. Modality
a. Problematic
b. Assertoric
c. Apodeictic

one cognition" (A77/B103). He linked the forms of judgment to the categories through his theory that they are but two different expressions of one and the same set of functions:

> The same function that gives unity to the various representations *in a judgment* also gives unity to the mere synthesis of various representations *in an intuition*; and this unity, generally speaking, is called the pure concept of the understanding. The same understanding thus and indeed even through the same operations by which it brought about, in concepts, the logical form of a judgment by means of analytical unity, also introduces a transcendental content into its representations, by means of the synthetic unity of the manifold in intuition in general. On this account these representations are called pure concepts of the understanding that extend a priori to objects. (A79/B104–5)

For Kant, the same concepts or functions provide both the logical form of judgments and the "transcendental content" of our representations, by which he meant a content that is not of empirical origin. This link between form and content represents a major departure from Aristotle, for whom the forms of judgment are considered in abstraction from their content and are quite distinct from the categories. Indeed, the notion of a form of judgment includes what were traditionally called the "syncategorematic" terms, that is, the copula, quantifiers, and logical connectives such as "if," "only if," "unless," and so forth. Syncategorematic terms, unlike categorematic terms, were thought to have no meaning independent of their use in propositions.[15] Kant's reference to the "transcendental

content" introduced by the logical functions of the understanding seems to suggest that these functions did have some independent meaning.

However, an ambiguity in Kant's notion of a logical function arises where he said that the purely logical functions of judgment are indifferent to what, for example in the case of categorical judgment, is the subject of a sentence and what is the predicate: "But as regards the merely logical employment of the understanding, it remains undetermined to which of the two concepts the function of the subject, and to which the function of predicate, is to be assigned" (B128). The *Metaphysical Foundations* provides an example. He said that in the categorical judgment that the stone is hard, we could "exchange the logical function of these concepts [*die logische Function dieser Begriffe umzutauschen*]" to yield "something hard is a stone" (1786 4: 475 n. 1). He then went on to say how these logical functions – now in the plural – become the pure concepts of substance and accident. These passages suggest that there is one function that synthesizes representations into concepts of substance and a second one that synthesizes them into concepts of accident. But then what would be the relation between these two functions and the (apparently) single function that provides unity to a categorical judgment? Kant is not at all clear on this point. As Paul Guyer suggests, the categories must somehow, "for reasons that therefore cannot arise from the logic of judgment alone, carve our experience up" into subjects and predicates (1992: 131).

Of course, Kant did not intend the metaphysical deduction alone to explain how forms of judgment relate to experience. This task would also require the transcendental deduction and the chapters on the schematism of the categories and the principles of pure understanding (cf. B167).

The Transcendental Deduction of the Categories

Where the metaphysical deduction argues that the categories and the forms of judgment rest on the same functions, the transcendental deduction argues that these categories make it possible for us to have knowledge that is not drawn from experience and yet applies to it (B159–60). The transcendental deduction of the categories attempts to show that our experience of objects depends on the same conditions as does the unity of our consciousness and that these conditions are given by the pure concepts of the understanding. By linking the categories to our ability to unify our conscious experience across time, the transcendental deduction connects these functions of the understanding to the schematized categories, which order our representations in time.

Kant contrasted a transcendental with an empirical deduction. An empirical deduction has to do only with questions of the origins of our concepts and does not suffice to justify their use. It "shows the manner in which a concept is acquired through experience and through reflection upon experience" (A85/B117). A transcendental deduction, on the other hand, concerns the justification of the use of these concepts. It must be able to show how these concepts can be valid of objects found in our experience as well as objects that we simply imagine, much as the transcendental aesthetic deals with how geometry can be valid both of imaginary space and of experience. A transcendental deduction starts with something as a given, in this case the cognition of objects and the unity of consciousness, and then proceeds from the given to its necessary conditions, the categories. As Kant said, if we can show that we can think about objects only by means of the pure concepts of the understanding, that will be a sufficient deduction of these concepts and will justify the objective validity of the categories (A97). The transcendental deduction is also supposed to make comprehensible the relationship of the pure concepts of the understanding to the sensibility and thus to all objects of experience (A128).

Because of the criticisms that were raised against the transcendental deduction in the first edition, Kant completely revised it in the second edition of the *Critique*.[16] The first or A edition itself presents two versions of the argument, sometimes called the "objective" (A95ff.) and the "subjective" (A115ff.) deductions.[17] The objective deduction begins with the question of how it is possible to have experience of objects and argues that it depends on our being able to unify our representations, which is made possible by the same conditions that make possible the unity of consciousness. The subjective deduction proceeds directly to the issue of the unity of consciousness and argues that representations can represent something only to the extent that they belong with all other representations to one consciousness (A116).

The objective deduction explains that the understanding unites representations by ordering them in time:

Whatever the origin of our representations, whether they are due to the influence of outer things, or are produced through inner causes, whether they arise a priori, or being appearances have an empirical origin, they must all, as modifications of the mind, belong to inner sense, and as such all our cognitions are yet finally subject to time, the formal condition of inner sense. In time they must all be ordered, connected, and brought into relation. (A98–9)

As Kant had explained in the Transcendental Aesthetic, time is the form of inner sense. In the chapters on the schematism of the categories and the principles of understanding, he went on to explain how the understanding orders representations in time according to rules supplied by schematized categories.

The objective deduction then proceeds to explain that in order to have a cognition of an object, all of our representations of that object must form a coherent whole: "For in so far as our cognitions refer to an object, they must necessarily agree with one another, that is, must possess that unity which constitutes the concept of an object" (A104–5). That is, in order to represent something as an object, such as an apple or an orange, our various representations of shape, color, texture, and other observable properties must be consistent with one another. However, this unity or consistency is not something we can simply perceive in the objects themselves or in what Kant calls a "manifold" or "multiplicity" of empirical intuitions. The unity of the object depends upon the unity of the consciousness that synthesizes or brings together this manifold of intuitions into one cognition (A105). This unity of consciousness, in turn, depends on the logical functions of the understanding: "For this unity of consciousness would be impossible if the mind in cognition of the manifold could not become conscious of the identity of the function whereby it synthetically combines the manifold in one cognition" (A108).

Kant makes the dependence of our cognition of objects upon the unity of consciousness perhaps more clear in the B deduction. The B deduction starts with the unity of consciousness and its necessary conditions and ends with an account of how empirical experience is organized. Here, Kant argued that the "I think" must be able to accompany all of our representations, for otherwise something would be represented without being thought, which would be impossible (B131–2). To say that they are all my representations, however, is tantamount to saying that it is I who unite them. As in the A deduction, Kant argued that the unity of objects of intuition is not in the objects themselves but is supplied by the understanding: "Combination does not, however, lie in the objects, and is not something that can be borrowed from them through perception and in this way first taken up into the understanding. It is, rather, solely something done by the understanding, which itself is nothing but the faculty of combining a priori and of bringing the manifold of given representations under the unity of apperception" (B134–5; cf. B137).

The B deduction attempts to make clear that the mind does not find the representations ordered in time by sensibility and then bring them under concepts. One could arrive at this impression from the objective A deduction, which proceeds sequentially through three different syntheses, one of intuitions, one of memory, and one of recognition under concepts (A98ff.). Rather, Kant intended to say that the pure concepts of the understanding are brought into play from the very start. Toward the end of the B deduction, he explained that even the synthesis of our intuitions of space and time requires the categories (B160–1).

Both the A and B deductions, however, attempt to show that the cognition of objects as well as what Kant called the transcendental unity of apperception depend on the same necessary conditions: that is, the categories. Kant distinguished transcendental from empirical apperception. Empirical apperception, which he also called "inner sense," is our consciousness of our constant flux of internal mental states (A107). It appears to be one of the sources of cognition or "capacities or faculties of the soul" along with sense and imagination (A94; cf. A115). Through empirical apperception, one knows oneself only as an appearance and not the self as it is in itself (B156–7). Transcendental apperception, however, which Kant also called "original" and "pure" apperception, is our consciousness of the unity of all of our representations and of the mind's activity in uniting them (B132). Unlike empirical apperception, transcendental apperception yields no intuition and hence no cognition and can show us at best only *that* we are active intelligences: "In the synthetic original unity of apperception, I am conscious of myself, not as I appear to myself, nor as I am in myself, but only that I am. This representation is a thought, not an intuition. . . . I have no cognition of myself as I am but merely as I appear to myself. . . . I exist as an intelligence that is conscious solely of its power of combination" (B157–9).

The Schematism of the Categories

The task of explaining how the categories relate to experience is not completed until the chapters on the principles of the understanding,[18] which are followed by the chapter on the distinction between noumena and phenomena in which the categories are limited in their application to the realm of appearances. The chapter on the schematism of the categories serves as a transition to these chapters. It seeks a way to mediate the pure concepts of the understanding and objects of experience. As I mentioned earlier, Kant posed the question of the schematism in a way that assumes the generic sense of a concept, that is, in terms of how

to subsume empirical intuitions under the categories, which, since they are *pure* concepts of the understanding, are thus "heterogeneous" with respect to empirical intuitions (A137/B176).

The mediators between the pure concepts of the understanding and the objects of experience are the schematized categories. As I mentioned earlier, these schemata provide the rules by which the understanding orders our representations in time: "Thus an application of the category to appearances becomes possible by means of the transcendental determination of time, which, as the schema of the concepts of understanding, mediates the subsumption of the appearances under the category" (A139/B178).

The schematism of the category of substance is the concept of an object that is permanent in time, while that of a cause is that of an object that precedes some other object in time and that of community involves coexistence in time. The schematism of the category of possibility has to do with the agreement with the conditions of time in general: for example, it specifies that opposites cannot exist at the same time. Actuality corresponds to existence at some determinate time and necessity to existence of an object at all times (A142–5/B182–4). Kant at first said that the schematism of quantity is number, but then in the chapter on the axioms of intuition, it became the notion of an extensive magnitude (A162/B202). The schematism of quality is degrees of reality, which, in the anticipations of perception, he also called "intensive magnitude" (A166/B207). There are only eight schematized categories and eight principles of pure understanding, with the three pure categories of quantity and the three of quality collapsed into one schematized category and principle each.

The schematism chapter opens with the notion of a category as a generic concept. It then characterizes the schemata as things that underlie concepts in a way that brings to mind the functions that underlie concepts (A141/B180). As the schemata are rules of synthesis that bring about the unity of the manifold of intuition (A145/B185), we can interpret these rules as specifying the functions that unite this manifold under concepts.

Problems of Interpretation

Philosophers who came after Kant, especially in France, often regarded his theory of the categories as belonging to a philosophical psychology, interpreting the categories as some sort of psychological capacities that

transform sensations into experience. Janet, for instance, read Kant's sensibility, understanding, and reason as three temporally successive stages in the mental processing of sense experience, for which the categories served as "molds" (Janet 1883: 810). Cousin interpreted Kant's philosophy as saying that his twelve categories are those that human beings just happen to have (1860: 58). Cousin is right in the sense that for Kant these are in fact the categories we have and we have no choice but to use them.[19] But it seems that for Cousin, this merely contingent fact about us had unacceptable skeptical implications. Hence, as I will show in the next chapter, Cousin sought a theological grounding of the principles of the understanding in order to ensure their necessity and universality (1860: 35, 54, 56, 61, 67ff.).

It would appear that many philosophers who came after Kant, at least in France, were mystified by his notion of a transcendental logic and could not grasp or accept the need for this discipline in addition to general or formal logic and rational and empirical psychology. The situation was not helped by the fact that Kant's transcendental logic included a transcendental deduction of the categories in which the transcendental unity of apperception played a significant role. It seems that those philosophers who were mystified by all this transcendentalism in Kant tried either to ignore or to do away with it, replacing it with or assimilating it to one of the more familiar branches of logic or psychology. To do so, of course, is to change entirely the nature of Kant's philosophical project.

As Patricia Kitcher points out, Kant's notion of the transcendental unity of apperception has been subject to a variety of interpretations. She argues that it is neither the first premise of the transcendental deduction, a version of Descartes's cogito, a claim about self-awareness, nor a claim about the self-ascription of mental states (1990, chaps. 4, 5). As she sees it, transcendental apperception is only "a theory about what must be true of cognitive states for them to be states of one mind," which is that their contents must be connected or at least connectable by synthesis (1990: 144). Nevertheless, she concedes that there are passages such as the ones from B157–9 that I quoted earlier where Kant appeared to identify transcendental apperception with the awareness or consciousness of the self as the spontaneous combiner of representations (1990: 122). However, in this passage Kant also distinguished this consciousness of oneself as the combiner of representations from any knowledge of oneself. To have any knowledge of oneself, even merely as one appears to oneself, requires an intuition. But the transcendental unity of apperception provides a mere thought with no intuition. It is difficult to see how such a thought, having

no content, could thus serve as the first premise of the transcendental deduction or of any other argument.

However, Kant's notion that one can be conscious of the self as a combiner of representations without self-awareness seems paradoxical. A way out of this difficulty is suggested by Wilfrid Sellars's distinction between absolute and relative spontaneity. He explained relative spontaneity through an analogy between the mind and a computer. A computer is only relatively spontaneous, as it must be set in motion by causes external to it. Once in motion, it follows a preset routine. Similarly, the understanding is set in motion by sensations and follows the rules that constitute the schematized categories. Whether there is in addition an absolute spontaneity raises the issue of the freedom of the will (Sellars 1974: 79; cf. Kitcher 1990: 253 n. 5). With Sellars's distinction in mind, we can see how Kant could have said that transcendental apperception reveals the synthesizing activity of the understanding without thereby committing himself to the view that we are capable of introspecting the self or will. For Kant, the self or will belongs to what he calls the "noumenal" realm of things about which we can merely think, which is distinct from the phenomenal realm of appearances. Even to speak of noumenal "things" is of course misleading, as the notion of a thing suggests that of an object, with all its Kantian apparatus of concepts, functions, and syntheses of intuitions that he went to great lengths to argue were limited in their application to the phenomenal realm. That is, only the phenomena and not the noumena are presented in either empirical or pure intuitions, and thus we can have cognition of objects only in the phenomenal realm. As Kant said, "I have no cognition of myself as I am but merely as I appear to myself" (B158), that is, through empirical apperception.

In his refutation of Mendelssohn's proof of the permanence of the soul, Kant made it quite clear that because transcendental apperception yields no intuition of an object, it cannot serve as the basis for a spiritualist philosophy (B413ff.). As he explained in a footnote, the proposition "I think" expresses an indeterminate empirical intuition, that is, an intuition that lacks an object yet is nevertheless real. Although the "I think" is empirical, the "I" in this proposition is not an empirical representation or appearance (B423 note). As Kant said in the passages I quoted earlier from B157–9, the transcendental unity of apperception yields no intuition and hence no cognition. Thus at best it can show us only *that* we are active intelligences. Because the "I" or the mere unity of our thought is not given in an intuition, we cannot subsume it under the category of substance. Similarly, this mere "that I am" must be distinguished from the

category of existence, which, as he explained in the schematism of the categories, has to do with the presence of something at some determinate time. Hence, the "I think" cannot be used in any proofs for the existence or permanence of the soul and Descartes's spiritualism is just as invalid as materialism (B420). However, as we shall see, these warnings were either overlooked or rejected by the first generation of Kant's interpreters in France.

Guyer claims that in spite of its ambiguities, the transcendental deduction nevertheless succeeded in setting a new agenda for philosophy. By showing that there is some connection between knowledge of objects and self-knowledge, Kant supposedly undermined the Cartesian philosophy that one could know the self independently of one's knowledge of the outer world, which had to be inferred (Guyer 1992: 155). Guyer's assertions, however, are not historically accurate, at least not for France, where we find Kant's transcendental apperception assimilated to Cartesian self-introspection, which was regarded as providing a foundation for our knowledge of the external world. As we shall see in the next chapter, many of Kant's subtle distinctions were lost upon his earliest French interpreters. Philosophers beginning with Maine de Biran tended to derive the categories from the introspection of the will as cause or the soul as substance. There are multiple differences from Kant here. First, by bringing the soul and the will under the categories of substance and cause, the French spiritualists appear to have ignored Kant's distinction between phenomena and noumena. They also seem to have assimilated Kant's transcendental deduction, which purports to show how the categories make possible the unity of consciousness and our knowledge of objects, with what he called an "empirical deduction" of concepts from their origins. Furthermore, their empirical deduction of the categories was grounded in an empirical apperception of the activity of the mind or will rather than in the transcendental apperception of the unity of thought.

One might object that when Guyer says that Kant transformed philosophy, he is not making a descriptive, historical claim so much as a prescriptive, normative judgment. That is, what he means to say is that, subsequent to Kant's transcendental deduction, philosophers should have realized that it is not possible to seek a foundation for our knowledge in the certainty of our own existence. Thus, if nineteenth-century French philosophers assimilated the critical philosophy to an introspective philosophical psychology, they were simply mistaken or confused.

However, to dismiss the early psychological[20] interpretations of the *Critique of Pure Reason* (1781) as ill-conceived would be to overlook the historical role that these interpretations actually played for about a century after the critical philosophy was first proposed. According to R. Lanier Anderson (2001: 297 n. 11), the psychological reading of the critical philosophy, according to which Kant grounds his epistemology in a theory of the human mind, was first challenged only in 1871 by Hermann Cohen.[21] Subsequent to Cohen's critique, philosophers in Germany began to give a purely epistemological reading to the *Critique,* according to which Kant is interested solely in the necessary conditions for objective knowledge. To cast aside philosophers who failed to recognize immediately what it took ninety years to achieve is not only unfair, but could present an obstacle to understanding some of Kant's works as well. Many of Kant's earliest critics, trying to understand a radically new and difficult philosophy by subsuming it under more traditional concepts, read the *Critique* as if it were offering up simply a new theory of how the individual mind processes its cognitions. This should hardly come as a surprise, given Kant's constant references to mental states, faculties, and processes, which subsequent purely epistemological readings are forced to reinterpret as metaphorical or otherwise explain away.

Kant tried to clarify his position first in the *Prolegomena to Any Future Metaphysics* (1783) and then in the second edition of the *Critique* (1787) at least in part in order to prevent this psychological reading of his philosophy. Toward this end, he began to place less weight on apperception in his later philosophy. As Guyer himself points out, Kant did not emphasize the transcendental unity of apperception in accounts of the transcendental deduction subsequent to 1787. Instead, Kant appealed to the use of the categories – especially those of substance, cause, and interaction – in making possible our knowledge of the positions of objects and events in a single space and time (Guyer 1992: 154). Even in the *Prolegomena,* dating from 1783, Kant did not mention the transcendental unity of apperception right away in his account of the categories. Instead, he stressed how the unity of the object makes it possible to have judgments of experience that are universally and objectively valid (1783 4: 298–9). The *Prolegomena* brings up the transcendental unity of apperception only later, in the account of how the laws of nature are possible (1783 4: 318–19). In this work, just as in the objective deduction in the *Critique,* Kant saw the categories as making possible the unity of the object of knowledge. This unity of the object, in turn, makes it possible to have judgments that are at once objectively valid and universally valid. There would be no reason in

the world for others' judgments to agree with one's own if they did not all refer to the same object – for example, if they referred to perceptions instead: "For there would be no reason why other judgments necessarily would have to agree with mine, if there were not the unity of the object – an object to which they all refer, with which they all agree, and, for that reason, also must all harmonize among themselves" (1783 4: 298). By referring our judgments to objects rather than to subjective perceptions, we try to ensure that they will always hold good for us and in the same way for everybody else. For a judgment to be objective, it must not be limited to a single subject in a single state at a single time, but everybody would have to connect the same perceptions in the same way under the same circumstances (1783 4: 299). Thus, if a judgment is valid of an object it must be valid for everybody, that is, universally valid. Similarly, if it is universally valid it must be objectively valid. What makes it possible for our empirical judgments to be objectively and universally valid are pure concepts of the understanding (1783 4: 299).

It is tempting to see a parallel between Kant's account in the *Prolegomena* of the role of the categories in making universal judgments possible and Durkheim's later emphasis on the social character of the categories. One could say that for both Kant and Durkheim, the categories make intersubjective agreement possible. However, there is an important difference between these two thinkers with regard to the role that the categories play in making this agreement possible. Whereas for Kant the categories are the logically necessary conditions of the unity of the object of agreement, for Durkheim the categories provide a common language or medium for thought and expression. For Durkheim they are thus psychological or social conditions in the empirical realm rather than logical conditions of universal judgments, as they are for Kant. Durkheim's conceptions of universality, necessity, and the categories reflect the philosophical tradition in which he was educated, which we will turn to in the next chapter.

There were other ambiguities in the *Critique* that Kant attempted to clarify in the *Prolegomena* as well. Perhaps the most well known involves Kant's concept of transcendental idealism. Kant defined this philosophy in the following passage: "We have sufficiently proved in the Transcendental Aesthetic that everything intuited in space or in time, hence all objects of an experience possible for us, are nothing but appearances, i.e., mere representations, which, as they are represented, as extended beings or series of alterations, have outside our thoughts no existence grounded in itself. This doctrine I call transcendental idealism" (A490–1/B518–19).

In a review published in 1782 in the *Göttingischen gelehrten Anzeigen*, written by Christian Garve (1742–98) and edited by J. G. Feder (1740–1821), Kant's transcendental idealism was assimilated to Berkeley's idealism. Hamann also found Kant's position to be like Berkeley's (Kuehn 1987: 227).

Kant was greatly annoyed by Garve and Feder's review, to which he replied in the Appendix to the *Prolegomena* (1783 4: 372ff.). The second and third notes to the First Part of the Main Transcendental Question in the *Prolegomena* (1783 4: 288–94) and the "Refutation of Idealism" in the second edition of the *Critique* (B274–9) are also directed against this interpretation. For instance, in the second note, after defining idealism as the view that denies the existence of anything other than thinking things, he said: "I say in opposition: There are things given to us as objects of our senses existing outside us, yet we know nothing of them as they may be in themselves, but are acquainted with their appearances, i.e., with the representations that they produce in us because they affect our senses" (1783 4: 289). In affirming the existence of objects existing independently of us, this passage seems to contradict the definition of transcendental idealism previously quoted from the *Critique*. However, Kant did not change this definition in the second edition, but simply added a footnote to it, in which he distinguished his own "formal" idealism from the "material" idealism that denies the existence of external things (B519).

Jacobi understood Kant perhaps better than did most of his contemporaries. At least he did not attribute Berkeley's metaphysical idealism to him (Lévy-Bruhl 1894: 186–7). Although he initially thought he could enlist Kant as an ally in his struggle against the Enlightenment faith in reason (ibid., 175–6), Jacobi soon came to find Kant's epistemological position unacceptable. Jacobi went so far as to say that Kant's philosophy, which he understood as concluding that all we can know are the products of our own intellectual activity, leads to "nihilism." Nihilism for Jacobi is a kind of skepticism or solipsism that doubts the existence of everything, including an independent natural world, God, other minds, and moral values, and even doubts the permanence of the self. That is, he read Kant as claiming that we can know no other reality than that which we ourselves have created.[22] According to Jacobi, Kant's postulation of the thing-in-itself was nothing but a desperate, inconsistent attempt to avoid this nihilism. As Jacobi saw it, Kant could not regard the thing-in-itself as some sort of independent reality that causes our sensations without violating his own stricture against taking the categories

of substance and causality beyond the realm of possible experience.[23] However, Kant could not regard the objects within our experience as the causes of our sensations either: "For according to the Kantian doctrine, the empirical object, which can only be an appearance, cannot be external to ourselves and thus be at the same time something other than a representation."[24] The only way out of this epistemological dilemma for Jacobi was to adopt something like the common-sense realism of Reid, according to which we have direct perceptions of external objects that are not mediated by mental entities of any sort (Kuehn 1987: 230).[25]

One could argue, as Samuel Atlas (1967: 236) has done, that Jacobi's objection rests on a misunderstanding of Kant's philosophical project. Jacobi was interpreting the first *Critique* as having presented a psychological theory of how sensations are processed rather than an epistemological theory of the necessary conditions for objective scientific knowledge. But once again, although there are professional philosophers today who would regard this psychological reading of Kant as mistaken, it was highly influential at the time. As we shall see in the next chapter, the interpretations of Kant by Jacobi and other German critics played an important role in the transmission of the critical philosophy into France. The eclectic spiritualists treated space, time, and the categories as individual psychological faculties rather than as the logically necessary conditions of experience. Durkheim assumed with the eclectics that the categories belonged to the empirical realm, but regarded them as social rather than psychological in character.

3

The Categories in Early-Nineteenth-Century
French Philosophy

The Introduction of Kantian Philosophy into France

Kant first came to the attention of the French as a moral philosopher during their Revolution. Many regarded him as a supporter of Republican ideals and a proponent of skepticism and atheism (Boas 1925: 165ff.; Vallois 1924: 34). The critical philosophy was only slowly introduced into France due to the difficulty of Kant's work and the fact that few French philosophers read German. Imbued with the French spirit of clarity and precision, many were simply discouraged by the obscurity of Kantian terminology from even trying to read Kant's works. The first French translation of the *Critique of Pure Reason*, by C.-J. Tissot, did not appear until 1835.[1] F. G. Born's Latin translation of this work was published in 1796 and was quickly followed by his translations of the *Critique of Practical Reason*, the *Critique of Judgment*, the *Prolegomena*, and other important books, constituting a four-volume Latin edition of Kant's works. However, this Latin edition was not widely cited by French philosophers at the time (Vallois 1924: 42–8).

For their knowledge of Kant's philosophy, the French at first relied on essays published in French by the Berlin Academy in the late eighteenth and early nineteenth centuries, written by Christian Gottlieb Selle (1748–1800), Johann Jakob Engel (1741–1802), Louis-Frédéric Ancillon (1744–1814), and his son Jean-Pierre-Frédéric Ancillon (1767–1837).[2] To the extent that they relied on the Berlin Academy philosophers for their understanding of Kant, the French were depending on writers who were either critical of Kant or using his philosophy for their own purposes. As Beiser (1987: 165ff.) explains, many of the philosophers in Berlin

and Göttingen at that time saw themselves as defenders of Enlighten-
ment values against what they perceived to be Kant's Humean skepticism.
Selle in particular was allied with Garve and Feder, who were responsi-
ble for the very negative review of the first *Critique*, equating Kant with
Berkeley, that I mentioned in the previous chapter. According to Beiser,
Selle preferred Kant's precritical philosophy and was disappointed in the
Critique, which he regarded as a return to rationalism and scholasticism.
Although Selle was an empiricist, he also wanted to defend metaphysics
against Kant's critical challenges. In his *De la réalité et de l'idéalité des objets
de nos connaissance* (1788), he argued that empirical justification is possible in metaphysics. Kant excluded this possibility because he restricted
experience to sense experience. But in addition to this sort of experience, Selle said, there is a self-awareness or reflection that cannot be
separated from perception but is a constitutive part of it. There is thus
no firm dividing line between the empirical and the metaphysical. To
justify metaphysical ideas, all we need to show is how they are constitutive
elements of experience (Beiser 1987: 179–80). Selle's position that the
transcendental apperception of the "I think" that accompanies all our
perceptions could reveal metaphysical truths was consistent with his preference for the precritical philosophy. Kant, at least in his inaugural dissertation of 1770, *De mundi sensibilis atque intelligibilis forma et principiis*,[3] did
not rule out the possibility of attaining metaphysical knowledge through
the use of the intellect alone. Selle's philosophy is also conducive to the
thought of French philosophers who came later, such as Maine de Biran
and Cousin.

These early accounts of Kant's philosophy also tended to give the
Critique a psychological as much as an epistemological reading, for instance by equating Kant's notion of the a priori with the innate. In the
Essai ontologique sur l'âme (1799) and the *Mémoire sur les fondements de la
métaphysique* (1803), L. Ancillon characterizes a priori principles and notions as "innate dispositions of our soul" that constitute simply our way of
seeing things. The same interpretation was promulgated by J. Ancillon in
his *Mélanges de littérature et de philosophie* (1809) (Vallois 1924: 23–4). However, to say that an idea or notion is "innate" is simply to make the claim
that it is inborn and implies nothing about its justification or warrant. "A
priori," on the other hand, is an epistemological concept, applied to concepts or judgments whose warrant is independent of experience. It would
appear that the confusion arises when the claim that a priori principles
or concepts are logically prior to experience is read as saying that they
are *temporally* prior and hence innate. However, all that is meant by the

claim that these principles are logically prior is that they are presupposed by or logically necessary conditions of experience.

Other early expositions in French of Kant's philosophy include Charles Villers's (1765–1815) *Philosophie de Kant*, which characterized Kant's philosophy as revealing the profound meaning of Protagoras's "man is the measure of all things" (1801: 352). Villers promoted a psychological interpretation of Kant's transcendental analytic, describing the categories as the "subjective and a priori laws of our understanding" (1801: 290). Madame de Staël (1766–1817) drew on this book in writing the chapter on Kant in her work *De l'Allemagne* (1813), which also provided a brief introduction to other German philosophers.[4] Johannes Kinker's (1764–1845) *Essai d'une exposition succincte de la critique de la raison pure* (1801), translated from the Dutch, is reputed to have been slightly better than Villers's book. Kinker, at least, explained Kant's account of the paralogisms involved in reasoning about the human soul (Vallois 1924: 148), which Villers omitted in his chapter on the transcendental dialectic (1801: 311–46). The chapter on Kant in Joseph-Marie Degérando's (1772–1842) *Histoire comparée des systèmes de philosophie* (1804) also presented an influential psychological interpretation of Kant's understanding and its functions (Vallois 1924: 205).

However, even these early expositions of Kant's philosophy were read initially only by a few philosophers. Kant's philosophy did not receive widespread attention in France until Cousin began teaching courses on Kant at the Faculté des Lettres (Vallois 1924: 49; Janet 1885: 5ff.). Cousin first taught Kant's moral philosophy in 1817 and then his critical philosophy in 1820.[5] Although Cousin endorsed Kant's moral philosophy, he was deeply critical of Kant's epistemology, as we shall see. Cousin's original exposure to Kant's thought was through a group of liberal scholars and former *idéologues* that used to meet regularly to discuss philosophy in Paris beginning around 1814. Cousin was probably introduced to this group by Pierre Paul Royer-Collard (1762–1845), his professor at the Sorbonne, who first introduced Reid's common-sense philosophy into France and for whom Cousin was appointed as a *suppléant* the following year.[6] The group also included Maine de Biran, his friend the physicist André-Marie Ampère (1775–1836), the previously mentioned historian of philosophy Degérando, the naturalist Georges Cuvier (1769–1832) and his brother Frédéric Cuvier (1773–1838), Philippe-Albert Stapfer (1766–1840), the former Swiss minister to Paris who had turned to intellectual pursuits, the historian François Guizot (1787–1874), who had formerly worked for Stapfer and who subsequently achieved fame in French politics, and

others (Boas 1925: 183; Hofmann 1995: 133, 147; Luginbühl 1888: 318–
20). Many in this group did not even read German and relied on secondary sources such as Villers's. Stapfer endorsed Villers's interpretation to this group, as he and Villers were friends, helping each other
with their writings (Vallois 1924: 98–9 n. 106). Cousin owed much of his
knowledge of philosophy to the members of this group and to another
Sorbonne professor, Pierre Laromiguière (1756–1837), as philosophical
instruction in the lycées had been suppressed under Napoleon (Janet
1885: 6–7; Kennedy 1978: 97). Cousin began his studies of Kant with the
French expositions, but he also read the Born translation and knew
enough German to at least check passages. He claimed to have spent two
years of his young manhood "buried in the vaults of Kantian psychology"
(Vallois 1924: 286). He no doubt was also familiar with Jacobi's reading of
Kant, since, as I mentioned in the previous chapter, he had spent a month
in the summer of 1818 with him and Schelling in Germany.[7] Cousin must
have felt an especial affinity for Jacobi's interpretation to the extent that
Jacobi, like Cousin's teacher Royer-Collard, was a follower of Reid.

In defending his theory of the categories, Cousin also drew some arguments from the work of Biran, who attempted to ground the categories in
the experience of willed effort. As I mentioned in Chapter 1, Cousin and
Biran were still setting the terms of debate regarding the categories as
late as the 1880s, when Durkheim began teaching philosophy (Durkheim
1884a; Janet 1883; Rabier 1884). Thus, it is important to consider Cousin
and Biran in order to understand Durkheim. As we shall see, Durkheim
shared with these philosophers the assumption that we are able to introspect forces or powers when he theorized that the category of causality
derives from our internal experience of social forces. Whether we are
able to have internal experience of force or power and whether this is
the same thing as causality, especially in the realm of human action, are
issues I will discuss later.

Victor Cousin's Eclectic Spiritualism

In his lectures on *The True, the Beautiful, and the Good*, Cousin said that
he preferred the name "spiritualism" rather than "eclecticism" for his
philosophy. By "spiritualism" he meant the philosophy that subordinates
the senses to the spirit and teaches the spirituality of the soul, the liberty
and responsibility for our actions, and the existence of God (1860: vi–
vii).[8] Nevertheless, Cousin's theory of the categories reflects an eclectic
mix of Descartes's rationalism, Reid's common-sense philosophy, Kant's

philosophy and the critical reactions to it in Germany, and Maine de Biran's philosophy of inner experience. Hence, the compound name "eclectic spiritualism" is perhaps the best name for Cousin's school of thought. I choose the term "school" deliberately, as Cousin, through his administrative positions, exercised a powerful influence on the philosophical curriculum in nineteenth-century France, as I explained in Chapter 1.

Cousin employed what he called the "*méthode psychologique*" in his philosophy, a method that he said was invented by Socrates, developed in modern philosophy by Descartes, and perfected by Kant. He appears to have meant two things by this method: First, he used this term to refer to the grounding of all philosophy, including logic, metaphysics, and ethics, in an introspective psychology that inquired into the laws, scope, and limits of our cognitive faculties (1846: 67, 313). For Cousin, to make psychology the foundational philosophical discipline was to follow the Cartesian tradition in modern philosophy, a tradition that he believed got fully underway with Locke and Condillac (1860: 3–6). He identified this foundational discipline with what the Germans called "rational" as distinct from empirical psychology. This rational psychology included the study of the universal and necessary principles of reason from which he believed the categories were derived. According to Cousin, the study of these principles was "nearly the whole of philosophy itself" (1860: 34).

In the second sense of the term *méthode psychologique*, Cousin used it to refer to the very method of introspection that this rational psychology employed (1846: 4, 313). For Cousin, the study of the universal and necessary principles of the mind rests on "the most certain of all experiences, that of consciousness" (1860: 36). This foundational psychological discipline must rest on neither hypotheses nor empirical laws (1860: 34). His strong opposition to the use of hypotheses in psychology reflects the influence of Reid, who in turn had adopted this stance from Newton.[9] Cousin thought that rational psychology must have the sort of absolute certainty that he believed Descartes was able to attain only through the method of internal observation (1860: 3):[10] "Between skepticism and hypothesis is the consciousness with the sovereign evidence of the facts that belong to it, incontestable facts that cannot be touched by any accusation of hypothesis and that are invincible to all the efforts of skepticism. There is the primitive and permanent certainty where man naturally rests and where the philosopher ought to return after all the detours and frequently the aberrations of reflection" (1846: 4).

Cousin held that people have a need for fixed, immutable principles. These include the principles that objects must exist in space, that events must occur in time, and that every event must have a cause. He argued that such universal and necessary principles concerning space, time, causality, and even final causality are required for science, mathematics, and morality. In morality, for example, if someone were to tell us that a murder had been committed, we would ask where, when, by whom, and why the crime was committed. Thus the concepts that are necessary to Cousin's universal and necessary principles are much like Aristotle's categories, in that they are the concepts that correspond to the most basic questions we can ask about things. If we are told that love or ambition committed the murder, we immediately think of a lover or an ambitious person, as we cannot think of an act without an agent or of a quality or phenomenon without an underlying substance. We also assume the concept of personal identity in considering the accused person to be the same as the person who committed the crime even if his actions and properties have changed. If the accused defends himself by saying that the victim was so unhappy that life was a burden to him, we respond by saying that even if the crime led to an increase in happiness, murder is an injustice and is never permitted (1860: 19–23, 27–8).

For Cousin, these universal and necessary principles are distinguished from merely general principles that are based on experience. Experience merely shows us what things are at the time and place we observe them; it does not show us what they necessarily are in all times and places (1846: 49). For instance, it is not a universal and necessary principle that day follows night, as we can conceive the possibility of being plunged into perpetual darkness. However, Cousin thought that we could not conceive alternative systems of mathematics, alternative moralities, or alternatives to the principle of causality, in which events would commence without any cause (1860: 23–4). According to Cousin, Kant held that the universality and necessity of these principles are marks of their a priori character (1846: 49).

However, in an argument that is picked up and repeated by French thinkers up through and including Durkheim, Cousin said that neither the Kantian critical philosophy nor traditional empiricism could account for the necessary and universal character of these principles. Empiricism could reveal at best only the origin of concepts like space, time, substance, and causality but could not at all explain how they are necessary for experience (1860: 38–9). Kant, on the other hand, did show how these concepts are necessary for experience, but limited our experience to the

phenomenal realm. To limit the universal and necessary principles of space, time, causality, and the other categories to the phenomenal realm, Cousin thought, is to restrict them to subjective experience and to deprive them of objectivity: "Kant . . . confines the power of [these principles] to within the limits of the subject who conceives them, and, to the extent they are subjective, declares them without legitimate application to any object, that is to say, without objectivity" (1860: 54).

Cousin recognized with Kant that from the fact that one must represent objects in space, it does not follow that they must exist in space or that space exists independently of us. In the same way, Cousin understood that from the fact that we represent things in time, we could not conclude that time exists in itself without making a hypothesis. Nevertheless, Cousin believed that Kant's denial that space and time existed independently of us entailed a kind of subjective idealism that led to skepticism about the existence of the external world independent of our perception of it (1846: 91–3). As Cousin understood it, Kant's philosophy that our knowledge is limited to the phenomenal realm also implies that we have no knowledge of ourselves as active beings with free will or even knowledge of God. Thus, borrowing a term from Jacobi, Cousin accused Kant of "nihilism," that is, of leaving us with nothing in which to believe (1846: 308).

One's first impression is that in order for Cousin to have argued that Kant deprived space, time, and the categories of objectivity, he must have willfully misread Kant. As I explained in Chapter 2, Kant's whole project was to give an account of the conditions that make our knowledge of objects possible. Indeed, Cousin went on to raise against Kant a point that Kant himself might have made: "In fact, when we speak of the truth of these universal and necessary principles, we do not believe that they may be true only for us: we believe them to be true in themselves, and still true if our mind were not there to conceive them. We consider them as independent of us; they appear to us to impose themselves on our intelligence by the force of the truth that is in them" (1860: 58).

However, Cousin's was not just a willful misreading of Kant. Rather, Cousin simply refused to grant Kant his concept of an object. For Kant, as we saw, an object was something that belonged to the phenomenal realm. However, he did not think of our representations of objects as merely subjective. In fact, it was our very ability to conceive objects in the phenomenal realm that made it possible for us to form universal or intersubjective judgments about our experiences. Cousin, on the other hand, appears to have used the term "object" to refer to things in the

world independent of anyone's possible experience of them. One could say that Cousin opposed Kant's philosophy from the point of view of the common-sense concept of an object. Indeed, Cousin accused Kant of having violated common sense by making space and time merely forms of our sensibility rather than things that exist in the external world (1846: 298). According to Madden (1984: 97–8), Cousin thought that the false premise in Kant's philosophy of space and time is that we are aware of only our own mental representations, an assumption that Kant supposedly shared with his empiricist predecessors. Cousin, like his teacher Royer-Collard and his friend Jacobi, adopted instead Reid's philosophy that we directly perceive things in the real world and that our perception is not mediated by such things as sensations, sense impressions, or representative ideas. In his lectures on the history of Scottish philosophy, given in 1819, Cousin considers Reid's refutation of the theory of representative ideas to be one of his most important contributions to philosophy (Cousin 1864a: vff., 275ff.).[11]

According to the common-sense philosophy, a person is not phenomenologically aware of sensations, sense impressions, or ideas. If we were aware of such entities mediating our perception of the world, we would never be in a position to compare them with real objects in order to determine whether these ideas adequately represented these objects. On the other hand, if we perceived physical objects directly, there would be no need of sensations to represent them. For Reid, the notion of a representative idea was a useless hypothesis that the philosophy of the human mind should dismiss, as it only leads to skepticism (Hatfield 1995: 208, 229 n. 119). Madden quotes from Cousin's *Elements of Psychology* the following passage that seems to be in essential agreement with Reid: "If by ideas be understood something real, which exist independently of language, and which is an intermediate between things and the mind, I say that there are absolutely no ideas" (Cousin 1864b: 280–1).[12] Cousin held similar views with regard to internal perception, denying that it is mediated by representations of any sort and thus rejecting Kant's claim that we can know ourselves only as appearances (1846: 102–6).

On Madden's reading, it appears that Cousin sought to avoid skepticism concerning our knowledge of the external world by affirming that we have direct perception of objects in the external world. As I will show in the following chapters, Janet and Durkheim also understood Cousin as having rejected the existence of representative ideas. Of course, even if we could directly perceive the external world without intermediates, this would be no guarantee of certainty in our knowledge of the world.

There are other ways in which we could be mistaken besides by having some sort of intermediary mental entity that misrepresents what is in the world. We could also be mistaken in our judgments about what it is that we directly perceive, for instance if what we perceive is very far away or very small, if the lighting is poor, if the sensation is short-lived, if we have been using drugs or alcohol, and so on.

A German influence on Cousin is reflected in his rejection of Kant's distinctions among the forms of intuition, the concepts of the understanding, and the ideas of reason. In an argument that brings Hamann's *Metakritik* to mind, Cousin saw no justification for these distinctions since all these ideas and concepts concerned the necessary conditions of experience and performed the same function of imparting unity to our experience (1846: 320–2).[13] Cousin agreed with Kant that space and time were forms of sensibility or intuition, but only in the sense that we cannot represent external objects except in space and that we cannot represent either external or internal objects except in time (1846: 79). He did not accept that they were forms of sensibility in the sense that they were a priori principles belonging to a faculty separate from the understanding or reason. He agreed with Kant that space and time were not derived from experience, but thought that this meant that they did not have their source in our sensibility. For Cousin, the sensibility was nothing more than our capacity for receiving sensations, as he thought that Kant's notion of a "pure sensibility" was a contradiction in terms (1846: 317–19; cf. 81–4, 88–90). Hence, for Cousin the notions of space and time, along with the categories and the ideas of reason, all belonged to what he called the "faculty of knowing" (1846: 138, 150–1).

Another of Kant's important distinctions that Cousin denied is that between empirical apperception and transcendental apperception. As we saw in Chapter 2, in the B deduction Kant had said that through empirical apperception, he knows himself only as an appearance, while through transcendental apperception, he is conscious of himself not as he appears to himself, and not as he is in himself, but only that he is (B156–7). Referring to this passage, Cousin asked whether this transcendental apperception is a consciousness of our own existence as beings or as phenomena. Since Kant rejects the latter, he must mean that we know ourselves as beings (1846: 102–3). Admittedly, there is some difficulty with Kant's position that he has a pure apperception of his own existence, since existence is one of his categories and thus would apply only to appearances. However, Cousin misused this opportunity to make a valid

criticism of Kant, insisting that since existence and substance are the same category, to know that we exist is to know that we are substances. He then went on for several pages raising polemics defending the idea that we apperceive ourselves as substances against the notion that we know ourselves only as appearances, arguing that the latter position leads to skepticism:

> Far from the self being a phenomenon, it knows itself as the self only by distinguishing itself as one and the same being from the various and changing phenomena with which it is in relation. To ignore that and to pretend without any proof that the unity of consciousness is empirical, and that the self, because it is witnessed by the consciousness, is only a phenomenon, in the strict sense of the word, is, by a superficial psychology, to lead philosophy astray down a path at the end of which, I repeat, is either absolute skepticism, if one wants to be rational, or chimeras and hypotheses. (1846: 105)

Cousin then charged Kant with having reduced the transcendental logic to empiricism through his changes to the second edition (1846: 106). Like Jacobi, Cousin preferred the first edition as a more genuine statement of Kant's views.[14]

Cousin's denial of the distinction between the categories of existence and substance is part of his larger critique of Kant's list of categories, which he found to be somewhat artificial or contrived. Cousin may be right that Kant appeared to have added certain unnecessary concepts merely to achieve the systematicity of having four groups of three. Hence, he regarded Kant's three categories of quality – that is, reality or affirmation, negation, and limitation – to be but three expressions of the same fundamental category of affirmation. Under the heading of relation, Cousin would not distinguish reciprocity from causality. These criticisms are fair enough. However, Cousin also refused to distinguish the category of existence under modality from that of substance under relation, since he believed not only that all substances exist but also that everything that exists is a substance (1846: 140–2), which just begs the question against Kant.

In his account of Kant on the paralogisms of pure reason, Cousin continued his polemic against the notion that we know ourselves only as appearances, accusing Kant of having raised only sophistical refutations against Descartes's argument that we know ourselves as substances. According to Cousin, Kant had set an impossible task in calling for a pure rational psychology that borrows nothing from experience. In trying to establish a foundation for this rational psychology, Kant came up with a mere "I think" that had no empirical content, a mere abstraction

consisting of the logical subject of our thoughts. However, Cousin argued, we can know about this abstraction only through the thoughts that are its attributes. This raises the following dilemma: we could begin with a consciousness of our thoughts, but this consciousness, since it would be empirical, could not provide the foundation for a rational psychology. Alternatively, we could begin with a transcendental "I think," but this "I think" cannot really be separated from our consciousness and experience. Either way, we could not achieve any knowledge of this I that thinks, a conclusion that was unacceptable to Cousin. Kant's mistake, he thought, was to try to separate rational from empirical psychology. Reason and experience cannot teach us anything in abstraction from each other. The subject of our thoughts can be known only through our thoughts. The unity and identity of the subject are known only by way of contrast with the multiplicity of our thoughts. From the fact that our consciousness contains empirical elements, it does not follow that it is exclusively empirical and thus that our knowledge of the self rests solely on an empirical basis (1846: 157–67).[15]

Cousin concluded that our consciousness or apperception shows us that we are the subjects of our thoughts, and hence substances, and also that we are the causes of our actions (1846: 327–8). Defending the idea that we know ourselves as causes, he criticized Kant for thinking that the freedom of the will could not be known through introspection. He regarded Kant's discussion of free will in the third antinomy of pure reason as purely artificial. For Cousin, whether or not we have free will was not a question to be answered through philosophical argument. Rather, he thought that it could be known "by the aid of that immediate apperception which we have of ourselves. I am conscious of the power to resist to a certain extent forces external to mine. What are all the arguments in the world in opposition to a fact like this?" (Cousin 1846: 195) Where else, Cousin asked, could we have obtained the idea of liberty except from consciousness? If our liberty were not a part of our consciousness, he argued, it would not be our liberty (1846: 195–6).

Cousin's appeal to the apperception of willed effort here derives from the French sensationalist tradition initiated by Étienne Bonnot de Condillac (1715–80). Its most recent representative was Maine de Biran, an older member of Cousin's philosophical circle in Paris. Cousin actively promoted Biran's work, republishing in 1834 his *Examen des leçons de Laromiguière* (1817) in a posthumous edition that also contains Biran's replies to his critics. Cousin reissued the 1834 volume in 1841 as the fourth and last volume of Biran's *Oeuvres philosophiques* (Maine de Biran

1841). Due at least in part to Cousin's efforts, Biran's philosophy was subsequently to prove as influential in France as Cousin's.

Maine De Biran

It would be less than accurate to say that Biran was a Kantian. Rather, Biran was developing his own views in opposition to what he took to be Kant's, based largely on his reading of secondary sources. Not knowing any German (Moore 1970: 47 n. 1), the only work of Kant's that Biran seems to have read was Kant's Latin inaugural dissertation of 1770, which, as I mentioned earlier, is far more sympathetic than the *Critique* to the possibility of metaphysical knowledge. He tended to rely on the French expositions of Kant's philosophy I discussed earlier, citing, for example, Degérando and Ancillon (fils) (e.g., 3: 43; 8: 139 n. 2).[16] He also relied on conversations with Ampère, Degérando, and Stapfer for his knowledge of Kant (Boas 1925: 173, 183; Hofmann 1995: 144ff.). In a letter written to Biran in 1812, Ampère accused him of not really understanding Kant and relying too heavily on the interpretations of Degérando, Villers, and Destutt de Tracy. These philosophers, Ampère claimed, had distorted Kant for their own purposes, twisting his words to make him say exactly the opposite of what he did say (7: 520).[17]

During the Revolution, Biran had been associated with the *idéologues* Pierre-Jean Georges Cabanis (1757–1808) and Antoine Louis Claude Destutt de Tracy (1754–1836), who was deeply unsympathetic to Kant. In the year X (1802), Destutt de Tracy had presented to the Académie des Sciences Morales et Politiques a memoir titled "De la Métaphysique de Kant," in which he attacked the very idea of a priori knowledge and defended French sensationalist empiricism as the best antidote to metaphysical dogma (Kennedy 1978: 117–20; Vallois 1924: 1125ff.). The *idéologues* sought to replace metaphysical inquiries into the nature of the soul with what they took to be the science of ideology, or the science of the formation of our ideas, which they were attempting to ground in a physiological psychology. Tracy summarized their philosophy in the slogan "Ideology is a part of zoology" (1801: xiii). Cabanis, who was trained in medicine, pursued this line of inquiry in his *Rapports du physique et du moral de l'homme* (1802).[18] Biran appears to have been more sympathetic to Kant, trying to reconcile the critical philosophy with the ideological program.[19] Biran's own physiological approach to philosophical questions is reflected in such writings as his "Observations sur les divisions organiques du cerveau" (1808), in which he suggested that the

phrenologist Francis Joseph Gall (1758–1828) should have taken Kant's forms of sensibility and categories into account in enumerating the cerebral organs (5: 101).[20]

Biran attributed to Cabanis and Tracy the identification of the self with willed effort (3: 180; 8: 178). Previously, Condillac had appealed to the experience of resistance to willed effort as a premise from which to argue for the existence of external reality. The *idéologues* gave this argument a new twist, pointing out that the experience of resistance first of all assumed the existence of the self (Kennedy 1978: 52–3). Biran developed this idea further, arguing that all of our knowledge, including that of our own existence, depended upon the experience of willed effort and the resistance to the will that effort entails.[21] In this early period of his career, Biran also proposed that the idea of causality or active force derives from "the internal sense of my own causality."[22]

In his later essays, Biran assimilated this internal sense (*sens intime*) to Kant's apperception and then tried to derive the categories from the introspection of willed effort. The best account of his views on the categories that Biran published was his *Examen des leçons de Laromiguière* (1817), with its two appendixes containing his replies to Hume and Engel on the origin of our idea of causality. In 1834, Cousin republished the *Examen* and its appendixes along with other, previously unpublished material, including Biran's reply to Stapfer's objections.[23] Biran actually published very little during his lifetime, but left behind a vast body of manuscripts. His most detailed attempt to derive the categories from willed effort appears in his *Essai sur les fondements de la psychologie et sur ses rapports avec l'étude de la nature*, which he worked on between 1810 and 1812 but never managed to complete or publish. What we have of it was cobbled together posthumously by Ernest Naville (1816–1909) and published as the first two volumes of Biran's *Oeuvres inédites* in 1859 (Moore 1970: 191–4). It is not clear whether Cousin knew these manuscripts. Perhaps needless to say, neither Naville's nor Cousin's editions of Biran's works would satisfy contemporary standards of scholarship. However, Naville's edition was known and cited by subsequent nineteenth-century writers, such as Paul Janet (1883: 109) and Élie Rabier (1884: 65).

Like Cousin, Biran made no distinction between transcendental and empirical apperception in his works. Indeed, he used the terms "internal sense," "apperception," and "reflection" interchangeably. He also seems to have identified apperception with the intellectual faculty of Kant's inaugural dissertation. In this early work, Kant distinguished the sensitive from the intellectual powers of the mind. The sensitive faculty presents things

as appearances or phenomena, while the intellectual faculty presents the noumena, or things as they really are (1770 2: 392). Of course, there is no such intellectual cognition of noumena in the *Critique*. As Paul Guyer and Allen Wood remind us (1998: 36), Kant made it clear that he was using "noumenon" only in the negative sense of something that is not an object of sensible intuition and not in the positive sense of an object of nonsensible intuition. There is no nonsensible or intellectual intuition in the *Critique* (B307). Nevertheless, Biran appears to have regarded apperception as a special intellectual faculty that reveals the self as noumenal object. For Biran, there must be some means of knowing or of "immediately apperceiving" what the self is (11: 407–8).[24] The method of apperception is to provide an indubitable Cartesian starting point for his entire philosophy. This indubitable starting point is our knowledge of ourselves as beings with the power freely to initiate action (8: 67–8).

According to Biran, a theory of the categories should be pursued as a "psychological" rather than an "ontological" inquiry. The ontological approach for Biran appears to be a purely philosophical or logical investigation into the necessary conditions of knowledge. The psychological approach proceeds from the internal observation of the self as an active being. Although Biran's internal sense is like Kant's empirical apperception insofar as it is supposed to give us knowledge of ourselves, it is also like his transcendental apperception in that it reveals the self merely as the subject that accompanies all of our representations: "By the internal apperception or the first act of reflection, the subject distinguishes itself from the sensation or the affective or intuitive element localized in space, and it is this very distinction that constitutes the fact of consciousness, personal existence" (11: 324).[25]

Like Kant also, Biran held that apperception reveals the spontaneous activity that accompanies all of our representations of objects. However, where Kant had identified this spontaneous activity with "I think" (B132), Biran identified it with "I will": "The connection between the will and the motion, which constitutes the internal immediate apperception, is not the object, but the proper subject of every external perception" (11: 411). Similarly, whereas for Kant it was the understanding that brings unity to the manifold of representations, for Biran it was the will that performs this task (8: 244). For Biran as for Kant, the unity of the objects of experience depends on the same conditions as does the unity of our experience. However, they understood these conditions differently, as Biran did not see the activity of the understanding as distinct from that of the will.[26]

Biran's apperception is also different from Kant's in that Biran used it in an empirical rather than a transcendental deduction of the categories, in which they are derived from our inner experience of willed effort. He saw the category of causality, as well as that of being, substance, or existence, as having its origin in our consciousness of our own efforts. We conceive causal forces in external bodies only on the model of the force that is constitutive of the self (8: 26–8). He took the category of causality to be more fundamental in an epistemological sense than the rest. For Biran, Leibniz, with his emphasis on the activity of the monad, came much closer to the primitive fact of apperception than did Descartes, with his emphasis on the substantiality of the soul (8: 219–22). Biran then proceeded to derive what he regarded as the categories of liberty, necessity (8: 249–50), unity (8: 243–4), and identity (8: 245) from the experience of willed effort as well. Biran's derivation of the categories from the apperception of the self departs from Kant in more than one way. In the transcendental deduction of the categories, Kant did not derive the categories from apperception. Instead, he attempted to justify their application to the objects of our experience by arguing that they are the same concepts that make possible the unity of our experience. It is this unity, not the categories, that is revealed by apperception, according to Kant, as I explained in the previous chapter.

Because the experience of willed effort is basic to his derivation of the categories, Biran felt it necessary to answer Hume's arguments that we do not experience the power of the will. The first empiricist philosopher to seek the source of our idea of power in our experience of the will was actually Locke, in *An Essay Concerning Human Understanding* (1690). According to Locke, our experience of external bodies shows us only the transfer of motion from one to another but never the beginning of motion. Hence, we obtain a much clearer idea of active power by reflecting upon what goes on inside us when we experience that we can move a part of the body merely by willing it (Book II, chap. 21, paragraphs 1–4). Like Locke, Hume argued in both *A Treatise of Human Nature* (1739, Book I, part iii, section xiv) and the *Enquiry Concerning Human Understanding* (1748, section vii) that the idea of power or necessary connection cannot be perceived in any single instance of the action of bodies on each other. However, Hume disagreed with Locke's conclusions about the source of this idea, arguing that we do not perceive any power in any single instance of the action of the will on either the parts of the body or ideas in the mind. Although we may experience the motion of the body or the calling up of an idea following the command of the will, we are not

conscious of the means or the power by which these effects are produced, and hence cannot obtain the idea of power from this source. Instead, Hume proposed that the idea of power or necessary connection arises from the repeated experience of one sort of event being conjoined with another. From the repetition of similar instances, the mind forms the habit of expecting one after the appearance of the other, and it is this feeling of expectation that is the source of our idea of power or necessary connection (1748: 74–5; cf. 1739: 163–4).

Biran recognized that, if valid, Hume's arguments would undermine any attempt to derive the category of causality from the internal experience of willed effort. Hence he felt it necessary to answer Hume's arguments that we do not experience the power of the will, particularly its power over the parts of the body. He did not quote Hume's actual arguments but only paraphrased them, distinguishing seven different arguments in Hume. I will not try the reader's patience by rehearsing all seven of Biran's arguments, for they all more or less turn on the same point. In reply to Hume's arguments that we are not conscious of the means by which the will acts on the body, Biran argued that the facts of internal experience are not known in the same way as facts about external experience (11: 367). In particular, he said, introspection is not mediated by any image, intuition, or representation of an object in the way that external perception is. Apperception yields an immediate sense of the power that initiates voluntary motion (8: 229ff.; 11: 369–70). Here again, Biran's apperception resembles the intellectual faculty of Kant's inaugural dissertation, which is a way of knowing distinct from the sensibility and which does not involve the representation of an object in an intuition (1770 2: 396). In reply to Hume's argument that anatomy suggests that the immediate effect of the will is on the nerves and muscles and not on the limb, Biran argued that in order to simultaneously perceive both the action of the will and that of the nervous system, one would have to be two people at once (8: 231–2).

There are several issues to sort out in Biran's replies to Hume. Not only does he assume that internal perception, unlike external perception, is unmediated by any sort of representative ideas, but he seems to think that this fact guarantees both that we have access to the action of the will and not just its effects and that this access yields certain knowledge. However, as I argued earlier in this chapter, the fact that a perception is unmediated by any sort of mental representation is no guarantee that it is not mistaken. Furthermore, why should we believe that an unmediated internal perception would give us access to causes and not just their

effects? If it could, why should not an unmediated external perception also reveal causal powers? Biran might insist that external perception is not unmediated, but this only raises the question of why the possibility of the perception of causal power should turn on the absence or presence of a mediating representation.

Furthermore, if the apperception of the activity of the self does not involve the representation of an object, it is not at all clear how it can serve as the model for our idea of external forces, as the very idea of a model suggests that of an image or object. Indeed, without an object of representation, apperception could not be the source of any idea at all, for what is an idea without an object? The most that apperception could reveal is simply *that* we willed to move a part of the body. In other words, apperception simply reveals the intentions behind our actions. Although there is a sense in which intentions can be causes, they are not causes in Hume's or Biran's sense, which includes the notions of power, energy, or force as well as that of a necessary connection between the cause and the effect. When we introspect a necessary connection between an intention and an act, we do not thereby introspect the causal power by which the will moves the body.

These objections were not raised against Biran in nineteenth–century France, however. Hardly anyone at that time distinguished the idea of causal power from that of necessary connection. Indeed, one of the relative strengths of Durkheim's sociological theory of the categories is that he provided separate accounts of the origins of these two ideas. Nevertheless, he retained from the eclectic spiritualists the idea that we experience causal power, except that he substituted the power of social forces for that of the individual will. According to Durkheim, social forces "are part of our internal life, and, consequently we not only know the products of their actions but we see them acting" (1912a: 522, t. 1995: 369).

During Biran's time, a different sort of objection to his theory of the categories was raised by Stapfer, one of the other members of Biran and Cousin's Parisian circle that I mentioned earlier. Stapfer argued that even if we originally had obtained the idea of cause from our experience of willed effort, we could not derive the principle of causality from it. That is, the apperception of our own willed effort could in no way establish that every event must have a cause. Any relation of cause and effect derived from willed effort would at best be contingent, particular, and finite, and not necessary, universal, and infinite (11: 403–4).

Biran's reply to Stapfer is essentially psychological, arguing that the principle of causality is necessary for thought. He distinguished this

"*necessité de conscience*" from logical necessity: logical necessity is that which is "imposed by the fixed conventions of language," while the *necessité de conscience* is that which is "imposed by the very nature of things or by that of the mind" (11: 425). According to Biran, we start with the causal relation between the will and its effect as necessary and invariable. External motions or changes are then attributed to causes that are conceived in imitation of the self. But because these external causes are modeled on the will, they are also conceived as necessary and invariable. He goes on to argue that not only causality but all the categories can only be understood as necessary and universal (11: 426–7). He regards this process by which we model external causes on the self as a kind of induction that is of a "higher order" than that used in the physical sciences and "often infallible" (11: 428). Biran thus claimed to have shown "the sort of hyperbolic universality and necessity of which this principle admits in its derivation from the fact of consciousness" (11: 433).

This psychological account of the principle of causality did not sit well with Cousin. In effect, Biran had only explained why it is that people believe in a universal and necessary principle of causality and had not tried to justify this principle. Such principles cannot be established by any sort of induction. An induction that led us to universally and necessarily associate a cause with every phenomenon would simply presuppose the principle of causality and thus beg the question. If the induction is not universal and necessary, it cannot replace the principle of causality and in fact destroys rather than explains this principle (Cousin 1860: 48). However, Cousin had no better solution to this problem than to assert that God is the source and foundation of this and other categorical principles (1860: 67ff.), and has given us the gift of reason to allow us to perceive their truth in "a sphere of light and peace" (1860: 61).

As I mentioned earlier, Kant, at least in the second edition of the *Critique*, explicitly denied that the categories were simply ways of thinking placed in us by the creator, as this would deprive them of their necessity and render them merely subjective and illusory (B167–8). To be fair, Cousin said that God placed in the human mind not these principles but only the ability to perceive their truth. These truths exist in God's mind, not ours (Cousin 1860: 70). Nevertheless, Cousin's attempt to justify the universal and necessary principles of reason by invoking God clearly mixes epistemological with metaphysical issues. Furthermore, to make them depend on God would seem to make them not necessary but merely contingent upon a cause, unless he wanted to argue that God necessarily had to choose just these principles and no other. But to

make this argument would be to mix different concepts of necessity. The necessity of the categorical principles is an epistemological necessity: that is, they are the necessary conditions of knowledge. Cousin appears to have confused this sense of necessity with some sort of either metaphysical, logical, or moral necessity. That is, if his intention were to ground their necessity by placing them in the divine mind, this would be to make them necessary in the sense of not dependent on any cause. But if his intention were to argue that these principles were necessary in the sense that God could choose no other, this would have to be because these principles were either logically necessary, in the sense that their opposites are contradictory, or morally necessary, in the sense that God had to choose these principles in order to achieve his ends.

In the next chapter we shall see how the following generation of eclectic spiritualists, as represented by Paul Janet, deftly avoided these problems with Cousin's metaphysical justification of the categories while following Maine de Biran's approach to deriving the categories from self-consciousness.

4

The Later Eclectic Spiritualism of Paul Janet

Academics sometimes trace their intellectual lineage in genealogical terms. If Cousin were to be called one of Durkheim's intellectual grandfathers, it would be because of the lineage that passes from Cousin to Durkheim through Paul Janet, who was one of the members of Durkheim's dissertation committee.[1] Although Janet was far too young to have studied with Cousin before Cousin left teaching for administration, Janet maintained a personal relationship with Cousin for twenty-two years, beginning in 1844 when he served a year as his secretary (Janet 1885: 483–4). Janet, who held the chair in the history of philosophy at the Faculté des Lettres, was the leading representative of the eclectic spiritualist school of thought during Durkheim's early academic career (Brooks 1998: 39). He was on the committee that drafted the 1880 philosophy *programme* or syllabus for the lycées. His textbook, the *Traité élémentaire de philosophie à l'usage des classes*, covers the prescribed topics and questions in that syllabus. It was widely adopted in the lycées, went through many editions, and was even translated into Spanish.[2] In what follows, I will be drawing my account of Janet's philosophy from this text.

Durkheim appears to have used Janet's text when he taught philosophy at the Lycée de Sens in the academic year 1883–4, the class in which André Lalande took the recently discovered notes.[3] The other main lycée philosophy text that Durkheim knew was Élie Rabier's *Leçons de Philosophie*. Both Janet's and Rabier's texts are representative of eclectic spiritualism at the time Durkheim began his career, and Durkheim cited both of them in his later published works.[4] However, the first two volumes of Rabier's text, on psychology and logic, appeared only in 1884 and 1886, respectively, and he never wrote the volumes on ethics and metaphysics to

complete a full set of texts for the year-long course in philosophy. Hence, Rabier's text would not have been available when Lalande studied with Durkheim, although Durkheim may have used it after he was transferred to the Lycée de Saint-Quentin in 1884. Janet's *Traité*, on the other hand, as I mentioned in Chapter 1, first appeared in 1879.[5]

In addition to being part of Durkheim's intellectual lineage, Paul Janet was the familial uncle of Pierre Janet (1859–1947), the well-known psychiatrist. Pierre was an exact contemporary of Durkheim, having begun the study of philosophy at the École Normale Supérieure the same year as Durkheim, 1879. While Pierre was a student there, his uncle encouraged him to pursue an interest in physiological and experimental psychology, introducing him to Dastre, the professor of physiology at the Sorbonne, and thus helping him gain a place in Dastre's laboratory. Paul also encouraged Pierre to go to medical school after he had completed his philosophical studies at the École Normale (Brooks 1998: 165; 1993: 133).[6] Although the *Traité* reflects Paul Janet's own interest in empirical work in psychology, as it opens with chapters on physiological psychology and endorses the study of animal and pathological psychology, the relationship between these parts of the book and the rest of it is not entirely clear. Nevertheless, Janet's mixing of philosophy with empirical science makes him conceptually as well as generationally intermediate between Cousin and Durkheim.

There are other intellectual affinities and relationships between Janet and Durkheim as well. For instance, Durkheim's terminology of moral and social facts can be found in Janet's *Traité* (1883: 7).[7] But perhaps more important for Durkheim, Janet endeavored to make the concept of representative ideas philosophically respectable again. His methodology, in which he defended the use of hypotheses in the sciences, was consistent with the postulation of these mental entities, which he found necessary for explaining the meanings of general concepts. Durkheim then did not have to defend the appeal to mental entities and was able to take the next step of distinguishing collective from individual representations, thus separating the subject matter of sociology from that of psychology. By identifying the meanings of general concepts, including the categories, with collective rather than individual representations, Durkheim transferred the categories from the eclectic spiritualists' philosophical psychology to the new discipline of the sociology of knowledge. Where Janet's and Rabier's texts followed Maine de Biran in deriving the category of causality from internal reflection on the individual will, Durkheim, as I will show in Chapter 6, substituted social forces instead.

Finally, Durkheim's eliminative mode of argument for his theory of the social causes of the categories in *The Elementary Forms of Religious Life* can be found in Janet's *Traité*. Durkheim, as I explained in Chapter 1, argued that neither empiricism nor rationalism could account for the universal, necessary, and variable character of the categories. This argument originated with Cousin, who, as we saw in the previous chapter, argued that neither the critical philosophy nor traditional empiricism could account for the universal and necessary character of the categories and, as we shall see, was picked up and developed at length in Janet's textbook.

Thus, through his accounts of method, representative ideas, and the categories, Janet – perhaps unwittingly – helped Durkheim to establish his sociology. One might object that I am placing far too much importance for the development of Durkheim's thinking on what would have been the equivalent of an American junior college philosophy textbook today. In reply, I would argue that few things other than writing for publication concentrate the mind on intellectual topics as much as having to teach them, and that Durkheim did in fact teach philosophy in lycées from 1882 until 1887, except for a one-year sabbatical. Janet's brand of eclectic spiritualism was thus on Durkheim's mind every workday at the same time that he was beginning to develop his sociological ideas. Janet's text is also indicative of the intellectual climate in which Durkheim defended his first major work in sociology, *The Division of Labor in Society* (1893b), as a philosophy dissertation. But the value of understanding Janet for understanding Durkheim's theory of the categories should become clear after I give an account of the relevant ideas in Janet's text and Durkheim's early philosophy course in this and the following chapter. I will begin with Janet's views on method.

Janet on Method

According to Janet, the antihypothetical attitude characteristic of the post-Newtonian period had begun to change in recent years (1883: 474). He differed sharply from Cousin on this issue, defending hypotheses as necessary to direct experimentation in the natural sciences (1883: 468). Janet willingly conceded the hypothetical status of Cartesian vortices, Stahlian phlogiston, and Ptolemaic astronomy, regarding Descartes's vortex hypothesis in particular as a work of scientific imagination and genius (1883: 152, 450). Nevertheless, he thought genius alone without method does not suffice for science. Hypotheses must be subject to the following

conditions: they must be based on the facts, not be contradicted by any fact, and be fecund in leading to new research and experiments. In addition, a hypothesis is good if it is simple (1883: 474–5).

These more liberal attitudes toward hypotheses were held by other philosophers in the generation that succeeded Cousin as well. Émile Boutroux (1845–1921), for example, who taught Durkheim while he was a student at the École Normale Supérieure, defended the hypothetical, contingent nature of science (Lukes 1973: 57–8). Rabier, who also taught at the École Normale Supérieure for one year while Durkheim was a student there,[8] expressed similar views in his textbook as well. The more open-minded attitudes toward hypotheses among the latter-day spiritualists may perhaps be attributed to their reading of Claude Bernard. For example, Durkheim cited him in the Sens lectures and followed him in defining the experimental method in terms of hypothesis testing rather than the manipulation or artificial creation of phenomena (1884a: 368–9; cf. 13–14).[9] Renouvier, who saw hypotheses as needed for directing experimentation at least in the physical sciences, may also have been influential in this regard.[10] Unlike the eclectic spiritualists, Renouvier was educated at the École Polytechnique, where he not only acquired some firsthand knowledge of the methods of science but also came into contact with Auguste Comte, who defended the method of hypotheses in his *Cours de philosophie positive* (1830–42).[11] These liberal attitudes toward hypotheses may have also been due to recent developments in the sciences, including the life sciences. Darwin and his supporters defended the use of hypotheses in science as part of their defense of evolutionary theory. For instance, John Tyndall defended evolution this way in his paper "The Scientific Use of the Imagination," which was published in Battier's French translation in the *Revue scientifique* in 1871 and cited in Rabier's textbook (1884: 206).[12]

Janet's liberal attitude toward hypotheses allowed for the postulation of representative ideas in psychology. He defended this hypothesis against the attacks of philosophers like Reid, Royer-Collard, and Cousin, pointing out that they had shown only that representative ideas do not mediate external perception. According to Janet, representative ideas were still useful in providing accounts of memory and the meanings of our general terms (1883: 369).

Although Janet disagreed with Cousin about the need for hypotheses and representative ideas, he nevertheless agreed with him about the need for philosophy to seek a psychological foundation in the introspective study of the faculties of the human mind (1883: 13). Psychology,

for Janet, is the part of philosophy that studies the human mind and its faculties. Although it is based on observation, it uses an entirely different method of observation than the natural sciences. Psychological observation is internal or subjective rather than external or objective. That is, psychological phenomena are perceived by conscious reflection or introspection (1883: 30). In psychology, "it is the same subject who observes and who is observed" (1883: 488). Whereas in the natural sciences the phenomena are studied from without as the effects of unknown causes, in psychology this method of internal observation "penetrates further than the phenomenon: it reaches right up to the affected subject" (1883: 488). Yet Janet did concede that a psychology that rested on introspection alone would be incomplete. "Subjective" psychology must be joined to such "objective" studies as animal, physiological, pathological, and "ethnological" or cross-cultural psychology. However, this objective psychology would be unintelligible if it were not grounded in analogies with ourselves, which make it possible for us to understand what is going on in the minds of others (1883: 490).

Janet on Meaning

As I mentioned earlier, Janet thought that the hypothesis of representative ideas was necessary for giving an account of the meanings of general terms. He distinguished two parts to the meaning of a term, which the scholastics called its "comprehension" and "extension."[13] The comprehension of a term consists of the elements shared by all the individuals that fall under the extension. It is the "collection of characteristics that distinguishes the represented idea from every other" (1883: 378). The extension, on the other hand, is the collection of individuals that present these characteristics. The extension of a general idea is in inverse proportion to its comprehension: the more general an idea, the fewer the number of their shared attributes (ibid.). This distinction is not the same as the philosophers' current distinction between sense and reference, which derives from Gottlob Frege (1892). At that time in France, the comprehension or sense meaning of a term did not appear to have been identified with anything like rules of usage or synonymy. Instead, it was identified with a mental entity or idea. Janet distinguished ideas, which come from the understanding, from images, which come from sensation, and then distinguished two sorts of ideas: First, there are concepts, which are "those that we call abstract and general ideas" and belong to the discursive understanding. Second, there are ideas that apply immediately to

immaterial and intellectual objects, such as the soul and God, and that belong to the intuitive understanding (1883: 154–5).

It may strike today's reader as very odd that Janet identified the meanings of general terms with abstract general ideas. After all, had not Berkeley and Hume long ago ridiculed and rejected this notion in Locke? Berkeley had challenged the reader to form the abstract general idea of a human being or an animal that would consist in what is shared in common by everything denoted by each of these terms. He suggested that we could not even form the abstract general idea of a triangle that would answer to everything from scalene to equilateral triangles. For Berkeley, a word becomes general not by being the sign of an abstract general idea but by standing for several particular ideas (1710: Introduction, secs. 9–13). Curiously, in his account of Berkeley's arguments for idealism, Janet made no mention of the role played in these arguments by Berkeley's rejection of such abstract ideas as the philosophers' notion of matter as being-in-general that supports properties (1883: 806–7; cf. Berkeley 1710, Part I, sec. 17). Although Janet did seem to recognize that there is some difficulty about the formation of abstract general ideas, he tried to get around this by suggesting that most of our general ideas are obtained through education and language (1883: 161).

Perhaps Janet's apparent acceptance of abstract general ideas can be explained as follows. As I mentioned earlier, Cousin had fancied himself a follower of the common-sense philosopher Reid, and Janet of course was a follower of Cousin. Reid (1983: 246), in the *Essays on the Intellectual Powers of Man* (1785), took up Berkeley's arguments against abstract ideas, but only to criticize him for drawing the wrong conclusion, that is, for rejecting abstraction rather than the hypothesis of ideas. In his endeavors to bring back the hypothesis of representative ideas, Janet may have accepted the common-sense philosopher's interpretation of the import of Berkeley's arguments and regarded them as a threat to ideas rather than to abstraction.

Also, Janet disliked the nominalist aspects of Berkeley's philosophy. For Berkeley to say that general terms do not signify abstract general ideas but are only names for classes of particular ideas would be, from Janet's point of view, to provide only the extension and not the comprehension of general terms. Janet argued that if words did not signify ideas, there would be nothing in our heads as we speak, and we would be talking the way parrots do, without meaning (1883: 162). It is difficult to say whether this argument is more unfair to Berkeley or to parrots. Janet anticipated the objection that it is possible at least in algebra to consider

signs in abstraction from the thing represented by each sign.[14] He replied that nevertheless the signs retain the degree of signification necessary to perform the operation. To wit, one sign may represent a known quantity, another the unknown that is sought, and so on. He rejected as incoherent what he called "absolute" nominalism, according to which signs do not signify anything. A "reasonable" nominalism, he added, would merely say that one could not have general ideas without words. But this view, he thought, is no different than conceptualism, the philosophy according to which general terms correspond to actual concepts or ideas (1883: 162–4).

A more detailed account of conceptualism was provided by Durkheim in his course at the Lycée de Sens. He explained that conceptualism was Peter Abelard's (1079–1144) middle way between nominalism and the Platonic realist doctrine that general ideas correspond to things such as essences or forms that are supposed to exist independently of us. According to conceptualism, general ideas are neither mere words nor independently existing substances, but exist "subjectively" or "substantially" as "concepts" in the minds of each individual who knows the meaning of the corresponding term (Durkheim 1884a: 207–8). These concepts are then shared mental entities much like Durkheim's later "collective representations," and one must seriously consider the surprising possibility that this central notion in Durkheim's sociology was suggested to him by his reading of a medieval philosopher. During the nineteenth century, Abelard's works had become accessible and familiar to French scholars through the efforts of Cousin, who had edited and published the *Ouvrages inédits d'Abélard* in 1836 and Abelard's two-volume *Opera* in 1848–59. However, as Cousin had dismissed the hypothesis of representative ideas existing independently of language, he presumably would have rejected the hypothesis of shared mental entities or concepts as well. Janet's methodology, on the other hand, is consistent with the postulating of shared mental entities in providing an account of linguistic meaning. Thus Janet through his philosophical arguments and Cousin through his historical scholarship provided Durkheim with some of the tools he needed to construct his sociology.

The Categories

Janet's theory of the categories is eclectic in two senses of the term. First, it synthesizes elements from several different philosophical systems, drawing on Aristotle's and Kant's accounts of the categories as well as Maine de Biran's derivation of causality and the other categories from our internal

experience of willed effort. Second, Janet's account of the categories resembles Cousin's in important ways. Like Cousin, Janet regarded an investigation of the nature and origin of the categories as a central part of a foundational philosophical psychology. Also, he followed Hamann and Jacobi in refusing to make Kant's distinctions among the forms of sensibility, the categories of the understanding, and the ideas of reason. Instead, like Cousin again, he located all these notions and principles in what he variously called the "faculty of reason" or the "understanding" (1883: 188).

According to Janet, it is the job of philosophy to investigate the universal and necessary principles that are presupposed by the sciences (1883: 872). These include the two purely analytic principles of identity and contradiction as well as such synthetic a priori principles as that every body is in space, every event takes place in time, every property presupposes a substance, and every thing that happens has a cause (1883: 192–3). These principles in turn presuppose the categories:

When one reflects on these principles of the sciences, one perceives that they imply a certain number of general, fundamental notions, which are in some way the very essence of the human mind. They are common to all the sciences and inherent in human thought. They are mixed in all our judgments, just as they are also mixed in all reality. They are, for example, the notions of existence, substance, cause, force, action and reaction, law, purpose, motion, becoming, etc. Thus these principles, which one finds at the root of all the sciences, are at the same time the principles of human reason, and whether one considers them as one or the other, there is a science of first principles. (1883: 8)

Janet, like Durkheim, did not present a systematic list of categories the way that Kant did, but left the set of categories rather open-ended. Elsewhere he also included space, time, unity, identity, infinity, perfection, necessity, the absolute, and even the true, the beautiful, and the good among the categories (1883: 188–9). However, he regarded five of these notions as the most fundamental: substance, cause, space, time, and the absolute (1883: 196). According to Janet, all of these notions share the following three distinguishing characteristics: (1) they are the highest of all concepts, which would make them either the most abstract and general for the empiricists or the "first and irreducible elements" of thought and being for those who assign another origin to them; (2) they are universal and necessary, that is, they are

universal in the sense that they are mixed in all our judgments, that they are implied in all our thoughts and that we cannot think without them. They are in all our thoughts, and in that very way I am led to believe that the

objects that they represent are *everywhere and always*: and it is for that reason that they are *universal*. I cannot think without them, and in that very way I am led to think that their objects cannot but exist in and through all the phenomena: and it is for that reason that they are *necessary*. (1883: 189; Janet's emphasis)

Finally, (3) they are the fundamental or first ideas of all the sciences. The category of space or extension is fundamental to geometry, as is number and quantity to arithmetic and algebra, motion and force to physics and mechanics, substance to chemistry, life to physiology, the good to morality, the beautiful to aesthetics, and the absolute to metaphysics or ontology (1883: 189–90, 872).

The Origin or Source of the Categories

Janet argued for his theory of the categories, according to which they derive from the activity of the human intellect, in the same way that Cousin before and Durkheim after him argued for theirs, that is, through the elimination of alternative empiricist and a priori accounts. Among the empiricists, Janet counted Epicurus, Gassendi, and Condillac, as well as more recent British associationists such as John Stuart Mill and Herbert Spencer.[15] He divided the empiricists into those who say that the categories are abstracted and generalized from external sense experience and those like Locke who recognize a kind of internal experience as well and who thus approach idealism. Janet contrasted the empiricists with the idealists, who hold that the categories have their origin in the mind itself independently of experience. Among the idealist theories he included Plato's doctrine of reminiscence, Aristotle's theory of the active intellect, Descartes's and Leibniz's theory of innate ideas, Malebranche's theory of vision in God, and Kant's theory of a priori principles (1883: 194–5, 891–3). Of these, Janet at least claimed to prefer Aristotle's theory that the active intellect extracts the intelligible forms from the sensible (1883: 216). Admittedly, it is difficult to see what makes Aristotle an idealist for Janet rather than an empiricist. It may be the fact that Aristotle did not regard the mind as merely passive. Indeed, Janet assimilated Aristotle's active intellect to Descartes's innate faculties. However, Locke resorted to such faculties as well. Be that as it may, for Janet, Aristotle's theory appears to have been a stalking horse for Maine de Biran's derivation of the categories from *internal* experience, much as Malebranche's theory that the categories are perceived by us in God appears to have been a stand-in for Cousin's theory.

Like Cousin, Janet rejected empiricism for its failure to account for the universality and necessity of the categories and first principles. Janet attributed this argument to Leibniz and Kant (1883: 205). To say that they are necessary is to say that their opposite is impossible, and to say that they are universal is to say that they are true everywhere and always. Experience, however, "can only give us that which is, and not that which cannot not be; that which is in a particular time and place, and not everywhere and always" (1883: 207).

For Janet, "substance" is the notion of that which remains of a being when one abstracts from it the phenomena by which it manifests itself. For an empiricist, however, a substance cannot be anything but a collection of phenomena. Against this empiricist notion of substance, he cited Royer-Collard's argument that in order for a substance to be a collection of phenomena, there must be somewhere that the unity or individual formed by the collection exists. Also, Royer-Collard argued that a collection presupposes a mind that makes the collection. However, the mind itself is a substance that cannot be just a collection of mental phenomena, for then there would have to be another mind to make this collection. Also, there would have to be somewhere for this collection of mental phenomena to exist. To these arguments, Janet added that the mind perceives itself as a unity and not as a collection of phenomena (1883: 196–8). Hence, the empiricist philosophy cannot explain the origin of the notion of substance.

Similarly, Janet thought that empiricism could not account for the notion of causality, either. For empiricists like Hume, Thomas Brown, and Mill, the cause is the invariable antecedent of a phenomenon. According to Janet, however, the notion of causality is not the same thing as that of relations of regular succession. Even in a world without regular succession, we would still believe in causality. The belief in causality is the belief that beneath the phenomena there is something else that leads to their existence. It is the belief that nothing comes from nothing. Even the freely willed actions of human beings or God are causes. A miracle involves the suspension of the laws of nature but not of causality (1883: 198–200).

Janet anticipated the empiricist reply that the belief that every phenomenon has a cause is generalized by induction from experience. That is, we begin in every case of the succession of phenomena by forming the habit of expecting the second after the first is perceived. We then arrive by induction at the law or principle that all phenomena belong to relations of regular succession, and conclude that every phenomenon is preceded

by an antecedent that is its cause (1883: 209–10). Janet responded to the empiricist that this process of generalizing from our expectations would at best give us only subjective, not objective, necessity. Habits are subjective and do not apply to the objective world: "How," he asked, "by a simple habit of my mind, am I able to impose a law on things?" (1883: 210) In other words, Janet appears to have identified the causal relationship with some sort of necessary connection among things themselves independent of our conceptions of them, and distinguished this sort of connection from a psychologically necessary connection among ideas as well as from the notion of invariable succession. Whether there genuinely are such necessary connections in things is a huge philosophical issue that Janet did not address. Be that as it may, Janet's argument here invokes a very different notion of causality than that in his previous argument, which distinguishes causality from laws of nature and attributes it to the human and divine wills.

In a perhaps less equivocal argument against the empiricists, Janet maintained that the number of even familiar phenomena for which we do not know the cause far surpasses the number of those where we do. He quoted Helmholtz to the effect that if the "law" of causality is based on experience, its inductive base is rather weak. Finally, he asked, if the principle of causality rests on the association of ideas, then what does association rest on? In order for our ideas to associate, the phenomena that suggest them must actually be related. That is, it is necessary for us to observe their constant succession. But what is the cause of that constant succession? Janet anticipated the suggestion that in asking this question, we are merely taking the principle of causality we formed by induction and applying it to the relations of succession from which we generalized it. However, he could not accept this answer, for he said that the very fact that we ask this question reflects that we cannot accept constant succession as a primitive or basic fact but must find its cause (1883: 211–12).

Another reason Janet gave that the association of ideas alone does not provide a sufficient explanation of the principle of causality is that, as every association supposes the connection of two ideas in the same consciousness, the association of ideas depends on the unity of consciousness (1883: 215). It seems then that for Janet, the concepts of causality and substance are equally the work of the human mind that holds ideas in itself and finds relationships among these ideas, and that empiricism cannot explain where these relationships come from. Instead of these empiricist and associationist accounts, Janet adopted Maine de Biran's derivation of the notion of causality from internal experience, a theory

that he also found in Locke (1883: 200). I will discuss Janet's derivation of this and the other categories later, after I finish explaining his reasons for rejecting empiricist and Kantian a priori accounts.

According to Janet, the categories of space and time are not derived from experience, either. He agreed with Kant that these notions have the following characteristics: First, they are not derived from experience but are the conditions without which experience would not be possible. Second, they are necessary in the sense that we can suppose the nonexistence of things in space and time, but we cannot suppose the nonexistence of space and time themselves. Third, they are not abstract general notions, extracted from particular things, since there are not several different spaces and times from which we can separate their common properties. Janet appears to have drawn this third characteristic from Kant's arguments in the Transcendental Aesthetic that space and time are not concepts, which I explained in Chapter 2. There is only one space and time, and particular spaces and times are only parts of this single space and time, which is, finally, infinite (1883: 202–3). Elsewhere, citing Mill's *An Examination of Sir William Hamilton's Philosophy* (1865), Janet explained that some empiricists have attempted to derive the notion of "extension and its various determinations" from the sense of motion that we get from a series of muscular sensations (1883: 127–8). For a Kantian, however, our sense of motion and our notions of the parts and directions of extension presuppose this single, infinite space.

The last of the five fundamental categories for Janet is that of the absolute. According to Janet, this and the related notions of infinity and perfection could not be derived from experience, either. He drew on Descartes's argument from the *Meditations* that we cannot get the notion of the infinite from experience because the infinite is not merely the negation of the finite. Nor, he continued, can we get the idea of an actual infinite from a potential infinite. For Janet, the notions of the absolute, perfection, and infinity, although distinct, are alike in being unconditional and part of the metaphysical idea of God. This idea comes from neither internal nor external experience. "It must come from a higher source, and that is that which one calls pure reason" (1883: 203–4).

Janet finally considered one last empiricist theory, a theory of the inheritance of acquired concepts that he attributed to Spencer, George Henry Lewes, and Robert Murphy[16] – and that Durkheim attributed to Spencer alone (1912a: 18 n. 2, t. 1995: 12–13 n. 15). According to this theory, our ideas of time, space, cause, and substance represent the accumulated experience of the species and are to be explained in the same

way as instincts: a series of generations contributes to the formation of associations or habits that are then transmitted in somewhat Lamarckian fashion to succeeding generations. Janet compared this theory favorably to Leibniz's innate ideas and Plato's doctrine of reminiscence. However, he also found fault with it as just another form of empiricism, except that in this case it is the species and not the individual that is the blank slate that is totally shaped by external relations. Even with the advantages that accrue to the empiricist theory from the accumulation of generations of experience, he believed, it cannot explain such notions as infinity or such principles as that of causality. The difference between individual and hereditary empiricism is only one of degree, and all the same objections still apply. Above all, he criticized hereditary empiricism for not being able to explain the notions of a substantial self and God (1883: 212–15).

For Kant, of course, the notions of God and the soul were not categories but ideas that result from an illusory theoretical use of pure reason. If we set aside Janet's criticism that these two concepts cannot be explained by the theory of the inheritance of acquired concepts, Janet's major objection to this theory is not that the categories are inherited, since innate ideas would be as well, but that they are the product of evolution. An evolutionary explanation of the categories would suggest a physiological, materialist basis for them that would be the very antithesis of eclectic spiritualism. Although it might be too strong to call it a contradiction, it is nevertheless curious that Janet began his text with a discussion of physiological psychology, alluded to mental pathologies in the medical literature, and yet resisted evolutionary accounts of the categories.

Janet's criticism that evolutionary theory could no more account for the necessity and universality of the categories than could any other theory that assigns them causes in experience is entirely valid. Such accounts could not serve as epistemological justifications of the applications of the categories to experience. However, a Darwinian account of the categories could at least escape Janet's objection to Lamarckian theories that assume that the entire human species rather than the individual is the blank slate that is written on by the environment. The ability to represent perceptions in space and time, to perceive causal relations and permanent substances, and so on could have been present although to a lesser degree in the primate species from which we evolved. For a modern-day Darwinian, these conceptual abilities are not produced by association or habit but are the result of natural selection acting on creatures actively engaged in seeking sustenance, safety, and sexual partners in their environment.

Janet on Kant

Although Janet rejected empiricism and seemed to accept Kant's account of space and time, he did not find Kant's theory of the categories wholly satisfactory. According to Janet, the basic problem of philosophy for Kant was that of explaining how thought agrees with its object. Kant rejected empiricism, according to which thought is modeled on the object, because it does not guarantee certainty in science. But he also rejected the idea of a preestablished intellectual harmony between the laws of thought and the laws governing objects, since it affords no guarantee that our thought will conform to objects and thus leaves us with a purely subjective belief in this conformity. According to Janet, that left Kant with the alternative that "it is the object that is modeled on thought and that takes its form from it" (1883: 809). On Janet's reading of Kant, all knowledge or cognition is composed of two elements: matter, from sensation, and form, which is given by the categories of the human mind: "Each of these concepts pre-exists in us, and, combining with the phenomena from without, constitute that which we call objects" (1883: 810). In describing the categories as "pre-existing in us," Janet was regarding them as innate psychological capacities. Indeed, he understood Kant as having held that the phenomena are processed sequentially in the mind by the sensibility, the understanding, and reason:

These phenomena coordinate, group, and classify themselves through taking the form of our mind. First, they enter into the form of space and time, and in that way coordinate themselves in *series*. Then they enter into the mold of the understanding and enchain or connect themselves by *causes* or *substances*. Finally the series form *wholes* of which the reason requires the completion, or rather that it completes itself by the idea of the *absolute*. (1883: 810; Janet's emphasis)

Janet then criticized Kant's philosophy on two counts. First he said that although he could accept that the phenomena must take the form of our sensibility, since the only way we can see things is in space and time, he could not see why the phenomena must agree with the laws of the understanding (1883: 811). Invoking the shopworn billiard-ball example, he asked why the motion of the second ball should be produced by the first "for the sole reason that our mind has need of it" (ibid.). According to Janet:

We do not find in Kant himself any response to the solution to this question; it is completely arbitrarily that he supposes that the lower faculty [viz., the sensibility] will take the form of the higher faculty [viz., the understanding]. The phenomena form a chaotic matter and they will remain chaotic matter whatever the laws

of the understanding may be. Doubtless, in this case, there would not be any science. But what makes it necessary that there be any science? (1883: 811–12; my parenthetical clarifications)

At the beginning of this passage, it appears as if Janet were simply about to rehash Hamann, Jacobi, and Cousin's argument that Kant could not explain how our mental faculties interact. As I suggested in Chapter 2, this argument anticipates Durkheim's criticism of the a priori philosophy for ascribing a "surprising prerogative" to the mind to give form to our experience.[17] But Janet pushed this line of objection further than these other thinkers did. With the billiard-ball example, Janet raised the issue of how Kant is able to justify not just synthetic a priori principles like the principle of causality but also particular causal laws, such as the laws governing the collision of billiard balls. As I explained in addressing this issue in Chapter 2, Friedman argues that such laws should be regarded as instances and not consequences of the principle of causality. The a priori principles and categories of the understanding are ultimately justified because they can be used to explain how the laws of science are possible. However, I do not think that this answer would satisfy Janet. For Janet, to argue that the categories are necessary because they make science possible is only to raise the issue of whether science is necessary. He was correct to point out that there is nothing necessary about science. There could possibly be no such creatures as us that have knowledge of the world. But to raise this objection is to misunderstand Kant's larger project. Kant did not want to argue that the categories must necessarily exist. The purpose of the transcendental deduction is merely to demonstrate that the categories are necessary for the sort of knowledge that we have. Kant's goal was simply to show how the sort of knowledge that we have applies to or is valid of experience, not to prove that there must be creatures who have such experience.

Janet attributed his second criticism of Kant to Jacobi. He asked, where do the phenomena come from? From the noumena? If so, then would this not be the application of the concept of causality to things-in-themselves, which Kant said one ought not to do? Janet thought that Kant regarded the phenomenal objects in space as the causes of our sensations, but believed that this answer led to a kind of idealism that revived the traditional dualism between knowing subject and known object (1883: 812). Once again, in this second objection Janet misunderstood Kant's project. Like Jacobi and Cousin before him, Janet read Kant as having presented an analysis of individual cognitive processes rather than an analysis of the necessary conditions for objective knowledge. It is

only their psychological reading of Kant that leads to subjective idealism. Kant's critical or transcendental idealism does not deny that there are objects existing outside us that affect our senses, but only that we know them other than as appearances in space and time (1783 4: 289). In other words, it is not objects but space and time that are ideal for Kant. This ideality of space and time explains how mathematics, and ultimately the categories as well, are valid of appearances, which is what he hoped to show. Although Kant may have left the relationship between the phenomenal and the noumenal world undefined, this was not what he was trying to explain.

Janet's Derivation of the Categories

Having rejected empiricist and evolutionary accounts of the categories as well as Kant's transcendental arguments, Janet had to seek an alternative theory of the categories. Of all the idealist theories, he claimed to find Aristotle's the simplest, least conjectural, and closest to the facts. In order to explain the categories, he said, it is not necessary to suppose that they are innate ideas or representations. It would suffice to say that what is innate is our ability to acquire them, which is how Janet understood Descartes's notion of innate ideas (1883: 216). As Leibniz was reputed to have said, to the old saying that there is nothing in the intellect that is not from the senses, we need to add only "except the intellect itself" (1883: 206). That is, in addition to the ability to sense, one has an intellect that knows and understands. This intellect perceives itself and insofar as it does, it is called "consciousness." Insofar as the intellect perceives the absolute, it is called "reason" (1883: 217). Of the five fundamental categories, Janet believed that substance and cause derive from consciousness or reflection upon our selves, while space, time, and the absolute have a "higher source" in the pure understanding or pure reason (1883: 196). Although he was inclined to side with Kant in regarding space and time as forms of sensibility, Janet added, "we do not see why the mind could not discover them by a sort of direct perception, as it discovers light and sound" (1883: 217).

In his derivation of the categories of substance and cause from consciousness, Janet borrowed some of the arguments that Maine de Biran had used in his attempt to derive these categories from our inner experience of willed effort. First, Janet defended the Biranian notion that we have direct self-knowledge. Previously, he said, philosophers assimilated self-knowledge to our knowledge of external things. In both cases,

we supposedly knew only the phenomena, and it is the phenomena that suggested to us the idea of an underlying cause or substratum, that is, the body in the case of external and the soul in the case of internal phenomena. However, he thought, this view of self-knowledge has been refuted by Maine de Biran and Théodore Jouffroy (1796–1842).[18] Quoting Jouffroy, he said: "It is necessary to erase from psychology this hallowed proposition: the soul knows itself only by its acts and modifications" (1883: 109–10). Janet then argued that a being that knows itself could not do so in the same manner as it knows external things, that is, by their appearances, "behind which there would be an unknown, an x" (1883: 110). To explain what would be wrong with that, he invoked the following argument from Maine de Biran: "If it were thus, the self would be an external thing to itself; it would see itself outside itself. It would be in some way the self of Sosie [a double], an objective self, a self who would not be myself" (1883: 110; my parenthetical explanation).

As I explained in the previous chapter, Maine de Biran had argued that one would have to be two people at once in order to perceive the action of both the will, which we know directly, and the nervous system, which we know by way of representation or appearance. It is indeed ironic that Janet should bring up this argument, for it would seem that the very existence of actual pathological cases of double personality would call many of his claims about self-knowledge into question.[19] Anticipating this objection, Janet insisted that in these cases it is not the Cartesian sense of one's own existence but only the patient's sense of individuality or social self that is in flux (1883: 111–12).

If he knew himself only by way of representation or appearance in the same way that he knew external phenomena, Janet added, then how would he be able to recognize phenomena as *his* phenomena, pain as *his* pain, or passion as *his* passion? (1883: 110, 488.) It is not clear, however, just what this rhetorical question is supposed to show. It is a giant leap from the premise that I can recognize a pain as my pain to the conclusion that I have direct knowledge of my *self*, if the word "self" is taken to refer to some sort of substantial entity, which is what Janet no doubt intended. One alternative would be that the word "self" is simply a kind of grammatical placeholder to which one ascribes mental states and other properties. On this reading, for a person to ascribe a pain to her *self* would just be another way of saying that she is in a state of pain. I do not think, however, that Janet would be satisfied with a merely grammatical as opposed to a metaphysical understanding of the term "self." My evidence includes the fact that he emphasized that the self is

something that is immediately perceived and not arrived at as the result of a judgment. According to Janet, in making a judgment, the subject is subsumed under an attribute that is always more general than it. However, this act of subsuming does not occur when one says, "I exist." Here, the attribute is not more general than the subject. He claimed that both terms are individual and that each refers to one's own existence (1883: 173–4).

Indeed, on the purely grammatical reading of Janet's claim to be able to recognize mental states as his own, his derivation of the categories would not follow. At somewhat breathtaking speed, Janet proceeded to derive from his supposed self-knowledge the category of being as well as other, what he took to be related, concepts:

I thus perceive internally something more than externally. This something more without which consciousness would be impossible, I call *being*. The human mind does not merely know the phenomena in itself, it knows its own proper being; it plunges into being, it has consciousness of it. It senses in itself *being* and *phenomenon*, *remaining* and *becoming*, *continuity* and *diversity*, *one* and *several*. All of these terms – being, permanence, unity, continuity, are equivalent; all the others – phenomenon, becoming, diversity, plurality, are equally equivalent. That which one calls the self, is that union of the one and the several rendered internal to oneself by the consciousness and by a continuous consciousness. (1883: 110)

Janet then derived the concept of activity from this opposition between being and phenomenon:

Consciousness does not give me only being and phenomenon, but the passage from one to the other: this passage is *activity*. The sensation of my internal being is not only the sensation of an inert existence. . . . No: the being that I sense in me is an active being, eternally reaching out, ceaselessly aspiring to pass from one state to another: it is an *effort*, a *tension*, an expectation, it is always something turned towards the future, an anticipation of being, a foretaste of the future. . . . The thinking subject is not only a being, it is an activity, it is a force. (1883: 110–11)

The debt to Maine de Biran, especially in the latter passage, is obvious. For Janet, these concepts of being and activity then yielded the categories of substance and causality. If the self knows itself as being, it knows itself as substance, he argued, "because substance is nothing else than being" (1883: 11). Substance is that which is, as opposed to that which appears. Janet added that we then "transport" this notion of substance by induction to things outside us (1883: 198). Similarly, if the self knows its own activity, it knows itself as cause, "because causality and activity is one and the same thing" (1883: 111). The cause is that which acts. One then takes the self as the model or type from which it draws these fundamental notions of

substance and cause. Conscious reflection on the self also furnishes the related notions of unity, identity, duration, and liberty (ibid.).

Janet credited Maine de Biran with the theory that the internal experience of willed effort provides the model for the notions of active power, force, and causality (1883: 200).[20] He also credited Biran with having satisfactorily discredited Hume's objections to Locke's derivation of the idea of power from internal reflection.[21] In addition, he defended Biran's theory of the categories against the charge that it is in fact an empirical derivation and thus does not support the claim that the categories are innate. In reply to this objection, Janet distinguished two sorts of consciousness, internal and external. The internal consciousness or consciousness of self or reflection is that "which attains being and which is one of the functions of the understanding" (1883: 202). Hence, Janet argued, Biran was not taking away from the innateness of substance and cause because, as Leibniz said, "being is innate to itself" (ibid.). But what Janet seemed to have overlooked is Cousin's objection to Biran that, even if the ideas of substance and cause were innate in us and perceived by reflection, that that alone would not justify their necessary or universal application to external experience. Or, to express this same objection in somewhat more Kantian terms, why would we then find these concepts presupposed in all our judgments and scientific laws?

Finally, Janet anticipated the objection to his own theory of the categories that it lacks unity, insofar as he derived substance and cause from reflection on the self and the notions of space, time, and the absolute from pure reason. In reply, he asked whether consciousness and reason are not "substantially identical," that is just the understanding applied to different objects (1883: 204–5). By this he seems to have meant that the categories of substance and cause derive from the understanding applied to the self, space and time derive from the intellect directly perceiving them, and the category of the absolute derives from the understanding applied to God (1883: 217).

Conclusion

Such was the philosophy that was taught to the generation that included the philosopher Henri Bergson, the sociologist Émile Durkheim, and the psychologist Pierre Janet. Of course, not all nineteenth-century French philosophers read Kant in exactly the same way. Renouvier, for example, recognized that Kant's making space and time the a priori conditions of the possibility of experience does not imply a kind of subjective idealism

(Renouvier 1875 I: 196–7). Renouvier, however, was not a part of the French educational establishment, never having held a university position. Boutroux may have been the first person to offer a course on Kant at the École Normale Supérieure and the Faculté des Lettres who recognized that Kant was not restricting space, time, and the categories to subjective experience (Boutroux 1912: 279ff.). But this course was first offered in 1896–7 (Boutroux 1965), when Durkheim was already a professor in Bordeaux. Thus, there is a good institutional explanation for Durkheim to have perpetuated the eclectic spiritualists' misplaced criticisms of Kant.

I think we can see now that many of the arguments that Durkheim presented in *The Elementary Forms* against empiricist and a priori theories of the categories are largely summaries of Janet's arguments. In light of the problems with the eclectic spiritualist tradition in French academic philosophy, Durkheim's attempt to derive the categories from social causes makes a kind of sense. Where Janet and others made the *conscience* the source of the categories, Durkheim turned instead to the *conscience collective*. Durkheim, of course, would argue that the very notion of a self, the soul, or consciousness is the product of social causes, and would probably deny Janet's distinction between a social self and a Cartesian self. He even argued that it is only through concepts taken from social life that people are able to think that our conscious introspection reveals the existence of a soul (1912a: 523, t. 1995: 370). By making the collective consciousness the source of the categories, Durkheim thought he could explain their necessity, or at least give them the same sort of necessity as moral and religious rules, laws, and customs. But just what sort of necessity is that? It is only a hypothetical necessity or the necessity of a means to an end, rather than an unconditioned or absolute necessity, as I will explain in subsequent chapters.

5

The Early Development of Durkheim's Thought

Durkheim suggested that the sociological study of religious phenomena would bring new life to the discussion of problems that previously only philosophers debated (1912a: 12, t. 1995: 8). This suggestion indicates that he perceived the eclectic spiritualist tradition as moribund. Of course, this philosophical tradition had already begun to change considerably if we take Paul Janet as representative of the generation of eclectic spiritualists that followed Cousin. The positions Durkheim took in his philosophy lectures at the Lycée de Sens (1884a) reflect this changing tradition. On the one hand, like Cousin, he regarded psychology as the philosophical discipline that provided a foundation for logic, ethics, and metaphysics. On the other hand, however, his views on scientific method and the role of representative ideas in philosophy mirror the later eclectic spiritualism of Janet. Also, Durkheim's interpretations of major figures in the history of philosophy such as Kant reveal an eclectic spiritualist influence.

The philosophical views expressed in Lalande's recently discovered notes from Durkheim's philosophy course at the Lycée de Sens suggest a new way to interpret Durkheim's career. In the Sens lectures, he was already seeking to replace the introspective psychology of his spiritualist predecessors with an empirical, hypothetico-deductive psychology as the foundation for the other three philosophical sciences. Although Durkheim shared with the spiritualists the goal of making philosophy scientific, conceptions of scientific method among French academic philosophers had shifted. For Cousin, science in general proceeded by induction from observations, and the observational base for the science of philosophy was supposed to be provided by internal perception

or reflection. Durkheim, however, sought to naturalize philosophy by applying the same experimental method of hypothesis and test that he found in use in the other sciences. Subsequent to the Sens lectures, Durkheim's goal was to replace even this hypothetico-deductive psychology with an empirical sociology that would then serve as the basis for the rest of philosophy. Questions of epistemology and ethics that had formerly been grounded in Cartesian certainties about the soul were now to be rethought in terms of sociological hypotheses about collective representations and social forces. Parts of psychology and logic would then be transformed into the sociology of knowledge. Much of metaphysics would be replaced by the sociology of religion. Ultimately, Durkheim had hoped to reestablish ethics on a sociological basis as well, a project to which he kept returning throughout his career but that he never completed.[1]

Although the Sens lectures never mention the word "sociology," they defend the method of hypothesis he used in that science, which permitted him to postulate the existence of mental entities, including both collective and individual representations. In these lectures, Durkheim endorsed the spiritualist conception of philosophy as the study of mental states over Auguste Comte's conception of philosophy as nothing but the synthesis of the other sciences with no distinct subject matter of its own (1884a: 20). His early rejection of Comte's conception of philosophy parallels his later rejection of Comte's conception of sociology. Durkheim's sociology was no longer a theory of social progress based on the three-state law of the history of science. Rather, it was to be an empirical science that used historical, statistical, and ethnographic data to test hypotheses about the collective representations that hold a society together. Thus Durkheim's project of reestablishing philosophy on a sociological basis involved the renovation of sociology itself.

The changing intellectual climate in philosophy may also help to explain how Durkheim was able to attract other young scholars, many of whom were also trained in philosophy, to his program of research in sociology. But ultimately, in order to win converts, he had to be able to argue that his sociology could explain all that eclectic psychology could explain and then some, and explain it better. Hence, for example, in *The Elementary Forms of Religious Life*, he made the argument that his sociological theory of the categories could explain their universality, necessity, generality, and variability better than any of the philosophical alternatives could, as I discussed in Chapter 1. As I then showed in Chapters 3 and 4, similar arguments can be found in Cousin and Janet, who maintained that they could provide better accounts of the universality and necessity of

the categories than could either the empiricists or the Kantians. The major difference in Durkheim's argument is that he claimed that he could explain the variability of the categories as well. Of course, it is precisely this claim that has led to so many misunderstandings and objections.

To be sure, there is nearly a thirty-year gap between the Sens lectures and *The Elementary Forms*, and during this time the philosophical climate had continued to change. Paul Janet had passed away, and Durkheim's former classmate Henri Bergson (1859–1941) had already emerged as the most important spiritualist philosopher of the new generation. Sociology, led by Durkheim himself, as well as a more empirical psychology, were encroaching on the traditional domains of philosophy. Although eclectic spiritualism's dominance of academic philosophy continued to be reflected in the official syllabus adopted in 1902, which followed the traditional Cousinian order of philosophical topics, positivism was enjoying an enhanced reputation. Sections of Comte's *Cours de philosophie positive* were included for the first time on the list of recommended readings along with the works of such canonical figures as Descartes and Leibniz (Brooks 1998: 256). Perhaps the most notable symbol of the rehabilitation of positivism was the statue of Comte erected in the Place de la Sorbonne the very same year. Also significant is the fact that whereas Lévy-Bruhl's first book was on the philosophy of Jacobi (1894), his second was on Comte (1900). Indeed, much of the new favor in which Comte's philosophy found itself can be attributed to the efforts of Lévy-Bruhl, through both his teaching and his publications. He taught a course on Comte first in 1895 at the École Normale Supérieure (Käsler 1991: 124) and then at the Sorbonne (Merllié 1989b: 498). In 1898 he published an article on Comte and John Stuart Mill in the *Revue philosophique* and then edited and published their correspondence the following year (Nandan 1977: 334). His *La Philosophie d'Auguste Comte*, published in 1900 (t. 1903), is still one of the best works on this philosopher. At a meeting of the Société Française de Philosophie in 1902, Lévy-Bruhl along with Boutroux defended Comtism as a living philosophy, one that they would like to develop in the Kantian direction of an investigation into the conditions of knowledge (Tardieu, ed., 1903). The year 1902 was also the year that Durkheim was hired to teach pedagogy in the newly reorganized university in Paris, in which the École Normale Supérieure was merged with the Faculty of Letters and Sciences (Clark 1972: 163).

Although the philosophical climate may have been changing at the time of *The Elementary Forms*, there are still good reasons to evaluate

Durkheim's arguments for his sociological theory of the categories as reacting more directly to eclectic spiritualism and only indirectly to Kant. One could interpret this work both as contributing to the critique of eclectic spiritualism and as appealing to a philosophical audience that was ready to welcome alternative points of view. Eclectic spiritualism was by no means dead at this time. Janet's textbook remained in print even after Durkheim passed away, with a new twelfth edition appearing in 1919. Also, the eclectic spiritualist tradition had profoundly shaped Durkheim's thinking about the categories, both during his own student years and through his teaching philosophy in the lycées. There is little evidence that Durkheim had given much thought to the categories from about 1887, the year he left teaching lycée philosophy, until about the time he and Mauss wrote their famous paper on primitive classification (1903a(i)). During this period his publications and his courses at the University of Bordeaux were devoted to other topics in social science and pedagogy. Durkheim's sociology of knowledge developed out of his study of ethnography and what it had to say about social structure and religion. In one of his earliest papers on the sociology of religion, he proposed that the concept of the sacred was social in origin, with the dichotomy between the sacred and the profane reflecting that between society and the individual (1899a(ii)). Other papers from about this same time dealt more specifically with dietary and sexual prohibitions and their relation to social structure, especially among Australian indigenes (1898a(ii); 1902a(i)). When this interest in the social origins of rules and concepts led to his taking up the categories again, it seems that he more or less picked up where he had left off in the 1880s.

In arguing for social causes of the categories, Durkheim was responding to the way in which Kant's critical philosophy was understood in the eclectic spiritualist tradition. There is little evidence that he ever carefully studied the works of Kant.[2] As I have tried to explain, the eclectic spiritualist tradition interpreted Kant as grounding his theory of knowledge in a psychology of the human mind, in which, for example, his a priori concepts were understood to be innate concepts. Indeed, Kant's use of terms like "faculty" only invites a psychological reading. His appeal to the transcendental unity of apperception in the transcendental deduction of the categories also led readers astray. The French, as we have seen, assimilated Kant's transcendental apperception to the Cartesian cogito, in spite of the fact that he explicitly denied that the unity of consciousness is presented as an intuition that can be brought under the categories (B421ff.), as I discussed in Chapter 2. Kant was interpreted in these ways

for a combination of reasons that had to do with both him and his readers. Some, like Maine de Biran, relied more on the secondary literature than on Kant's own work. But to be fair, we should keep in mind that Kant is notoriously difficult to understand. Through changes to the chapter on the paralogisms of pure reason in the second edition, Kant had tried to clarify the differences between his use of "I think" and Descartes's, but Cousin had followed Jacobi in dismissing these changes and preferring the first edition. Cousin may have been correct to criticize Kant for equivocating in saying that apperception could reveal that one exists without yielding an intuition of the self that comes under the category of existence. Nevertheless, Cousin went on to beg the question by concluding that one apperceives oneself as substance. Also, as I suggested in Chapter 2, Kant himself was apparently less than pleased with his appeal to the unity of thought, as he placed less emphasis on it in his later works.

For all these reasons and more, by the time Durkheim had entered academic philosophy, the French had developed a tradition of deriving the categories from internal reflection. That Durkheim was answering the spiritualists at least as much as Kant will become most obvious when we examine his argument in *The Elementary Forms* for the social causes of the category of causality itself. For Durkheim, just as for Maine de Biran, Cousin, and Janet, this fundamental category derives at least in part from our inner experience of power or force. The major difference is that for Durkheim, it was the inner experience of social forces or the power of society over the individual, rather than that of the individual will, that gave rise to the concept of causal force or power. These social forces are generated in us by collective representations.

The argument of this chapter will focus on the Sens lectures and that of the next on *The Elementary Forms*. Because the Sens lectures were so recently discovered, they are still relatively unknown compared to Durkheim's other works. Hence, rather than jump right into what the Sens lectures say about the categories, I will first try to put his theory of the categories in context by explaining some of the metaphysical and methodological views he expressed in these lectures. Although his later writings reflect a more thoroughgoing empiricism, the seeds of his methodology can be found right here in these early lycée lectures. There are other ways as well in which the views expressed in these lectures, such as those concerning the role of representative ideas in the meaning of general terms, illuminate his later writings. It should become clear that Durkheim's mature thought developed out of and in response to the eclectic spiritualist tradition.

Eclectic Spiritualism in the Sens Lectures

As I have indicated, Durkheim's philosophy lectures at the Lycée de Sens follow Cousin's prescribed order, beginning with psychology and proceeding through logic, ethics, and metaphysics. In fact, following his fellowship year in Germany, Durkheim reported that he was "astonished" to learn that the Germans had an entirely different conception of philosophy, in which psychology did not provide an epistemological grounding for the rest of philosophy. German students of philosophy began their studies with logic, which for them included epistemology. Psychology was regarded as a closely related but distinct discipline (1887a: 324).

In his lectures on psychology and metaphysics, Durkheim defended a position he called "spiritualist realism." This term was not unique to Durkheim but was used by other philosophers, including Félix Ravaisson-Mollien (1813–1900) and Jules Lachelier (1832–1918) (Brooks 1998: 59, 157). For the spiritualist philosophy, nothing exists except as a spirit or, presumably, as an object of representation. What we call matter, along with its three-dimensional extension and motion, as well as its color and other more obviously mind-dependent qualities, is only an ensemble of appearances, according to Durkheim (1884a: 503).[3] Unlike Cartesian dualism, spiritualism is a monist realism that is not faced with the problem of how two essentially different sorts of substance, mind and matter, are able to interact with each other (498). But unlike idealism, spiritualism does not deny the existence of the external world, either. It says that external reality consists in forces or spirits analogous to ourselves, but with perhaps less consciousness: "The only thing real is force, forces similar to that which we are and which have no need of extension in order to act. . . . There is no break in continuity in nature; from the perfect spirit to inorganic matter, everything is spirit, everything is force. There is only a question of degree of consciousness" (101). Atoms, for example, are conceived by analogy with ourselves, that is, as formed of elementary forces. Spiritualism has its historical antecedents not in Descartes's dualism or Berkeley's idealism but in Leibniz's metaphysics of monads of varying degrees of consciousness (101–2). Durkheim also connected spiritualism with the vitalist philosophy that there is some sort of organizing or directing principle in living matter (509).

The philosophy that three-dimensional extended matter exists only as the content of a mental representation, it should be pointed out, was not just something that the young Durkheim was paid to teach but rather a view that continued to be present in his mature works. As he explained

both in *The Elementary Forms* and in a published draft of the introduction to it, "nothing exists for us except through representation" (1912a: 493 n. 1, t. 1995: 349 n. 55) and "the world exists for us only to the extent to which it is represented" (1909d: 756, t. 1982: 238). Of course, Durkheim found similar positions expressed by positivists like Hippolyte Taine (1828–93), for whom the world of sense experience is not just an appearance but reality itself (1897f: 288; Schmaus 1994: 65), and perhaps by other philosophers as well. All of these ontologies appear to be but varieties of the monism that characterized much of nineteenth-century thought. This philosophy, for which there is only one kind of stuff that is neither Cartesian mind nor matter, often took the form of energeticism, the view that all is energy. When Durkheim in his later works began to speak of the "duality" of human nature,[4] he was not affirming a duality of substances, entities, souls, or any other such metaphysical substrata. All that he meant was that there were two sets of mental states, individual and collective, in each one of us, a position he had been defending ever since *The Division of Labor in Society* (1902b: 74, t. 1984: 61). Durkheim emphasized that the collective or social consciousness is not to be thought of as some ghostly entity but rather as merely the collection of shared mental states that exist in the minds of the individual members of society.[5] However, in these later works Durkheim left unexplained the nature of the human mind in which individual and collective representations were supposed to exist. After all, a mind is not just a collection of ideas or representations, for a book or even an art museum could also be described in that way.

As I indicated in the previous chapter, Durkheim's use of the hypothesis of representative ideas also reflects at least the later form of eclectic spiritualism defended by Paul Janet. Both Durkheim and Janet found this hypothesis necessary for explaining where words get their meanings. In their accounts of meaning, they distinguished the extension of a general term from its comprehension (1884a: 316). Durkheim identified the comprehension of a general term with a representative idea or concept formed by comparison and abstraction from particular ideas. As we have seen, he rejected both nominalism and realism in favor of the "conceptualist" solution to the problem of universals, according to which general ideas exist in the minds of all the individuals who understand the meaning of the corresponding general term (206ff.).

Durkheim's views on the relation between representative ideas and meaning are perhaps best revealed in his discussion of whether the use of language is either necessary or sufficient for thought. He took the

philosophy of Condillac, who was sympathetic to abstract ideas, rather than the unsympathetic views of Berkeley, Hume, or Reid, as his point of departure. If anything, Durkheim went even further than Condillac in his endorsement of abstract general ideas.

First, Durkheim divided the question of whether language is *necessary* to thought into three parts, concerning particular, abstract, and general ideas, respectively. *Particular* or concrete ideas, he argued, are the only ideas of which we can think without naming them. However, even this process is facilitated by the use of language. Turning to *abstract* ideas, he reported that Condillac had held that language is necessary for thinking about abstract ideas, since abstract ideas could not exist without their signs. Durkheim disagreed with Condillac and argued that abstract ideas *could* exist independently of language or signs. For example, he said, we can mentally separate the extension (*étendu*) of a table from the table and do so without the use of signs. But every time we wanted to think about such an abstract thing without its sign, he added, we would have to go through the laborious mental operation of abstraction all over again. This is so arduous a task that the sciences, given the major role that abstract ideas play in them, would be nearly impossible without language. The word "fixes" the abstract idea so that we do not have to form it again every time that we need it (394–7). He then turned to the question of whether the having of *general* ideas required the use of language. He took as his example the general idea of humanity, which for purposes of argument he defined as the collection of beings that are intelligent and free. The only way to represent these qualities without signs, he argued, would be to represent to ourselves a being who had them. However, we would then have the idea of an individual, not of humanity. It is true that one could attempt to consider in this individual only, say, intelligence, without concerning oneself with the various manifestations this faculty could take. However, this would be difficult. The word would decrease the effort required to retain the general idea of humanity. Thus, with regard to the question of whether language is *necessary* to thought, Durkheim concluded that we could think without signs, but not as well (397–8).

When he turned to the question of whether language alone was *sufficient* for thought, Durkheim made it clear that ideas were also necessary. He considered Taine's theory that we can think with signs alone, abstracting from any ideas, but only to reject it:

It is always necessary to think about something and we are able to think about only an idea. It is thus necessary that we see something beneath the words. This

idea will be very vague, if one wants, but it will exist nonetheless. We are not able to think of the word except under the condition of seeing at least the shadow of an idea under the word.

But this shadow of an idea could not be sufficient for thought. Thanks to the word, it takes on a sort of body: it thus aids thought, but without substituting entirely for the idea. (399)

Durkheim's position here closely resembles Janet's argument in the previous chapter that without ideas in our heads we would be speaking like unthinking parrots. For Durkheim, both language and ideas were necessary for thought.

As I suggested in the previous chapter, the shared concepts or mental entities to which Durkheim and Janet appealed in their accounts of the meanings of general terms could have served as the inspiration or model for Durkheim's later notion of collective representations or states of the collective consciousness. It seems that Durkheim and Janet thought that what allowed them to postulate the existence of such shared mental entities was the method of hypothesis that they endorsed.

The Method of Hypothesis in the Sens Lectures

Durkheim's account in the Sens lectures of the role of imaginative hypotheses in science should put to rest once and for all the view that he was an utterly naive inductivist who thought we could simply generalize laws from an unbiased study of the facts.[6] In these lectures he defended a fallibilist position according to which putative laws never lose their hypothetical character no matter how many supporting facts are found. Although this hypothetical character will diminish, especially if the hypothesis leads to the discovery of new, still unknown facts, he thought, it is impossible to observe all the phenomena relevant to one's hypothesis. Furthermore, a single phenomenon that contradicts a hypothesis will suffice to refute it (13–14, 380 n. 2).

According to Durkheim, "Hypothesis is necessary in all the physical sciences: without it no discovery is possible" (366). He was aware that other philosophers, such as Alexander Bain, had argued that the true scientific method consists in observing the facts without adding anything to them and that this was the method least likely to lead to error. Durkheim, however, found the method of hypothesis to be "dangerous but . . . necessary" in the physical sciences (367). Doubtless we can be deceived by a hypothesis, he added, but we cannot arrive at the truth

without one. The laws governing the phenomena do not "leap to the eyes." A hypothesis, for Durkheim, is simply a law that has not yet been verified. He provided the example of Pascal observing the height of mercury in a column and forming the idea that it is caused by the variable weight of the air. This hypothesis became a law when it was verified by the method of concomitant variation (366–7). According to Durkheim, observation alone was not sufficient to lead to new discoveries in the sciences, since observation shows us merely the facts as they happen and is not sufficient to yield the law that governs them. Anticipating the objection that there are sciences of pure observation like natural history that do not require the use of imaginative hypotheses, he replied that such sciences merely describe and classify; they do not explain the phenomena and thus are not true sciences (370–2). Durkheim thought that error is to be eliminated not by avoiding hypotheses altogether but through the process of verification. He laid down four conditions for the acceptability of new hypotheses: (1) they must be simple; (2) they must explain the known facts; (3) they must be precise; and (4) they must lead to the successful prediction of new facts (367–8).[7]

For Durkheim, it was an exaggeration to say that new discoveries in science are due to the application of method. In particular, he thought that there was no method for generating new hypotheses. The invention of a new hypothesis "is due to that which is not given by a method, the force of genius" (357). Method may be necessary to the process of invention, he added, but it is not by itself sufficient for doing science since that method itself would first have to be discovered without the use of method (357). Although one cannot say in a rigorous way how someone invents a new hypothesis, he believed, one can say that analogy is the procedure that is usually followed and that gives the best results (365). However, even though the appeal to the use of analogy may allow us to explain how a hypothesis was invented, it is no help to us in explaining the fact that one scientist rather than another invented it: "But that which we cannot explain, is why such and such a hypothesis was made by such and such a scientist rather than by such and such another; even in the very case of a hypothesis drawn from an analogy there is a place for creation, which is entirely a work of the imagination; everything in analogy is not the work of logic, there is in the invention of every hypothesis a large share of contingency" (366). Apparently, then, Durkheim thought that although analogy plays a role in the formation of hypotheses, the scientists who had more of this force of genius would be better able to exploit analogies to invent hypotheses.

In his lectures on psychology, he associated genius with what he termed the "creative imagination." He distinguished three forms of imagination: (1) the memory or "reproductive imagination," which creates nothing new; (2) the faculty of combination, which can create no new materials but only recombine elements drawn from the memory, as in dream images; and (3) the creative imagination, which, although it may borrow elements from the memory, can actually add new things, drawing its materials from itself. As an example of this last form of the imagination, he provided Newton's gravitational hypothesis. Although Newton may have been pushed in that direction by Kepler's laws, Durkheim argued, there is nevertheless a break in continuity between these laws and Newton's hypothesis. This gap was filled by Newton's creative imagination. What the creative imagination adds to the elements drawn from observation and memory is unity, according to Durkheim. He then drew an analogy between art and science. The artist may draw his or her elements from observation, but this supplies only the matter. The form comes from the artist, however, and the form gives the work of art its unity. Both in art and in "the great scientific hypotheses," the imagination unifies into groups the elements provided by observation. In his second example, Durkheim cited Galileo's observation of the swinging of a chandelier. Others may have noticed that it was isochronous, but it took the genius of Galileo to imagine that this could be a general law for all pendulums (186–9).

Durkheim then argued that the imagination is one of the most important sources of knowledge. Reason alone may suffice for the abstract sciences, such as mathematics, he said. But we can know about concrete reality only through the use of the imagination: "we can know reality only by divining it [*qu'en la devinant*]. However, the only faculty that permits divination [*de deviner*] is the imagination" (191).[8] He then hazarded the guess that there may not be a single law in the sciences that did not originate as a hypothesis formed through an act of the imagination. The imagination is then needed for the growth of science: "In a general way, one can say that the imagination is *the only faculty that augments our knowledge.* We owe to it everything new that enters the mind" (192). Logic alone allows us merely to draw out the consequences of the ideas that we already have. Without the use of the imagination to generate new hypotheses, he concluded, reality would escape us (192). Today, a philosopher of science might want to criticize this last argument for running together issues about the growth of knowledge with questions about ampliative inference. Durkheim is perhaps more convincing where he draws upon

examples from the history of science to defend the use of imaginative hypotheses in science.

Durkheim's Conception of Philosophy and Psychology in the Sens Lectures

In Durkheim's Sens lectures, we find a more thoroughgoing defense of the use of hypotheses in psychology and in philosophy generally than we find in Janet's philosophy text. Although Janet and Rabier had each defended the use of hypotheses in the natural sciences at least to some degree, in philosophy they still subscribed to Cousin's *méthode psy-chologique*, or the method of seeking a foundation in internal reflection.[9] For Durkheim, philosophy was an empirical, experimental science that proceeded through the method of hypothesis and test. Breaking with tradition, he rejected the Cartesian cogito as a foundation for philosophy (210–11). He also dismissed as too vague the eclectic method of accepting what other systems affirm and rejecting what they deny. As Durkheim pointed out, it is not at all clear how to distinguish what is affirmed from what is denied. He also criticized the eclectics' appeal to common sense, maintaining that common sense is but a collection of prejudice and error (8–9).

According to Durkheim, the goal of science is to provide explanations (*explications* [16]). He laid down three conditions for some body of knowledge to be considered a science. (1) First, it must have its own object to explain, an object distinct from that of any other science. This first condition is subsequently reflected in the way in which he began *The Rules of Sociological Method* (1895a) by seeking a definition of social facts in order to establish that there is a distinct subject matter worthy of its own science. For Durkheim, there are two types of explanation in science: a mathematical explanation is a demonstration of a theorem by means of relations of identity, while in the physical sciences, one explains a fact through relations of causality. This distinction leads to his second condition: (2) The object of study must submit either to the law of identity or to the law of causality. (3) The third condition for something to be considered a science is that this object must be "accessible" to us in some way; that is, there must be some method appropriate for studying the object. According to Durkheim in the Sens lectures, philosophy fulfills these three conditions and is thus a science: (1) it takes states of consciousness as its object, (2) these states are subject to causal relations,

and (3) it has the experimental method or method of hypothesis testing (17–19).

For Durkheim, philosophy is the study of our internal conscious states and the conditions on which they depend. It commences with psychology, which provides a description, enumeration, and classification of the different types of mental states. These include everything from our concepts of space, time, and causality to our inclinations, passions, and emotions (6, 26). Psychology did not include for him an account of the soul. He agreed with the spiritualists that the self is apperceived at the same time we perceive the phenomena and is not a merely constructed notion, as it was for Taine (111–14). However, he rejected Maine de Biran and Cousin's identification of the self with a substantial soul that serves as a substratum to our conscious lives but that escapes our conscious awareness and is only known through the use of reason (116–17). For Durkheim, logic differs from psychology in that it concerns only those mental states connected with our intellect. Also, logic is not merely descriptive but explains "the rules that the mind ought to follow to arrive at the truth" (282). Logic, like moral philosophy, is an art as well as a science. Moral philosophy concerns those mental states relevant to our active lives and the laws to which we should submit (26–7, 285–6). Metaphysics, finally, is concerned with the conditions on which our mental states depend, that is, whether they depend on the existence of the soul, the body, or God (493).

Durkheim thought that the experimental method of hypothesis and test was needed in philosophy to get beyond the mere internal observation of mental states and to discover the laws that govern them.

Philosophy is a science, and there is no true science, seeking to explain its object, that can live by observation alone. This procedure by itself is, if not absolutely sterile, at least little fecund. Observation is only the establishment of facts: generalization, which is the necessary complement of it, can only extricate the common characters of the phenomena. It is still necessary that these characters be very apparent, and even then one will be able to obtain only very simple laws. Observation shows that bodies are heavy, but it cannot give the law of gravitation. As soon as the facts become ever so little complex, observation can no longer suffice to find the law. In order to find it, it is thus necessary for the mind to intervene and make what one calls a hypothesis. (13)

To be sure, this passage may seem a little vague, as Durkheim did not specify just how complex the phenomena must be before a hypothesis becomes necessary. But he was more clear with regard to the physical sciences, arguing that hypotheses were always necessary, as I explained earlier.

According to Durkheim, not only psychology but all the branches of philosophy, including logic, ethics, and metaphysics, were experimental sciences. In saying that Durkheim endorsed the method of hypothesis in philosophy and psychology, I do not mean to suggest that he always used it all that well there. To begin with, Durkheim seems to have thought that his justification of the method of hypothesizing laws would also suffice to justify the use of hypotheses that postulate entities, including mental entities. This may be because he believed that all genuinely explanatory laws in the empirical sciences were causal laws, and did not distinguish hypotheses that postulated putative causal laws from those that postulated unobservable causal entities. A more serious weakness, perhaps, is that he seems to have understood the method of hypothesis as allowing him first to classify mental states into types and then to postulate a mental faculty responsible for each type. For Durkheim, these faculties were "activity" or the will, sensibility, and intelligence. To be sure, he said that these faculties were not to be thought of as distinct entities, but only as the "powers" of a single entity, the self. But, of course, the real problem is whether this sort of faculty psychology in fact exemplifies the experimental method and involves genuinely testable hypotheses (44–7). This problem continues to be exemplified today by those functionalist psychologists who would simply postulate the existence of a mental "module" for each of our cognitive abilities without providing an account of the underlying neurophysiology.[10]

Nevertheless, Durkheim at least claimed to have used the experimental method even in his moral philosophy (489). However, we do not find him actually testing hypotheses in his lectures on ethics. The empirical character of his ethics amounts to little more than his claim to have drawn from experience the fact that we are morally responsible agents (405–8). He in fact rejected the empiricist ethics of the utilitarians, arguing that it fails to issue in universal moral principles. This rejection of empiricism in ethics is surprising, given his later attempts to ground ethics in an empirical sociology. He endorsed instead the Kantian view that morality is grounded in the principle that one should always treat others as ends in themselves and never only as means. However, he also criticized Kant for not being sufficiently empirical, accusing him of having produced an imaginary ethics and not one of real human beings (489–90).

The exclusion of unconscious mental states from the domain of philosophy and psychology in the Sens lectures is also puzzling. For Durkheim, the notion of an unconscious mental state was contradictory. The unconscious had to do with the physiological states of the nervous system, which

he regarded as distinct from psychological states (32–3).[11] He rejected Eduard von Hartmann's (1842–1906) suggestion that conscious mental states are grounded in unconscious states, insisting that everything that could be explained in terms of the unconscious could be explained just as well in terms of a very weak consciousness. Besides, Durkheim asked, how would anything in the unconscious ever be able to return to the conscious self? (107–8) Such a stand against unconscious mental states would perhaps have made sense for someone, like Cousin, for whom psychology relied on conscious introspection alone. However, if Durkheim thought his methodology of hypothesis and test justified the postulation of mental faculties, it is not clear why he would have balked at unconscious mental states.

Furthermore, Durkheim did not make clear what he meant by excluding unconscious states from psychology, other than to exclude physiological states. He certainly could not have meant to include in the domain of psychology only those states of which one is presently conscious. Consider, for example, his conceptualism, according to which the meanings of general terms consisted in ideas present in the minds of all who understood these terms. Given the number of words an individual knows, it seems unlikely that one could be even weakly conscious of all of their corresponding meanings all the time. One might argue that Durkheim meant that philosophy was the study of all those mental states of which we could potentially be fully conscious. But how many would that be? Would he include only those mental states that we have explicitly represented at some time in the past, of which we are now only weakly conscious, but of which we could be fully conscious again at some point in the future? Then what about the status of those new ideas produced by the creative imagination of which he made so much in his account of method? Where do such ideas come from before one is conscious of them, and when do they become part of the domain of psychology? Would he then also include in the domain of psychology all those states of which we could possibly be conscious at some future time? This number would be limitless. Durkheim never clarified these issues in his later works, either. In addition, these works seem to equivocate on whether individuals could be conscious of collective representations or only of their effects, as I will argue.

In spite of these problems with interpreting the Sens lectures, it is nevertheless clear that Durkheim, at a very early point in his career, conceived philosophy as making use of empirically testable hypotheses about shared mental states. For Durkheim, this method of hypothesis applied not only

to philosophy but also to the rest of what he called the "moral sciences," which included for him the social, philological, and historical as well as the philosophical sciences. By the social sciences, he meant politics, law, and political economy. Some of the moral sciences, such as philology, he characterized as using the inductive or comparative method, and others, such as law, he regarded as purely deductive. However, he regarded even the science of politics as having abandoned the geometrical method of demonstration for the method of observation and experimentation, with history furnishing the empirical basis (376–7). He also characterized a role for experimentation in the historical sciences themselves. These sciences do not simply recount the facts they have discovered but "reconstruct the past" through the use of the imagination (384–5). With the aid of a few surviving words or facts, a historian may reconstruct a constitution, a belief, or a practice. For Durkheim, historical reconstruction and interpretation involves an experimental method of hypothesizing laws and testing them: "But once the law is invented, it is necessary to demonstrate it. The historian demonstrates it in showing that his hypothesis conforms to the laws already discovered and that it explains the facts well. This proof will be especially good if the hypothesis leads to the discovery of new facts. It is in that which consists what one may call *historical experimentation*" (385). This method of historical experimentation thus appears to be one of testing hypotheses about beliefs and practices against what are often the very few facts and documents available to the historian.

Hence, although Durkheim had not yet included sociology among the moral, social, and historical sciences, much of his later sociological methodology is already implicit in these lectures. To arrive at his conception of sociology, it remained for him to generalize his method of historical experimentation in two ways: (1) First, he had to make explicit the use of historical data to test hypotheses about collectively shared mental states. He appears to have already thought that the experimental method allowed him to postulate shared mental states, as we saw in his conceptualist account of the meaning of general terms. The notion of shared mental states subsequently constituted the subject matter of his sociology, first under the name "states of the collective consciousness" and later under the name "collective representations." (2) Second, he had to allow the use of statistical and ethnographic as well as historical data to test hypotheses about these collective representations.

The Sens lectures thus reveal that Durkheim was in exactly the right frame of mind to benefit intellectually from his trip to Germany in

1885–6. On this trip he met with scholars such as Wilhelm Wundt, who was endorsing a role for historical and ethnographic evidence in testing hypotheses about shared mental states. Durkheim then went on to use historical data in his *The Division of Labor in Society* and statistical data in *Suicide* to test hypotheses about shared mental states. After 1895, with the additional urgings of his nephew Marcel Mauss, he also began to use ethnographic data for this purpose.

The Categories in the Sens Lectures

Like the eclectic spiritualists, Durkheim regarded an investigation of the categories or "principles of reason" as the central task of psychology. His account of the categories in the Sens lectures reflects both similarities with and differences from accounts given by his eclectic spiritualist predecessors. According to Durkheim, there are certain necessary principles of reason that make it possible to have knowledge of things. These necessary truths, such as that every event has a cause, are due to the faculty of reason and are distinguished from merely contingent judgments based on experience. Durkheim recognized that others have called these "universal" principles, but since even an empirical judgment can be adopted universally, he thought it made more sense to call them "necessary" principles. He then inquired into how there could be such necessary principles. If they are necessary, he said, their opposites cannot be conceived. Hence, they cannot be derived from experience, which can never show us that the opposite of something is not possible. They must therefore derive from the very nature of the human mind. For Durkheim, these necessary truths are thus the laws of the mind. Reason is but all of these laws taken together (122–4).

Durkheim then derived these necessary principles of reason by starting from the premise that the nature of the mind is such that it has a need for unity, order, and simplicity. The principles of reason are there because they satisfy this need. They bring the order and unity to our representations of things that are required by the nature of the human mind. However, the representations of things given in experience, both internal and external, are multiple. To give order to this experience, the mind arranges its internal experience in time and its external experience in space. But even this ordering in space and time is not sufficient. The mind, finding certain relations among the things represented in space and time, forms groups among the phenomena in accordance with these relations, with some sort of being or entity at the center of

each group. In this way, the mind is led to conceive the phenomena as modifications of an independently existing thing called a "substance." Hence, it arrives at the necessary principle "All phenomena are modifications of a substance."[12] However, because the phenomena also have relations among themselves and not just to substances, it is necessary to order the phenomena themselves. The mind finds itself unable to conceive a phenomenon without assuming some other phenomenon that is the condition of the first and calls these phenomena "cause" and "effect." Hence, it arrives at the principle "Every phenomenon has a cause." However, even this ordering is insufficient. Relationships must be established among these various causal series of phenomena. The mind is thus led to represent these series as all converging toward a common goal or purpose. Hence, it arrives at the principle "Every phenomenon or series of phenomena has an end." For Durkheim, there are thus five necessary principles that, in Kantian terms, are constitutive of experience: the principles of space, time, substance, causality, and final causality. These five principles are constitutive of our knowledge with its laws. However, these laws also have certain relations among themselves. From these relations one draws what Kant called the "regulative principles" of knowledge, the principles of identity and contradiction (128–32).

Durkheim's list of categories here resembles the eclectic spiritualists' more than Kant's list insofar as it includes space and time. As we saw in Chapter 3, Cousin had followed Kant's early German critics in denying the distinction between the categories and the forms of intuition. Similarly, Durkheim saw no distinction between the forms of intuition and the concepts of the understanding, regarding them as equally subjective (164). Also, like Janet, Durkheim listed only five categories in addition to the regulative principles. Unlike Janet, however, his fifth category is final causality rather than the absolute. Although he agreed with Janet in subsuming the concepts of infinity and perfection under the concept of the absolute, Durkheim did not believe that the concept of the absolute is a priori. For Durkheim, all thought is relative and the absolute plays no role in human knowledge (140–1).

In the Sens lectures, Durkheim held that the necessary principles of reason are a priori. Like the eclectic spiritualists again, he rejected empiricist accounts of the categories, arguing against Herbert Spencer (1820–1903) and John Stuart Mill (1806–73) that these concepts could not be constructed from external experience (135–7, 145–51, 157–62). However, he also rejected what he took to be Maine de Biran's attempt to derive the categories from introspective experience (88, 138).

Apparently Durkheim was not convinced by Janet's defense that for Maine de Biran the categories were innate and not empirically derived. He also rejected Cousin's theory that these principles have a divine source, arguing that this makes them dependent upon a cause external to them. Presumably, Durkheim thought that this would deprive them of their necessity. Durkheim at least claimed to share instead Kant's view that these principles are solely the expression of our own nature. Turning to the question of whether these a priori principles are innate, he denied that there are innate ideas in us in the sense of ideas engraved upon the mind prior to any experience. For Durkheim, there are no ideas in us prior to experience. However, as soon as experience commences it is forced to follow these laws, which are as necessary to the mind as gravity is to body. Thus, they are innate only in the sense that we discover them through the use of reason, which is innate in us. Through the use of reason, we find that the terms of these principles are indissolubly linked to each other, such that one term cannot appear without the other (125–6). Thus, although Durkheim may have rejected the doctrine of innate ideas we find in Descartes, he could not accept the empiricists' blank slate theory of the mind, either. Durkheim subscribed to a French tradition of ascribing to Aristotle the "axiom" that "there is nothing in the intellect that was not first in the senses" and then adding that Leibniz improved upon this axiom by adding "except the intellect itself" (161–2; cf. Janet 1883: 206).

The argument in the Sens lectures that the categories could not depend on external causes obviously raises questions about Durkheim's later theory in *The Elementary Forms* that the categories depend on social causes. As I have been saying, something that results from a cause is contingent upon that cause and thus is not necessary, at least not in some ontological sense of necessity, unless its cause could be said to exist necessarily. However, like Cousin and others, Durkheim appears to have equivocated with respect to what he meant by the necessity of the categories. When he argued that they could not be derived from experience because their opposites cannot be conceived, he was appealing to a concept of logical necessity. But in his derivation of the categories from the nature of the human mind, what he showed instead is that they are necessary for some end, that is, for achieving order among our mental representations. As I read it, the necessity he attributed to the categories in *The Elementary Forms* is also of this latter sort, except that in this work he characterized the categories as serving social rather than merely psychological purposes.

Durkheim's reasons for rejecting empiricist accounts of specific categories also illuminate parts of his later sociological theory of the categories. Let me begin with his discussion of space and time. According to Durkheim, empiricism is unable to explain the fact that, when we have a sensation of color, for example, we immediately infer the existence of a colored object in external space. As soon as we experience a sensation, "we spontaneously objectify it and situate its cause in space" (89). As we have seen, Durkheim believed that the mind does this so as to give order and unity to our manifold sensations. According to Spencer, on the other hand, we form the idea of time from our experience of one thing succeeding another and our idea of space from things coexisting at the same time, which allows us to reverse the order in which we experience them. As Durkheim pointed out, Spencer's account is subject to the problem of circularity, in that one would need the category of time in order to recognize relations of succession and coexistence in the first place (135–6). It is ironic that he makes this criticism of Spencer, since from the earliest days Durkheim's own critics have raised this very same problem of circularity as an objection against his sociological theory of the categories in *The Elementary Forms*. The categories could not be derived from social life, it is said, because they are the necessary conditions of the experience of social life in the first place. For instance, the category of time could not have its origin in the periodicity of religious rites since the mind must presuppose the form of time in the act of perceiving this periodicity (Dennes 1924: 39; cf. Schaub 1920: 336–7). As I mentioned in Chapter 1, this charge continues to be raised against *The Elementary Forms* today. To be sure, Durkheim's critics are arguing that the categories are logically presupposed by experience, while in Durkheim's criticism of Spencer, he appears to have said that the categories are the psychologically necessary conditions of experience.[13] However, even on the psychological reading of the categories, they could not be derived from social life without begging the question. It seems highly unlikely that Durkheim could have been unaware of the problem of circularity in 1912 if he had made this objection to Spencer's theory of the categories in 1883–4. Whether in fact Durkheim's mature sociological theory of the categories successfully avoids this problem we will take up again in the following chapter.

The problem of circularity also arises in Durkheim's explanation of the inadequacy of empiricist accounts of the origins of the categories of substance, causality, and final causality. First, Durkheim argued against Mill's attempt to explain the principle of causality in terms of

experience, association of ideas, and habit that these things do not give us necessity. The past tells us nothing about the future. Any attempt to argue that regularities that have been observed in the past will continue to hold in the future in effect assumes the principle of causality (149–50). Then Durkheim made a similar criticism once again of Spencer's evolutionary account of the categories. According to this theory, as we saw in Chapter 4, the categories are explained in terms of the inheritance of acquired habits of mind. Durkheim first objected that this theory suggests that there could be some peoples in whom not all the principles of reason had evolved, which he found to be contrary to fact. Then, like Janet, Durkheim argued that Spencer's evolutionary account simply pushes back to the beginning of our species the problems generated by empiricism's assumption that the mind is a blank slate. A blank mind is incapable of forming judgments. For any thought or judgment to form, there would already have to be some thought there (160–1).[14] Thus we return to the vicious circle problem once again.

However, Durkheim was not fully satisfied with Maine de Biran's and Cousin's accounts of the categories, either. The principle of causality could not be generalized from internal any more than external experience, in spite of Biran's attempts. Although Cousin maintained that the principle of causality is a priori, according to Durkheim, Cousin contradicted himself in holding that the "idea" of causality is given experientially. How, Durkheim queried, could the principle of causality be a priori if the idea of causality contained in it is not? Similarly, how could the principle that every attribute presupposes something in which it inheres be a priori if the idea of substance is not? To resolve this contradiction, Durkheim distinguished these ideas as given by reason from the same ideas given by experience. For example, reason merely tells us to relate phenomena to something else, but does not tell us what that something ought to be. Experience intervenes and provides the concrete representation of the idea of substance. Also, reason provides the idea of a necessary antecedent of a phenomenon, while only (internal) experience can yield the concrete representation of a cause. Finally, reason gives us the abstract idea of a point of convergence of several series of phenomena. Experience gives us the concrete idea of an intelligent being deliberating and acting toward some end. In sum, according to Durkheim, reason provides the conditions of experience in an abstract and general manner, while experience alone – whether inner or outer – allows us to represent them in a concrete way (138–40). In a similar manner, in his account of the category of space, Durkheim distinguished the a priori concept of

exteriority, by which we spontaneously locate the causes of our perceptions outside of us, from the concept of a spatial ordering, which is introduced by experience (89).

In resolving this contradiction in Cousin's philosophy, Durkheim had in effect distinguished two senses of the categories, one in which they are regarded as universal and necessary principles of reason and another in which they are regarded as concrete representations, drawn from experience, that fall under these principles. Durkheim assumed something like this distinction in his criticism of Spencer's evolutionary theory, where he said that while no observed tribe lacks the rational principles, a tribe may be in an underdeveloped state and apply these principles in a naive way. For example, the tribe may not understand causality the way our scientists do (160). In other words, Durkheim appears to have been suggesting, the principle that every phenomenon has a cause may be universal, while the concrete representation of causality may nevertheless be culturally variable. In a way, this prefigures his later position that the collective representations of the categories are culturally variable. However, his later theory differs from that in the Sens lectures in that he attempted to provide an empirical, sociological account of the universality of the categories, rather than to explain it by saying that they are somehow given by reason.

The Sens Lectures on Kant

Although Durkheim claimed to agree with Kant that the categories or principles of reason are a priori, there are important differences between Durkheim and Kant in addition to the ones noted earlier. His discussion of Kant's theory of knowledge appears to be strongly colored by the eclectic spiritualist tradition reading of Kant and does not seem to be grounded in a careful study of Kant's own texts. For example, Durkheim interpreted Kant's position that the principles of rationality apply only to a world of phenomena that we have constructed as implying that these principles are merely subjective in their application (164). For Kant, however, as I explained in Chapter 2, the forms of sensibility, the categories of the understanding, and the principles that follow from them are constitutive of our experience of objects in the first place. That is, such principles as that substances are permanent in time and that every event has a cause are part of what makes it possible for us to have experience of objects. To consider the world of appearances or phenomena as merely subjective is to suggest that one is identifying the "objective" with something that

exists independently of the mind's experience or with the noumenal world. Durkheim appears to have done precisely this in using the term "object" to refer to things in the external world that serve as a substratum for the world of phenomena (165).

An eclectic spiritualist influence is also apparent in Durkheim's reading of Kant's antinomies of pure reason. In the antinomies, Kant had argued that we arrive at contradictory conclusions when we illegitimately try to apply our concepts to questions that are beyond the realm of any possible experience. For example, we are able to demonstrate both that free will exists and that it does not exist. According to Durkheim, Kant's solution to the antinomies is that in each pair of opposing propositions, one applies to the noumenal and the other to the phenomenal world (167). However, this is Kant's solution only to the third antinomy, regarding the freedom of the will, and the fourth, regarding whether or not there exists a necessary being (Kant 1783 4: 343–7). It is not how he dealt with the first antinomy, which concerns whether or not space and time are infinite, and the second, which concerns whether or not matter is infinitely divisible. In the first two antinomies, the possibility of proving contradictory propositions is due to the mistaken assumption that there are objects existing in space and time independently of our experience of them, when in fact for Kant space and time belong only to our representations of the world (1783 4: 341–2). For Kant, spatial and temporal objects exist only in the phenomenal world of appearances. As he explained, "the concept of the noumenon is not the concept of an object" (1781/87 B344/A287). Nevertheless, as we have seen, Cousin had refused to grant Kant his concept of an object and instead followed the Scottish common-sense tradition of talking about objects independently of anyone's experience of them. He then criticized Kant for failing to explain how we can have objective knowledge. I submit that Durkheim understood Kant in a similar fashion.

Durkheim's account in the Sens lectures of Kant on free will also bears the mark of the spiritualist tradition. According to Durkheim, Kant imprisoned the will within the noumenal world, where it is unable to influence the phenomenal world (275). However, one could with at least equal justice argue instead that Kant imprisoned causality within the phenomenal world. For Kant, the relation between will and action is not causal in the sense of being a temporal, before-and-after relationship. Causal, temporal relations apply only to the phenomenal realm, the realm of objects constituted by the understanding and the sensibility. The will, for Kant, stands outside of the phenomenal realm and thus outside of experience,

spatial and temporal relationships, and the categories of the understanding. Of course, one would hardly expect to find in the spiritualists' texts a sympathetic discussion of Kant's notion that the will is outside the realm of experience. After all, Maine de Biran had tried to ground the concept of causality in our introspective experience of the power of the will over the body. For Biran, it was possible to have direct experience of the will as causally efficacious and not merely indirect experience of the will through the effects of its actions. Cousin went so far as to use Biran's arguments as a basis from which to defend a traditional notion of a substantial soul with causal powers. One can also see Durkheim thinking along these same lines when he rejected Spinoza's position that we experience only our actions and not their causes (260).

A lack of sympathy for Kant's account of the will, one could argue, is also reflected in Durkheim's subsequent conception of sociological explanation. The eclectic spiritualists taught Durkheim to think of the will as *causing* action. For Kant, on the other hand, the relationship between the will and the action has more to do with the reasons than with the causes for the action, if causes are understood as temporal and reasons are understood as logical antecedents. As Kant explained, "the relation of the action to the objective grounds of reason is not a time-relation" (1783 4: 346). For Kant, to explain an action in terms of its reasons is to say that the action makes sense in the light of these reasons. In other words, to explain an action is to give the *meaning* of that action for the agent. Of course, we may regard reasons as causes also if we either consider our reasons as mental states that exist temporally antecedent to our actions or broaden our conception of causality beyond mere relations of temporal succession. Durkheim, however, never gave sufficient attention to the philosophical issues surrounding the meaning of human actions and the explanation of these actions in terms of the agent's reasons for them. In *The Rules*, he simply relegated to psychology explanations that appeal to an agent's intentions or goals (1895a, chap. 5). To the extent that many other early French social scientists had a philosophical training similar to Durkheim's, it is perhaps no accident that interpretive sociology that focuses on the meaning of actions developed and took hold in Germany rather than in France.

6

Durkheim's Sociological Theory of the Categories

It should be clear by now that Durkheim's sociology of knowledge was developed in reaction to and borrowed heavily from the eclectic spiritualist tradition in philosophy. One of the elements Durkheim adopted from this tradition can be seen in the argument by which he introduced his sociological theory of the categories in *The Elementary Forms of Religious Life* (1912a). As we have seen, French thinkers beginning with Cousin presented their theories of the categories by offering first an eliminative argument criticizing all previous empiricist and a priorist accounts of them. They maintained that the empiricists could not account for the universality and necessity of the categories and that their Kantian rationalist opponents could not explain or justify the way in which the categories are imposed on our experience of the external world. Durkheim added to this eliminative argument that the Kantians could not account for the cultural variability of the categories, either. But in making this change, he thus appeared to have imposed rather conflicting demands on a theory of the categories, requiring that it explain both their universality and their variability. In order to remove this conflict, I have distinguished the categories from their collective or cultural representations and argued that it is only the cultural representations of the categories that are variable. That is, each culture has the same set of categories, including space, time, and causality, but has developed different systems of representations for thinking and communicating about them.

The same distinction between the categories and their collective representations would seem to be necessary in order to avoid the problem of circularity in a sociological theory of the categories. The categories could not be derived from social or any other sort of experience without

begging the question since the categories are the necessary conditions of experience. However, as I argued in Chapter 1, it is not clear that even the collective representations of at least some of the categories, in particular causality, could be derived from social experience. Durkheim's claim that the collective representation of causal power is derived from our experience of social forces rests on the problematic assumption that we are able to experience these forces and not just their effects.

In this chapter I will be examining in greater detail Durkheim's arguments for the social origin of the collective representation of causality. But before I do, I should emphasize that my distinction between categories and their collective representations departs from his sociology of knowledge. Durkheim explicitly said that the categories are both universal and culturally variable and that these characteristics were to be explained in terms of the social causes or functions of the categories. Furthermore, he identified the categories with their collective representations. In *The Elementary Forms* (1912a: 619–20, t. 1995: 435–6), the pragmatism lectures (1955a: 204, t. 1983: 104), and elsewhere (e.g., 1914a: 331, t. 1960c: 338; 1973: 162), he said that all general ideas and concepts, which would include the categories, are collective representations. Also, where I propose to resolve the conflict between the demands of universality and variability by distinguishing the categories from their collective representations, Durkheim, in the year following the publication of *The Elementary Forms*, simply resolved the conflict in favor of the variability of the categories. In his lectures on pragmatism, he said: "We can no longer accept a single, invariable system of categories or intellectual frameworks. The frameworks that had a reason to exist in past civilizations do not have it today" (1955a: 149, t. 1983: 71). In sacrificing the universality of the categories to their cultural variability, Durkheim was sacrificing their necessity as well, for how could a category be necessary to social life if it were lacking in some cultures?

Durkheim was led to conclude in favor of the variability of the categories by two premises that he held: (1) that collective representations are culturally variable and (2) that the categories can be identified with collective representations. The second premise seems to be based on his assumption that the meanings of the categories and of concepts generally can be identified with their collective representations. He simply took it for granted that words refer to their meanings as some sort of entity, much as a proper name refers to a person or place. These views on meaning reflect the philosophical tradition in which he was educated. As we have seen, Durkheim, in the Sens lectures, drawing on Abelard's contribution

to the medieval debate between the realists and the nominalists, had identified the comprehension of a general term with a mental representation of the characteristics shared by all the things that fall under the extension of this term (1884a: 209–10). He appears to have thought that when members of the same society share moral or other general concepts, they all have mental states with the same representational content.

This assumption about shared meanings struck even Durkheim as wildly implausible for modern, complex, highly differentiated societies. As I have argued elsewhere (Schmaus 1994), he was thus motivated to turn his attention instead to the study of collective representations in so-called primitive societies, in which he thought that people, due to their limited range of experience, had the most similar ideas. However, the move to primitives does not avoid the problem of cultural incommensurability to which his views on meaning give rise. As I argued in Chapter 1, if the meaning of a category is identified with a collective representation, and if collective representations depend on variable social causes, then people who have been exposed to different social causes would have different collective representations and thus give different meanings to the categories. In this situation, how then could we even say that two different cultures represent the same category, only with two different representations? In what sense would they be representations of the same category? How could we then distinguish there being completely different categorical frameworks from there being merely different cultural representations of one and the same universal framework? Durkheim never addressed these questions and thus left his position unclear.

To avoid the incommensurabilist implications of Durkheim's sociological theory of the categories, I am proposing that the meanings of the categories be understood at least in part in terms of their social functions.[1] My proposal is rooted in Durkheim's arguments about the categories making certain necessary social functions possible. If two different representations from two different cultures nevertheless have similar functions or uses in their respective cultures, they are to that extent similar in meaning. I do not mean to identify the meanings of the categories entirely with their social functions, since I do not think that their social functions exhaust their meanings. I will illustrate this way of thinking about the meanings of the categories through a reinterpretation of Durkheim's account of the category of causality in *The Elementary Forms*. The category of causality is of central importance to Durkheim's theory of the origin of religion in this book, and it is thus the category that receives the greatest amount of attention.

Causality in *The Elementary Forms of Religious Life*

In *The Elementary Forms of Religious Life*, Durkheim, unlike his philosophical predecessors, distinguished two parts to the concept of causality and sought the separate origins of each. These were the idea of a causal power or force and the idea of a necessary connection between cause and effect (1912a: 524, t. 1995: 370). His account of the idea of power or force, according to which it derives from our experience of social forces, is subject to the same objections as the spiritualists' derivation of this idea from our experience of willed effort, as I will explain. However, there is a part of his account of the idea of a necessary connection that is not subject to these objections. In addition to his somewhat implausible hypothesis about the origins of this concept, he provided a more interesting functional hypothesis that emphasizes the important social role that this idea plays in making moral rules possible. This functional account suggests that we should think of the meaning of the idea of a necessary connection, and perhaps other categorical concepts as well, in terms of their social functions rather than in terms of a shared set of mental entities.

As I will explain, Durkheim's account of the social function of the idea of a necessary connection is not defeated by the objections one could raise against his account of the origin of the idea of power. Indeed, I would argue that Durkheim could have dropped the entire discussion of the idea of power from his sociology of knowledge and concentrated solely on the idea of necessary connection and still have made a very good case for the social function of the category of causality. His account of the collective origins of the idea of power is needed only for his sociology of religion. It must be pointed out, however, that contemporary anthropologists no longer favor his theory that totemism is the earliest form of religion. Many in fact have questioned the empirical evidence Durkheim adduced in support of his theory of religion, arguing that he was reading too much into ethnographies of indigenous Australians, Pacific Islanders, Native Americans, and other peoples.[2] However, his theory of the social function of the idea of necessary connection does not depend on his theory of the origin of religion and is thus not subject to its empirical shortcomings.

The Idea of Power

In presenting his argument for the social origins of the idea of power or force, Durkheim appears to have been challenging not the Kantian metaphysical and transcendental deductions of the categories so much as

Maine de Biran's spiritualist philosophy that the concept of causal power is derived from our internal experience of willed effort. Durkheim was defending the collective origin of the way in which we represent causality to ourselves as some sort of efficacious strength or energy. At least in this argument, he was less concerned with demonstrating the collective origin of Kant's concept of causality, which is concerned with such things as temporal relationships and hypothetical judgments.

Durkheim began with the straightforwardly Humean argument that our experience of the external world through the five senses does not give us the idea of power: "The senses enable us to see only the phenomena that co-exist or that follow one another, but nothing of what they perceive can give us the idea of that constraining and determining action that is characteristic of what one calls a power or a force. . . . the internal process that links these states escapes [the senses]" (1912a: 519–20, t. 1995: 368). However, although Durkheim also rejected our internal experience of the operation of the will as the source of the idea of power, he did not do so for the reasons that Hume gave. As I mentioned in Chapter 3, Hume had argued that just as we receive no impressions of power from external bodies, we are similarly unable to observe any power in any single instance of the operation of the will upon either the body or the mind itself. All of our ideas and sense impressions are wholly passive and inert for Hume. Instead of giving Hume's arguments, Durkheim first associated this theory of the origin of the idea of power with the theory that animism, or the belief that the universe is ruled by wills or spirits analogous to ourselves, was the earliest form of religion. He then argued that totemism and not animism was the earliest form of religious belief and that the idea of power owes its origin to the experience of collective totemic powers rather than the power of individual wills.

The animistic theory of the origin of religion was closely allied with the spiritualist philosophy that Durkheim sought to reform, renew, or replace. Rabier's philosophy text, for example, says: "Primitively, all the external causes that we conceived were conceived by us on the model of this internal activity, desire, or will, that we grasp within ourselves: thus all of nature is animated; we see life everywhere, everywhere efforts, tendencies, forces; and these invisible forces are for us the secret spring that unfolds all the visible phenomena of nature" (Rabier 1884: 296–7). As Durkheim explained, it has often been thought that the action of the will served as a model for our idea of force. He went on to describe what is clearly the spiritualist view that "In the will, . . . we perceive ourselves directly as a power in action" (1912a: 520, t. 1995: 368). As this idea was

then extended to other things, it became the idea of force. According to Durkheim, "As long as the animistic theory passed for a demonstrated truth, this explanation could appear to be confirmed by history" (ibid.). In arguing for the theory that religion originated in totemism rather than animism, Durkheim was thus attempting to strike another blow at spiritualism.

Durkheim argued against the animistic theory of the origin of religion by citing two important disanalogies between the primitive idea of force or power and the idea of the will as it is at least currently conceived. First of all, he said, the earliest way in which human beings conceived forces was as "anonymous, vague, diffuse forces" that were impersonal, like cosmic forces, and hence quite unlike human wills (ibid.). As evidence for this claim, Durkheim brought forth examples such as the Sioux notion of *wakan*, the Iroquois notion of *orenda*, and the Melanesian notion of *mana*, all of which, he said, were conceived as some sort of principle, energy, or power that underlies all the phenomena of nature (1912a: 290–2, t. 1995: 205–6). Furthermore, these cosmic forces, due to their impersonal character, were conceived as able to pass from one thing to another, making them again unlike the human will, which cannot change its substratum (1912a: 521, t. 1995: 368–9). The prototype for the idea of force, he said, was "mana, wakan, orenda, the totemic principle, various names given to collective force objectified and projected on to things. The first power that men have represented to themselves as such thus seems to have been that which society exercises over its members" (1912a: 519, t. 1995: 367).

He then concluded that the origin of our idea of force must satisfy two conditions: it must come from our internal experience and yet it must be impersonal. The only forces that satisfy these two conditions, he thought, are the social forces that arise from collective life. On the one hand, they are internal because "they are entirely psychical; they are made exclusively of ideas and objectified sentiments." On the other hand, it is true by definition that they are impersonal, since they are the products of cooperation (ibid.). Physical forces may satisfy this latter condition but they are not experienced internally. When we collide with an obstacle, we perceive only the effects and not the causes of these sensations. In the case of social forces, however, Durkheim argued that "they are part of our internal life, and, consequently we not only know the products of their actions but we see them acting" (1912a: 522, t. 1995: 369). Furthermore, he added, the idea of force bears the mark of its social origin, including within itself the idea of domination and subordination (1912a: 522, t. 1995: 369–70).

Far from deriving the concept of force or power from the will, Durkheim went on to argue that the very idea that the will has power over the body is borrowed from social life, that is, from our experience of the power by which society dominates the individual:

> Thus man could not have arrived at conceiving himself as a governing force of the body in which he resides except under the condition of introducing, in the idea that he makes of himself, concepts borrowed from social life. . . . In fact, it is indeed under the form of the soul that he has always represented the force that he believes himself to be. But we know that the soul is something entirely other than the name given to the abstract faculty of moving, thinking, or sensing; it is, above all, a religious principle, a particular aspect of the collective force. After all, man is conscious of a soul and, consequently, a force because he is a social being. (1912a: 523, t. 1995: 370)

Durkheim's argument that we can actually perceive social forces in action is puzzling, for Hume's point that we do not experience powers or forces directly but only through their effects would seem to apply just as much to social as to physical or any other forces. Thus it would appear that Durkheim had missed the point of Hume's arguments. In fact, there is no evidence that Durkheim had any direct knowledge of Hume. At least, Durkheim never cited him.[3] Instead, Durkheim appears to have relied on the eclectic spiritualists for his knowledge of Hume's arguments. Their lycée texts present Biran as having effectively refuted Hume and defend the idea that we can introspect forces or powers in action. As we have seen, Janet's text is sympathetic to Biran. So is Rabier's. Rabier went into great detail about Hume's argument that the idea of power does not derive from external sensation. However, he did not take the trouble to explain Hume's arguments or Biran's replies regarding the question of whether this idea derives from our internal experience of the will's effect on the body (Rabier 1884: 295). It appears that Rabier took it for granted that Biran had refuted Hume on this point.

Curiously, in *Suicide* Durkheim himself seems to have taken a more Humean position on the issue of the perception of force or power. In defending the claim that collective forces are just as real as physical forces, he said that collective forces, like physical forces, act on the individual from without, and are known in the same way as physical forces, that is, through the constancy of their effects (1897a: 348, t. 1951a: 309). However, he did not say that social forces are known *only* in this way. One possible interpretation is that Durkheim, regardless of whether he actually sided with Hume or Biran, in writing *The Elementary Forms* assumed that his audience thought that Biran had bested Hume on this question.

Taking for granted along with his audience that we can perceive forces in action, he then offered what he thought was a better account than the spiritualists' of the origin of the idea of causal power, insisting on the impersonal character of such forces. However, it would seem that Durkheim could have made a much more powerful argument against the spiritualist philosophy and the animistic theory of the origin of religion if he had taken a more Humean position in *The Elementary Forms* on the perception of forces. If we could not directly perceive the will in action but only indirectly perceive it through its effects, it would then appear to be less likely for religion to have originated in our peopling the world with active forces analogous to the human will. The idea of an active power would then have to have had some other origin than the human will.

One might object that I have not presented a fair account of Durkheim's theory of the origin of the idea of causal power. Durkheimians may argue that these collective forces are not merely perceived but also created in social life. In particular, a Durkheim scholar may say that I am overlooking Durkheim's account of how collective forces are born during periods of what he called "collective effervescence," which occur on those special occasions when the tribes gather and there is a heightened sense of being a part of something larger than oneself (1912a: 397ff., t. 1995: 216ff.). Anne Rawls, for instance, has written about how these collective forces are supposedly created through religious rites. According to Rawls, Durkheim believed that participation in rites provides one with "the experience of necessary force" (1996: 446). This experience creates feelings of well-being and "moral unity" that can be known by "direct" internal reflection. Participants in religious rites are able to directly perceive a causal relation between their participation and these feelings, she says, and it is the perception of this causal relationship that is the source of our category of causality (Rawls 1996: 447–9). On Durkheim's view, our internal experience has some advantage over external experience that allows us to perceive causal forces as well as causal relations:

Durkheim argues that, because these feelings are manifest internally, they are immediately available and, therefore, can be known directly rather than indirectly as with external objects. Knowledge of these internal states is, therefore, better and more valid than knowledge of external states or affairs. . . . Whereas natural forces cannot be perceived directly, social forces can, and the perception of them can therefore be validly shared with others. (Rawls 1996: 450–1)

It is not at all clear, however, that the appeal to the direct experience of social forces is sufficient to answer Hume's argument that "no

impression, either of sensation or reflection, implies any force or effi-cacy" (1739: 160). First of all, we need to know what is meant by direct or immediate perception. Second, we need to clarify exactly what it is that is supposedly being directly perceived. When Maine de Biran, Cousin, and Janet claimed that we have direct or immediate perception of the will's effort, for example, they meant that this perception was not medi-ated by any mental representations or ideas. It is not clear, however, how unmediated perception is supposed to solve Hume's problem. A Scottish common-sense philosopher, for instance, could argue that he has a direct perception of a compass pointing north, unmediated by any mental rep-resentation of any sort, yet still maintain without contradiction that he does not perceive the forces acting on the needle, but only their effects. If unmediated perception of the external world does not reveal forces, why should we think that unmediated internal experience would do so, regardless of whether the source of these forces is the individual will or society?

If internal reflection does not reveal forces, this raises the question of exactly what it does reveal. In my critique of Biran in Chapter 3, I argued that the apperception of willed effort reveals at best the necessary connection between an intention and an act, which is quite a different thing than causal power and force. This connection is revealed not by internal perception so much as by reflection upon the logical relation that exists between an intention and an act when the one is simply a re-description of the other. That is, there is a necessary connection between willing to raise your arm and raising your arm because these are nothing but two different ways of saying the same thing. On Rawls's reading of Durkheim, what internal reflection reveals is a feeling of well-being and a connection between that feeling and participating in a religious rite. This is only an empirical and not a logical, necessary connection. Feeling good and participating in a rite are not merely two descriptions of the same thing. To affirm a necessary connection involves an act of reflection or judgment. Perception alone can reveal only how things actually are and not how they necessarily must be. Thus, the idea of a necessary connec-tion cannot be simply derived from immediate perceptual experience, social or otherwise. Indeed, as I mentioned already and will explain later, Durkheim distinguished the idea of necessary connection from that of force or power and gave a separate account of the origin of the idea of a necessary connection.

I would go Durkheim one better and also separate the notions of force and power. The idea of power has the sense of a potential or capacity. A

potential or capacity is understood as the ability to do some specific sort of thing, such as a capacity to use language, and is thus very different from a force. The force of gravity, for example, can cause the tides or the swinging of a pendulum or any number of other things. Thus one could say that there is a sense in which we directly experience the power or capacity of society to produce a feeling of well-being in us. But to conclude that we therefore have direct experience of social forces and not just of their effects is merely to equivocate on the concepts of force and power. For Rawls to speak of "necessary force" as "immediately available to perception" (1996: 441) is for her to lump together the ideas of force, power, and necessary connection under a univocal concept of causality much as Hume and Biran and other philosophers have done in the past. There is nothing to recommend that we run these very different concepts together today.

The Idea of a Necessary Connection

In addition to the notion of force, the principle of causality also contains the idea of a necessary connection between the cause and the effect, according to Durkheim (1912a: 524, t. 1995: 370). Unlike his account of the idea of power or force, his account of the origin of the idea of necessary connection is not necessarily tied to any particular theory of the origin of religion. Nor does it depend entirely on claims about what is available to introspection. For Durkheim, the idea of a necessary connection between cause and effect is more like a principle of reason that makes social life possible than an idea or mental representation derived from social life. He characterized it as an a priori postulate: "The mind lays down this relationship in advance of any proof, under the empire of a sort of constraint from which it cannot free itself; it postulates it, as one says, a priori" (ibid.). The task of a sociology of knowledge, as he saw it, is to account for the a priori character of this principle.

Empiricism, Durkheim thought, has failed to account for the a priori and necessary character of the causal relationship. The association of ideas and habit alone can yield nothing but a state of expectancy. The principle of causality, however, is more than that. It has a normative character that rules the mind, which shows that the mind is not its creator (1912a: 524, t. 1995: 371). In addition, he explained that an individual state of expectation is not to be confused with "the conception of a universal order of succession that imposes itself on the totality of minds and events" (1912a: 630, t. 1995: 442). The individual may form from experience an idea of regular succession, but this is not the category

of causality. The sensation of regular succession is individual, subjective, and incommunicable, while the category of causality is "a framework in which empirical verifications arrange themselves and which allows us to think about them, that is to see them from a point of view that allows us to understand one another in regard to them" (1912a: 526, t. 1995: 372). Durkheim saw the principle of causality as universally valid, that is, as valid for all minds. The problem with empiricism, however, is not just that its premises are too individualistic to explain the universal character of our concepts, but also that it cannot explain their obligatory character. Durkheim also rejected the hypothesis that the idea of a necessary connection is inherited, arguing that an inherited habit of mind, simply by extending beyond the life of a single individual, does not acquire any normative or regulatory force (1912a: 524, t. 1995: 371).[4]

Instead of deriving the idea of a necessary connection from a feeling of expectation, Durkheim located the origin of this concept in the obligation of the members of a society to participate in things such as fertility rites. In certain rites exemplified by indigenous Australians, for instance, one imitates a certain species of plant or animal at an appropriate time of year in order to make it reproduce and flourish. However, it is not simply a matter of the group performing the rite and then collectively expecting the result to follow. Society imposes the obligation to imitate this species because a social interest is at stake. To obligate the members of a society to imitate an animal or a plant so that it will reproduce is to presume that performing the rite necessarily leads to the flourishing of the species that is being imitated. If society allowed people to doubt this causal relationship, Durkheim argued, it could not compel them to perform the rite (1912a: 524–5, t. 1995: 371).

One might object that Durkheim has overstated his case. Surely in order to compel all the members of a society to participate in a religious rite, it is not necessary for society to quell all doubts about the rite's efficacy. As Margaret Gilbert has argued, a group belief is not necessarily a belief that every, or even any, member of a group personally holds. Rather, a group belief is one that the group will agree to let stand as a group belief. Individuals may have all sorts of different reasons for allowing such a group belief to go unchallenged other than the personal belief that this group belief is actually true. One may prudently keep one's doubts to oneself (Gilbert 1989: 289ff.). For instance, Durkheim may have publicly adhered to the group belief among academic philosophers of his day that Biran had effectively refuted Hume, yet nevertheless harbored private reservations about it. Even if one grants Gilbert's point, however,

Durkheim's argument that the idea of obligation presupposes that of a necessary connection is still valid. Indeed, one could add that even for people to argue that they are not obligated to participate in a rite because it does not work would involve their making at least a negative use of the concept of causality. That is, such skeptics would be denying the existence of a necessary connection between the performance of the rite and the flourishing of the totemic species.

To be sure, Durkheim may have been less than clear about whether he was providing an account of the social origins or the social function of the concept of necessary connection or perhaps both. To link the idea of a necessary connection with that of moral obligation and derive both from the authority of society over the individual, as he did (1912a: 525, t. 1995: 371), is to raise the issue of the original source of this authority. As I mentioned in Chapter 1, Durkheim attempted to explain the moral authority of society over the individual in terms of the greater power, force, or vivacity of collective as opposed to individual representations. Collective representations are supposed to have the combined strength of the individual representations from which they are formed (1912a: 297–8, t. 1995: 209–10). It is not necessary for the individual to be able to perceive the power of these collective representations in action in order for them to exert their constraining power over the individual. Indeed, he said that the pathways by which they act are "too circuitous and too obscure" for the individual to perceive the source of their power (1912a: 299, t. 1995: 211). This claim would seem to contradict his account of the source of our idea of power or force. But even if we set that problem aside, and even if we are willing to leave unchallenged his theory that individual representations fuse into collective representations of greater strength, Durkheim has at best explained only the coercive power of society over the individual. He has said nothing about what gives this power any moral or normative character. At least since Rousseau, it has been a philosophical commonplace that yielding to superior force is not the same thing as restraining oneself in accordance with the moral law.

Durkheim's account of the social origins of the idea of a necessary connection also seems to run together more than one sense of "necessity." At least, he made no attempt to distinguish the different senses of the term. To recognize that one's action falls under a moral rule involves the use of a concept of logical necessity. That is, one may recognize that a moral rule entails that one faces certain obligations. To do the opposite of what one is obliged to do would be to act in a way that contradicts the moral rule. Similarly, to understand that there are certain things

that one must do in order to achieve some morally desirable end may also involve a concept of logical necessity. However, it is not clear what sort of necessity is involved in Durkheim's notion of the coercive power of society. When someone yields to a superior force, one is acting in a way that appears to be logically necessary in order to preserve one's life, which one takes to be a morally desirable end. But Durkheim's appeal to the action of unperceived powers or forces seems to involve a different, physical, mechanical, or natural notion of necessity. Yet he did not explain this notion or make clear how there could be such a thing as physical or natural necessity. It would seem that to say that some physical relationship among events is a necessary relation would be to say that this relationship could not be other than it is. But whether any laws of nature actually enjoy this status or whether the universe could have had an entirely different set of laws remains an open question. In sum, before attempting to explain the origin of our idea of necessary connection, Durkheim should have first provided an analysis of the different things that necessity could mean and then told us which concept of necessity he was trying to explain. This ambiguity regarding the concept of necessity also infects his repeated argument that the categories are necessary and universal. To be fair to Durkheim, French philosophers at least as far back as Cousin had been making ambiguous claims about the necessity of the categories, as we saw in Chapter 3. But we also saw that unlike these philosophers, he did not conflate necessary connection with power or force. So it is not unreasonable to wish that he had pursued his analysis of causality a little further and made clear what he meant by a necessary connection.

If we are willing to assume that Durkheim was talking about the concept of a logically necessary connection, his account of the social function of this concept makes a valid point, even if he was less than convincing with regard to the social origins or causes of this concept. That is, his account suggests that the idea of a necessary connection is itself necessary for the individual members of a society to understand the obligations that their society imposes on them. Society cannot obligate its members to do something unless they have some concept of a necessary connection. Where Kant saw the categories as necessary for there to be universally valid judgments about the objects of our experience, it seems that Durkheim was implying that the category of causality, and perhaps the other categories also, are needed for there to be universally valid moral judgments as well.

However, it appears to be only the notion of necessary connection, not power or force, that is required for the idea of moral obligation. That the idea of force or power is no part of the idea of moral obligation coheres

with the fact that people are held morally responsible for actions or states of affairs that do not necessarily involve any effort on their part, such as a failure to do something. H. L. A. Hart and Anthony Honoré (1985), for instance, have shown this in their analysis of the use of causal language by ordinary people, lawyers, and historians. According to them, the central concept of causality to be found in ordinary and legal discourse is that of some sort of human intervention in the normal sequence of events that results in the effect to be explained. Related commonsense concepts of causality include that of one person by word or deed providing another with a reason for doing something and that of one person providing an opportunity for harm to be done. They also find negative uses of these concepts, including that of a failure to intervene or to provide a reason or opportunity (Hart and Honoré 1985: 2–3). The commonsense or legal notion of causality as something equivalent to voluntary action, as Hart and Honoré point out, is not Hume's notion of causality (ibid., 2, 13ff.). It does not involve an invariable relationship between cause and effect. When we say that someone caused something to happen, we are not committed to something like the claim that under similar circumstances, she would do it again (ibid., 51, 55–6). What does seem to matter for our ordinary moral and legal sense of causality is intentionality. For instance, in holding someone responsible for poisoning another's food, it matters whether the victim knows he's being poisoned. If the victim knows this, and if he is not coerced into eating the food, he causes his own death. On a Humean analysis, on the other hand, what the poisoned person knows is irrelevant (ibid., 77). In other words, what matters for our ordinary moral and legal sense of causality is not so much a physical relation between cause and effect as a logical relationship between an intentional state and an action.

Regardless of whether we accept Durkheim's analysis of the concept of causality, we can still agree that some concept of a logically necessary connection between an agent's intentions and her actions is required for there to be moral and legal obligations and thus for there to be human society. The idea of a necessary connection is also assumed when one is held to account for some harm caused not through one's intentional acts but through one's negligence. For example, if you are held liable for an injury resulting from your icy sidewalk, there is a chain of necessary relations connecting you to that sidewalk. Owning a house entails the obligation to clear the sidewalk of ice. Of course, there may be extenuating circumstances such as injury or illness that would excuse you from your obligations. However, the very fact that we feel that exceptions to the

rules must be spelled out only supports the claim that these obligations are conceived as necessary.

In agreeing with Durkheim's claims about the social, moral, or legal functions of the concept of a necessary connection, we obviously need not go all the way with him and affirm that the origin of this idea was in the obligation of our ancestors to participate in totemic imitation rites. The concept of a necessary connection could have had some other origin and still perform the same function. Hence, Durkheim's account of the social function of the idea of a necessary connection does not depend on his theory of the origin of religion in totemism. It is not the specific nature of the obligation but the general concept of moral obligation that is necessary for the maintenance of a social group and that requires the concept of a necessary connection. Shared beliefs or interests do not alone suffice to transform a set of individuals into a social group. In order for a population to constitute a social group, they must perceive themselves as forming such a group, which would include accepting certain mutual obligations. The specific nature of their obligations matters less than the fact that they have some obligations. For example, even the obligation to follow certain rules of dress helps to maintain a collection of individuals as a social group. Hence, the sociological question is not how society was able to achieve universal assent that a certain religious rite yielded its intended effect and thus was able to achieve universal participation in this rite. Rather, the question is how it was that a group of people came to feel sufficiently obligated to one another that they would set aside their personal doubts about the efficacy of a rite in order to join together in the performance of that rite. In a similar manner today, one might suppress one's religious skepticism in celebrating the holidays with one's relatives or in-laws. The joint participation in religious rites may then help to maintain the social group in existence even if it did not create the society from a population of individuals in the first place. As Durkheim recognized, in order for religious rites to perform this function, it is not necessary that they work in the sense of bringing about their intended effect. What matters is that individuals are bound by the obligation to participate in them. In order for individuals to act in accordance with and understand their obligations to participate, however, they must have the concept of a necessary connection.

In sum, human society as we know it would not be possible without the idea of moral obligation. This means that people must be held accountable for their actions, which in turn assumes that in some sense they are the causes of their actions. Some may wish to object that societies are

maintained in existence through the exercise of social control through sanctions or the threat of sanctions. Sanctions, however, are applied as the result of the violation of a rule. Also, even the threat of sanctions is not always immediately present, and in their absence most people nevertheless continue to follow the rules. Of course, many of these rules may be only implicitly understood and not carefully articulated in a legal or moral code. However, it would not be possible to have even implicit moral rules without some notion of obligation and responsibility.

If the ideas of moral obligation and responsibility for one's actions presuppose the concept of a necessary connection, this concept should prove to be a cultural universal. The idea of a causal power or force, on the other hand, does not appear to have any necessary social function and thus may not be found in all cultures. Although I have criticized Durkheim for not carefully separating the idea of a logically necessary connection from various concepts of physical causation, in fairness to him it must be pointed out that these concepts are combined in many cultural representations of causality as well. Cultures may start off with rather confused ideas of causality and then subsequently introduce all sorts of distinctions among different sorts of causal and logical relations. This process is reflected in the development of the common law. As swindlers invent ever more sophisticated ways in which to cheat their fellow human beings, for instance, the courts must constantly articulate new grounds for holding them responsible for their misdeeds.

The idea of moral responsibility also involves the notion of ascribing intentional states to others. These may include beliefs as well as desires, goals, or purposes. A person may be held responsible for some harm not only because she intended it, but also because she knew (or should have known) that some harm was about to occur that she could have prevented but did not. Social life in humans, and perhaps other species as well, depends on our being able to ascribe such mental states to others and to hold them responsible for certain states of affairs on the basis of some necessary connection between these mental states and states of affairs in the world. Different human cultures may have different ways of communicating about these mental states and their connections with events in the world, as long as they all have some way of conceiving them. It is because different cultural or collective representations can perform this same function in their respective societies that we are able to recognize them as causal concepts.

For instance, Lévy-Bruhl, in his many books on so-called primitive mentality, described a social or moral function for what he took to be an

early causal concept, that is, the concept of participation. In accordance with this notion of participation, people are held responsible for all sorts of things for which we would not blame them. For example, there is supposedly no such thing for the primitive as an accidental death or death by natural causes. All death is due to witchcraft. Witchcraft assumes a notion of participation, according to which one is supposed to be able to harm one's intended victim through actions taken against his or her bodily fluids, hair, nails, footsteps, image, clothing, utensils, and so on, because all these things "participate" in the victim. People who perform such witchcraft may be held responsible for the death of their victims (Lévy-Bruhl 1910: 321ff., t.; 1985: 276ff.; 1922: 20ff., t.; 1978: 37ff.; 1927, t.; 1928: 114ff.). Although we may not hold people accountable for murder through witchcraft, nevertheless the relationship between the notion of participation and that of moral responsibility allows us to recognize this notion of participation as a causal concept.

Conclusion

In closing, I would like to remind the reader that Durkheim recognized that "The principle of causality has been understood differently in different times and countries; in the same society, it varies with the social milieux and with the reigns of nature to which it is applied" (1912a: 527, t. 1995: 373). As he explained in a footnote, the concept of causality is not only different for the ordinary person than it is for the scientist, but is even different in different branches of science, such as physics and biology. I suggested in Chapter 1 that a single individual may even use different concepts of causality on different occasions. From the discussion in this chapter, it should be clear that even in everyday discourse, the concept of physical causation that is used is different from the concept of causation involved in human action. Physical causation is more closely tied to the idea of force, while human agency is bound up with the idea of a necessary connection between intention and the act or even with a capacity or power to act. Thus we may want to give different accounts of the historical and cultural development of collective representations of each of these concepts. How such an inquiry into the collective representations of the categories would proceed and what the sociology of knowledge today can draw from Durkheim are topics for the concluding chapter.

7

Prospects for the Sociological Theory
of the Categories

In the preceding chapters I have shown that in arguing for the social causes and functions of the categories, Durkheim was responding to the way that the Kantian categories were understood in the eclectic spiritualist tradition. Kant's logically necessary conditions of experience were understood as psychologically necessary conditions, which led to the subjectivist reading of the critical philosophy according to which it was unable to explain or justify the application of the categories to our experience of the external world. The eclectic spiritualists then sought an epistemological grounding of the categories in an empirical apperception of the mind's activity, rather than in Kant's transcendental deduction of the categories, in which the transcendental apperception of the unity of consciousness plays a central role. Among the early eclectic spiritualists, the theory of the categories was thus thought to belong to a foundational introspective psychology.

During the late nineteenth century in France, however, psychology increasingly came to be seen as an empirical, hypothetico-deductive science. Durkheim's purpose was to show that a theory of the categories should rightfully belong to an empirical sociology instead. To make sense of his arguments, however, we have had to introduce a distinction between the categories and their collective representations. With this distinction in mind, we can then extract two different theses from his sociology of knowledge: (1) that there is a set of categories that is found in all human cultures because they are necessary to the moral rules and obligations that hold individuals together in a society; and (2) that a person's ways of thinking and communicating about these concepts are acquired from his or her culture. Whatever intrinsic interest these hypotheses may hold,

neither of them was what Kant was trying to show. His goal was to demonstrate that the categories were valid of experience because these are the very concepts that make possible the unity of judgments, consciousness, and the objects of experience.

Insofar as Durkheim's sociological theory of the categories emphasizes the role that the categories play in making possible social discourse about everything from objects in the real world to moral rules, it may be regarded as an improvement over the eclectic spiritualist tradition in philosophy, which considers only the role of the categories in processing perceptual experience. At the same time, however, his theory is still encumbered with many assumptions that derive from this philosophical tradition. Durkheim's belief that we can have direct experience of forces can be traced to Maine de Biran. The notion that the meanings of general concepts can be identified with mental contents of some sort Durkheim shared with Paul Janet. Durkheim's way of formulating his sociological research program has some unfortunate consequences. First of all, by identifying the categories with their collective representations and then distinguishing sociology from psychology as the study of collective rather than individual representations, he made psychological studies of cognition wholly irrelevant to the sociology of knowledge. Second, his position that these collective representations of our most fundamental categories of thought were culturally variable led to an unacceptable incommensurabilism and cognitive relativism. In this concluding chapter I want to investigate what remains of value that can serve as a fruitful guide for further research, once we disencumber Durkheim's theory of the categories of assumptions inherited from his philosophical predecessors.

One might think that the cultural variability of the categories does not necessarily lead to cognitive relativism. Even if different cultures had vastly different categories, that would not prevent them from saying things that are true in some nonrelative sense. For instance, if people from a different culture were to say that an elephant is larger than a mouse, it would still be true regardless of their categorical framework. Whether or not a statement is true has to do with the way the world is, not the way the human mind works. The existence of nonrelative truth does not depend on a universal human nature (McGinn 2002: 41). Fair enough. But the problem that cognitive relativism poses is not about what statements are true so much as what statements people take to be true. Whether people from different cultures are able to agree on the evaluations of putative truth claims depends on whether they share certain concepts. If not, they may have incommensurable standards of truth.

Moreover, Durkheim was already heading down the path to an antirealist philosophy as a result of his assumption that the objects of our thoughts and perceptions are representations, regardless of whether these are individual or collective representations or both. The assumption that the objects of our perceptions are mental representations derives from the early modern philosophers who were in thrall to a picture of perception that assumes some sort of homunculus observing images on a screen. On this picture, we always have before us the skeptical challenge of whether there is anything behind those representations other than Descartes's evil genius. Even if there is, why should we think that it resembles our representations or constrains them in any way? As Philip Kitcher (2001: 14) suggests, if we add to this picture the assumption that part of the image is supplied by the human mind, the goal of perceiving reality becomes hopeless. Kant himself was not entirely free of the representational model of perception held by Descartes and Locke, which explains why his earliest critics drew antirealist implications from his philosophy. The desire to avoid these implications was the motivation behind the philosophy of direct perception of Reid, Jacobi, and Cousin. It was bad enough that Janet reintroduced representative ideas in order to give an account of meaning. Durkheim unfortunately extended this hypothesis to explain perception as well and in fact compounded the problem by introducing collective in addition to individual representations, thus permitting an antirealist reading of his sociology of knowledge. In Durkheim's defense, one could say that at least he did not postulate a homunculus. But he thereby left unexplained exactly whom these representations were present to and who or what processed them. He would have been better off without these mental entities entirely and with the physical brain processing sensations from objects in the real world. I do not mean to suggest that the world is exactly as we perceive it. For instance, we obviously see different colors, not photons of different energies. However, it does not follow from the fact that the way things appear to us is different from the way science says they are that there are nonphysical mental representations that mediate perception.

To rescue what is of value from the Durkheimian tradition in the sociology of knowledge, we need to free it from all these mentalistic assumptions. We should jettison the assumption that shared meanings consist in shared mental entities of some sort. Instead of identifying the categories with collective representations, we should define them at least in part in terms of their social functions, as I have explained. We also need to give up the notion that a collective representation is a type of mental entity

distinct from individual representations. We can then reconceive the relationship between the sociology of knowledge and psychology in a way that would allow for more fruitful exchange and cooperation between them.

It is not necessary to drop the notion of collective representations from the sociology of knowledge entirely, however. Rather, we need to distinguish two different senses of "collective representation," both of which can be found in Durkheimian sociology. The term originally referred to a shared mental entity. But it has also been used to refer to such public representations as works of art, songs, dances, spoken words, emblems, symbols, and so forth. It is through such public representations that people are able to communicate about objects in the world or even about their fantasies. Perhaps it would be better to call these things cultural rather than collective representations in order to avoid the confusion with Durkheim's mental entities. What makes it possible for us to communicate with people in other cultures and to learn the meanings of their cultural representations is that they can be used to refer to objects in the real world, not just to objects that exist only in collective mental representations. As Durkheim showed us, they can be used for other functions as well, such as holding people responsible for certain actions or states of affairs. It is because there are certain functions that are necessary in all societies that people are able to interpret what is going on in cultures other than their own. We are able to recognize that someone from another culture is either giving someone directions or accusing him of causing some harm because these are things that we do in our culture. Through recognizing these functions, we can come to learn the meanings of the cultural representations associated with them. The problem of incommensurabilism then does not arise.

The Relation between Sociology of Knowledge and Psychology

Durkheim is often interpreted as holding that human nature is eminently plastic and shaped by cultural and social factors. On this interpretation, he supposedly held that the human mind is little more than a blank slate at birth and that most of its contents are written there by the social and cultural environment. In support of this reading of Durkheim, his critics typically quote passages such as the following one from *The Rules of Sociological Method*:

Every time that a social phenomenon is directly explained by a psychological phenomenon, one may be assured that the explanation is false.... But one would be strangely mistaken about our thought, if, from the foregoing, he drew the

conclusion that sociology, according to us, must, or even can, make an abstraction from man and his faculties. It is clear, on the contrary, that the general characteristics of human nature enter into the work of elaboration from which social life results. However, it is not these that give rise to it nor that give it its special form; they only make it possible. Collective representations, emotions, and tendencies have for their generating causes not certain states of the consciousness of individuals, but the conditions in which the social body finds itself as a whole. Doubtless, these can be realized only if individual natures are not refractory to them; but these individual natures are only the indeterminate matter that the social factor determines and transforms. Their contribution consists exclusively in very general states, in vague and consequently plastic predispositions, which, by themselves, could not take on the definite and complex forms that characterize social phenomena, if other agents did not intervene. (1895a: 128, 130, t. 1982: 129, 130–1)[1]

However, in this passage Durkheim was saying merely that the characteristics of human nature are only necessary and not sufficient conditions for the collective states that constitute social life. He was not arguing that there is no such thing as a human nature that is independent of the way it is shaped by society. Durkheim wanted only to distinguish the subject matter of sociology from that of psychology, not to deny that psychology had one at all. *The Rules* is a polemical work first published as a series of articles in the *Revue philosophique* in 1894 as a manifesto for the still new science of sociology. Although it is true that Durkheim argued in this work that sociological theories could not be derived from theories of human nature, in the chapter from which these passages are taken he took Comte and Spencer as his principal targets. Before Durkheim, theories of human nature were still largely philosophical. As I explained in Chapter 1, Durkheim was attempting to distance sociology from psychology as part of his strategy for defending the empirical status of sociology. Durkheim's more substantive works in sociology reveal a belief in individual psychological characteristics that are independent of social causes. For instance, in *Suicide*, Durkheim explained only social suicide rates and not individual suicides in terms of social causes. He did not think that individual suicides could be explained simply by narrowing down through sociological factors alone the reference class to which the individual belonged. Instead, he said that due to an individual's "mental constitution," one member of a high-risk group, such as elderly Protestant bachelors, may be more or less resistant to suicide than another (1897a: 366, t. 1951a: 323). In *Moral Education*, he argued that human nature requires discipline and restraint and thus gives rise to our need to belong to society ([1925a] 1961: 50–1).[2] Even in *The Elementary Forms*,

he never denied that the human mind has some content that is independent of culture. As we saw in Chapter 1, he allowed for the existence of
psychological capacities that correspond to the categories but are distinct
from them and even make the collective representations of the categories
possible.

However, as I have explained, neither these collective representations
nor these psychological capacities are what Kant meant by the categories.
Yet, when Kant said in the *Prolegomena* that his theory of the categories
is about the concepts that are necessarily found in experience and not
about the way in which experience is generated, he did not rule out the
possibility of an empirical investigation of these psychological processes.
He merely argued that his critique of cognition and the understanding
would have to precede such an empirical psychology.[3] Even if one were
to insist, contra Kant, that such things as spatial, temporal, and causal relations exist in nature independently of the human mind, we would still
need to have the appropriate cognitive mechanisms to perceive these
relations. If Kant were right that the categories are the necessary conditions for universally and objectively valid judgments, this would suggest
the empirical question of how these conditions are met by members of
our species. To what extent has either cultural development or the evolution of our linguistic and cognitive capacities – or both – been responsible for meeting these conditions? Perhaps needless to say, Durkheim
cannot simply use Australian ethnographies for evidence of how our
spatial, temporal, and causal thinking first originated. The indigenous
Australians are of course not our ancestors but fully modern human beings with fully evolved linguistic and cognitive capacities like everyone
else's.

The distinction between a cultural representation of a category and an
individual psychological capacity that corresponds to a category in effect
distinguishes the domain of inquiry of the sociology of knowledge from
that of the cognitive neurosciences. The cognitive neurosciences look for
evidence of underlying mechanisms that can explain the perception of
permanent objects and spatial, temporal, and causal relations. The sociology of knowledge investigates the culturally variable representations
that make it possible for people to communicate about things in their
perceived environment, including permanent objects as well as spatial,
temporal, and causal relationships. These cultural representations make
it possible to formulate claims about objects, events, and processes in this
environment that others can then criticize and test. Through this sort of
mutual dialogue, human beings are able to acquire a more reliable form

of knowledge than if they were each reduced to their own individual perceptions.

Evolutionary Perspectives and the Sociology of Knowledge

Once the cognitive neurosciences have unveiled the perceptual processing mechanisms that explain the appearance of the categories in experience, evolutionary science may then seek for evidence that these mechanisms are adaptations that have been produced by natural selection. This study may include comparisons with the cognitive equipment of other species in order to understand how less complex systems may have provided advantages at every step of the way. If Kant were right that the categories are necessary conditions for conscious experience, then other species of animals that appear to be conscious would also have to possess psychological capacities corresponding to the categories at least to some degree.

An evolutionary approach can help to explain how our concepts of space, time, causality, permanent object, and other categories apply to the real world, at least in a descriptive, psychological sense if not in a justificatory, epistemological sense. Simply to postulate the existence of corresponding psychological capacities in the way that Durkheim did is only to raise the question of why we should trust them and not regard them as illusory. We may say instead that these psychological capacities are adaptations that have been naturally selected because they help us to track certain features of the external environment that are important to us, much as the different colors we perceive track real differences in the energies of light. Natural selection explains that what the mind contributes to perceptual experience is not arbitrary. Other species may pick out different things from the environment. But what each picks out must track actual objects, properties, events, or processes. Such natural selection accounts will not answer Kant's epistemological questions concerning the validity of the categories, of course. But they can explain how it is that the corresponding psychological capacities are reliable for all practical purposes.

One might object that it is hard to believe that all of our complex notions of space, time, causality, and classification have biological functions or are evolutionary adaptations. After all, of what possible use to anyone are the physicists' notions of curved space or the biologists' debates over the proper way to classify the different sorts of reptiles? How could anyone's chances of survival and passing on his or her heredity depend

on such concepts? In reply, we can take our cue from Ruth Millikan's response to a similar objection to her view that the beliefs and desires of folk psychology have proper biological functions. It is true, she says, that we have apparently useless beliefs about things like dinosaurs. Nevertheless, she argues, we can say that the system that produces beliefs and desires has a biological function, as long as it has produced some beliefs and desires that have aided survival and reproduction and the system was naturally selected for that reason (Millikan 1993: 94–5). We could defend claims about the functions of spatial or temporal cognition in a similar fashion. Although it may be hard to see the function of the super string theorists' ten-dimensional space-time, nevertheless our ability to conceptualize space and communicate about it may have functions that aid survival and reproduction. Ten-dimensional space-time is simply a subsequent cultural development. Dan Sperber (1996: 66) similarly points out that to say that human cognitive abilities have been naturally selected is not to say that all of their effects are adaptive.

Millikan shares with Steven Pinker and Paul Bloom the belief that our innate cognitive mechanisms have resulted from natural selection. Indeed, how else could they have been produced? These authors argue that it is difficult to believe that complex physiological mechanisms are either mere spandrels or the result of genetic drift, pleiotropy, or allometry. Such random and accidental processes would hardly be particular about whom they benefited, and would be just as likely to result in mechanisms that benefited species other than the one in which they appeared. If we therefore accept that a complex organ such as the eye was produced by natural selection, then by analogy we should also accept that complex cognitive mechanisms, such as the ones responsible for language acquisition, were produced by natural selection.[4]

However, it is one thing to defend the general thesis that the human brain includes innate cognitive mechanisms designed by natural selection and quite another thing to provide evidence that any particular concept, such as space, time, causality, belief, or desire, represents an evolutionary adaptation. Not everything that appears to be useful or adaptive is therefore an adaptation. It may be that certain concepts that are adaptive developed through cultural processes and do not represent evolutionary adaptations. Even if certain concepts may be found in all human cultures, the universality of these concepts may be due to convergent cultural development rather than to some inborn cognitive mechanisms that have been naturally selected. As Donald Symons (1989, 1990, 1992) argues, to say that something is adaptive is merely to say that it has some current

beneficial effects, while to say that it is an evolutionary adaptation is to imply that there is a history of natural selection behind it. Thus to say that a trait is an adaptation is to make an empirical claim that must be supported by evidence. For instance, there could be evidence that the population that lacked the trait in question went extinct due to the relative advantages of the population that possessed the trait.

The possibility that a useful concept may appear in all cultures because of convergent cultural development is a reason that cognitive and evolutionary approaches to the mind need to take the sociology of knowledge into account. All these disciplines need to work together in order to sort out the relative contributions of evolution and culture to our cognitive resources. I am using the term "sociology of knowledge" here in a large sense, which would include historical studies and cross-cultural comparisons of the ways in which people have represented the categories. Thus the domain of inquiry of the sociology of knowledge overlaps with those of social and cultural anthropology, which in fact derive at least in part from Durkheim's sociology of knowledge and religion in *The Elementary Forms*. In this work, Durkheim recognized that our cultural representations might help us to adapt to the natural as well as the social environment. This is implied in his account of how the concepts representing the categories can be constructed on social models and yet apply to things in nature. He explained that if some artifice enters into the categories because they are constructed concepts, it is an art that approaches nature by degrees. For Durkheim, the categories are comparable to other sorts of tools that societies have improved over time (1912a: 25–7, t. 1995: 17–18).

Human beings of course are not the only social species. Hence, if Durkheim were right about the social functions of the categories, we would expect other species to have evolved ways of communicating about them as well. This prediction is borne out by studies in cognitive ethology of such things as the ways in which honeybees communicate with each other about the direction and distance of pollen-bearing flowers.[5] Similarly, our prelinguistic ancestors may have used various means to communicate about spatial, temporal, or other relationships. Darwin's *On the Origin of Species* (1859) is full of examples of how species may evolve new behaviors while the evolution of biological structures that facilitate these behaviors lags behind. For instance, he talked about woodpeckers that feed on insects on the ground and web-footed geese that have adopted a purely terrestrial way of life (Darwin 1859: 471). In a similar manner, our hominid ancestors could have been communicating with each other

about things like spatial distances and directions before the cognitive mechanisms that make human language possible evolved to facilitate this sort of communication. That our language is full of spatial metaphors, as evidenced for instance in the fact that all of our prepositions seem to suggest spatial relationships of one form or another, may be a clue to the evolution of language.

Cultural representations of the categories may actually allow us to improve upon the cognitive resources that natural selection has bequeathed to us. Natural selection has a way of jury-rigging things, taking advantage of what is already there rather than starting anew. For instance, an engineer designing a bipedal mammal such as ourselves would probably not use the same basic skeletal plan found in quadrupeds, nor would she provide a giraffe with the same number of neck bones as an elephant. The evolution of the human nervous system and its cognitive mechanisms no doubt displays the same pattern, adapting preexisting structures to new purposes. Hence there is no reason to believe that the cognitive mechanisms bequeathed to us by natural selection are the best they could be. Thus it would be possible for human beings through the development of culture to find ways of representing space, time, or causality that are more coherent or less ambiguous than the ways in which our naturally selected cognitive mechanisms represent them. Also, natural selection can adapt the mind only to relatively stable features in the environment, whereas the development of cultural representations may allow us to think and communicate about rapidly changing circumstances. Finally, cultural representations make possible an intellectual division of labor in which not everyone needs to carry the full load of a culture's system of representations. As Scott Atran says, cultural representations amplify human conceptual abilities (1995: 218). It then becomes the task of the sociology of knowledge to understand how our cultural representations may have improved upon the innate cognitive abilities with which natural selection has endowed us.

To be sure, cultural representations may give rise to ambiguities in our conceptual repertoire as well. Consider again our concepts of causality. As Pinker (1997: 315) points out, cultural representations of causality in animistic explanations of natural phenomena and in anthropomorphic tales often mix two very different notions of causality, the intentional and the physical. However, cultural representations may also make it possible to introduce finer distinctions into our concepts of causality. For instance, it is only through the development of a system of cultural representations that philosophers such as Hume have been able

to distinguish the notion of an invariable sequence from that of force or power. Cultural representations allow us to refine our concepts of intentional causality, as well. As I suggested in the previous chapter, much of the development of the English and American common law tradition can be regarded as refinements in our concepts of that for which people may be held responsible. That one can be held causally responsible for some harm through one's words alone shows how much our understanding of causality depends on cultural representations such as are found in language.

Causal Cognition

The variety of causal concepts provides a good example of the need for an interdisciplinary approach to sorting out the relative contributions of culture and our innate cognitive capacities to our conceptual repertoire. The recent cognitive science literature distinguishes at least two different mechanisms for perceiving causal relations, one for physical causality and the other for intentional or animate causality. Alan Leslie (1994: 127), for example, calls the one for physical causality "ToBy," for the "Theory of Body," and the one for animate causality "ToMM," for the "Theory of Mental Mechanism."[6] ToMM is supposedly that which makes possible what is often called "folk psychology." It is thought that this mechanism allows us to understand, explain, and even predict the actions of people, animals, and perhaps other things by attributing intentional states such as beliefs and desires to them.

There is a long research tradition investigating the perception of physical causality that begins with Albert Edouard Michotte's (1946) work with adults and continues today with studies by Leslie, Renée Baillargeon, and Elizabeth Spelke of human infants as young as four months old.[7] These psychologists use a looking-time methodology that is based on the assumption that infants will look longer at displays that violate their expectations than at those that are consistent with them. They found, for instance, that infants do in fact expect one billiard ball to communicate its motion to another and that they show surprise when this does not occur. Of course, these cognitive scientists do not use actual billiard ball collisions in these experiments but only movies or other projected images of them. Indeed, it is only through such media that they can produce billiard ball interactions that violate our expectations. Nevertheless, when the film shows the expected interaction, even adults are subject to a perceptual illusion of causality. The fact that adults

continue to see the illusion even when they know how it was produced is evidence that the illusion is due to our hard-wiring (Leslie and Keeble 1987: 266, 285).[8]

Leslie (1995: 124) thinks that this illusion of causality is the result of an evolutionary adaptation by which the mind applies a primitive notion of force to such situations. He agrees with Hume that we do not literally "see" the power, force, or necessary connection in things themselves. Rather, he says, we have this primitive notion of a "force" that is an evolutionary adaptation, not a product of science or culture, which we apply to these sorts of situations.[9] However, evidence that a perceptual illusion is due to a hard-wired cognitive mechanism is not evidence that the ability to perceive the illusion is an adaptation. Consider the well-known "moon illusion," in which the moon is perceived to be larger when it is near the horizon than when it is directly overhead. Even if it could be shown that the cognitive and perceptual mechanisms responsible for this illusion are adaptations, it hardly follows that the moon illusion itself is an adaptation. Similarly, we need to ask what, if anything, is an adaptation in the mechanisms responsible for the causal illusion. Leslie (1982: 186) is more cautious in his earlier papers on causal perception, in which he claimed only that his experiments revealed the perception of spatiotemporal continuity, which he said hardly constitutes even a primitive conception of causality but is at best an ingredient in physical causality. One could argue that the illusion of causal force or power is not an adaptation, as it confers no additional advantage over and above that yielded by our ability to perceive spatiotemporal continuity and invariable sequences. But again, natural selection does not always work in ways that make sense to us. We need evidence of exactly what innate cognitive mechanisms are responsible for the causal illusion and of how these mechanisms have been shaped by natural selection.

While ToBy is supposed to be an adaptation to the physical environment, ToMM or the concept of intentional causality is thought to be an adaptation for social life. The adaptive value of being able to attribute beliefs and desires to others is that it helps one to predict the behavior of both friends and enemies. In addition, as Leslie Brothers argues (1995: 1112), the ability to represent the intentions of others facilitates the development, social learning, and spread of technologies. That is, to learn the use of some technical device involves being able to recognize the intentions of the person who is demonstrating its use. This is true both for the child learning the adult culture and for the adult learning a new technology from its innovator.

The idea that there may be some sort of innate theory of mind mechanism goes back to David Premack and Guy Woodruff's paper "Does the chimpanzee have a theory of mind?" They call this a "theory" of mind because the mental states that one primate supposedly attributes to another are unobservable and because these attributions can be used for predicting another's behavior (Premack and Woodruff 1978: 515). There are two questions we need to consider here: whether there is an innate mechanism responsible for folk psychology and, if there is, whether this innate mechanism is an adaptation designed by natural selection. Evidence for such innate capacities in humans comes from studies of cognitive development in childhood, especially pathological cases, and evidence for the presence of these capacities in nonhuman primates could be relevant to the question regarding the evolution of these capacities.

The developmental evidence for ToMM involves one version or another of the following test: one takes two children, Amanda and Bob, and shows them some candy in a red box. Next, one sends Bob out of the room and switches the candy to a green box in plain view of Amanda. Then one asks Amanda where Bob will look for the candy when he returns. If Amanda is less than four, she will answer with the green box, where she last saw the candy, rather than the red one, where Bob last saw it. In other words, she is not yet able to understand the connection between what Bob believes and what he perceives and thus to attribute a false belief to Bob. The very young Amanda answers the question from the point of view of what she knows to be true of the candy and the boxes, rather than from the point of view of what Bob is capable of knowing.[10] However, Leslie (1991) reports that many autistic children even well past the age of four will persist in giving the same response as three-year-olds, although even children with Down's syndrome will pass this false belief test starting at about the age of four. He explains these results through the hypothesis that childhood autism involves some sort of impairment or delay in the development of ToMM. The fact that ToMM takes so much longer than ToBy to develop in human children may indicate that it is a much more complex mental mechanism that is perhaps tied to the development of language abilities.

The evidence for an innate concept of mind in nonhuman primates is less clear. Premack points out that an ape is able to attribute to others only those mental states that it has itself. These will be very close to sensation, such as seeing, wanting, or expecting; it is doubtful that a chimpanzee has beliefs (Premack 1988: 175). One of the reasons it is difficult to find unequivocal evidence of the existence of an innate theory of mind

in nonhuman primates may be that the propositional attitudes that folk psychology employs are so closely tied to human language. Just as the chimpanzee has only the most primitive linguistic abilities, it has only the most primitive abilities to ascribe propositional content to another individual. However, even if there were evidence of an innate theory of mind mechanism in nonhuman primates, this evidence would not necessarily show that natural selection had produced the same cognitive mechanism in humans or in a common ancestor to humans and chimpanzees. Birds and bats both fly, but they do not have a common ancestor that could fly. Whatever ability chimpanzees may have to attribute intentional states to others could have evolved after the chimpanzee and hominid lines diverged, after which humans may have evolved a capacity for folk psychology more closely tied to language. Whether or not this is true is an empirical question for which it could be very difficult to find evidence.

Kim Sterelny questions whether natural selection could have produced a mechanism such as ToMM adapting us to the social environment in the same way that it could have produced a mechanism like ToBy adapting us to the physical environment. As he puts it, "when evolution is driven by features of the social structure of the evolving species, it transforms the adaptive landscape of the evolving organism. The evolution of language, of tool use, of indirect reciprocity, or solutions to the commitment problem, are not solutions to a preexisting problem posed to the organism. There are no *stable* problems to which natural selection can grind out a solution" (Sterelny 1995: 372). Natural selection is a slow and gradual process, and in order for it to work, there must be some fairly stable, preexisting conditions in the environment. Unlike ToMM, ToBy or whatever innate mechanism is responsible for the causal illusion is responding to relatively stable features of the physical environment.

Nevertheless, one could argue that there is at least some empirical evidence for ToMM, whereas Durkheim's theory that the concept of a necessary connection is required for social life is based on a purely philosophical analysis. That is, it is only from a logical point of view that moral rules and obligations, and hence society, require that we all have some concept of a necessary connection in order to understand our obligations. Simply from a philosophical analysis of what is needed for social life, we cannot conclude that the brain has the corresponding cognitive mechanisms. The idea of a necessary connection in particular would seem to depend on language and may even be a cultural product. Fair enough. But the very possibility that the idea of a necessary connection is a cultural product and not innate once again argues for the need for cooperation

between psychology and the sociology of knowledge. Both disciplines are necessary to answer the question concerning the relative contributions of nature and culture to our ability to understand obligation. If the concept of a necessary connection turns out to be largely a cultural product, we may want to investigate why and to what extent cultures have introduced it into their systems of moral rules. Perhaps it has helped us make improvements in our ideas of personal responsibility in the same way that cultural representations of causality have. If this were the case, we could turn to the cognitive neurosciences to find out about the limitations of our natural endowments for understanding social relationships and then turn to the study of how cultural representations may have refined this understanding. For instance, it is probably the case that our innate endowment leads us to treat kin and others who are like us differently than we treat other people, and that the idea of a rule that necessarily applies to everyone alike is a subsequent cultural development.

Conclusion

In sum, the answer to the question concerning the relative contributions of culture and our innate cognitive mechanisms to the conceptual requirements for social life requires a cooperative effort between the sociology of knowledge and psychology. The sociology of knowledge should investigate just how diverse the representations of the categories in different cultures may be and what these representations from different cultures appear to have in common. From this study, it should then try to derive some conclusions about the cognitive or conceptual requirements for social life. It may then investigate the extent to which the common features of different cultures' representations of the categories can be explained by convergent cultural development. The degree to which the cognitive requirements for social life are met by our innate psychological mechanisms is a question for the cognitive neurosciences. Evolutionary science may then address the issue of how these mechanisms may have evolved. I do not mean to suggest a strict division of intellectual labor among these disciplines or that the psychologists and biologists must wait for the sociologists to complete their task. Rather, there should be constant cooperation and sharing of results.

In the past two chapters I have concentrated almost exclusively on the role that causal concepts play in human social life. As Durkheim recognized, concepts such as space and time and our ability to classify also have social functions. Hence the sociology of knowledge and the

cognitive neurosciences should investigate the relevant cognitive mechanisms and cultural representations for these concepts as well. Once we have a sense of the range of cognitive mechanisms at play in the diverse cultural systems of representations, we can then ask how these mechanisms evolved. The answer might just be that we evolved a flexible system of cognitive capacities that could be readily adapted, through culture, to various physical and social environments. This is the very answer suggested by Durkheim in *The Elementary Forms of Religious Life*.

Notes

Notes to Chapter 1

1. I usually provide my own translations from Durkheim's French texts. Page numbers for the most recent English translations of each work are provided for the convenience of the reader. For references to Durkheim's writings, I have adopted the numbering system invented by Steven Lukes (1973), which is the standard practice among Durkheim scholars. A recent bibliography of Durkheim's works that updates this system can be found on the Durkheim web pages at http://www.relst.uiuc.edu/durkheim/Bibliography/Bibo1.html.

2. Pickering (1993) argues that the classificatory concepts that concerned Durkheim and Mauss in their 1903 paper must be distinguished from the categories that concerned Durkheim in *The Elementary Forms*. In biology, too, systematists today distinguish classificatory concepts or "taxa" from categories. Categories include kingdom, phylum, class, order, family, genus, and species, while taxa may include animal, chordate, mammal, primate, hominid, and Homo sapien. As I mention in the following text, even biological taxa are not all that culturally variable.

3. My text is a paraphrase of Douglas (1970: 20). An earlier statement of the thesis is to be found in Max Gluckman: "From infancy, every individual is moulded by the culture of the society into which it is born. All human beings see, but we know, for example, that how they see shapes and colours is to some extent determined by this process of moulding. More than this, their ability to describe their perceptions depends on the categories contained in their respective languages" (Gluckman 1949–50: 73–4). On the following page he attributed the notion that our thoughts are shaped by "collective representations" to the French sociologists (ibid., 75). Edmund Leach makes a similar claim about the construction of perceptual reality:

I postulate that the physical and social environment of a young child is perceived as a continuum. It does not contain any intrinsically separate "things." The child, in due course, is taught to impose upon this environment a kind of discriminating grid which serves to distinguish the world as being composed of a large number of separate things,

each labeled with a name. This world is a representation of our language categories, not vice versa. Because my mother tongue is English, it seems self-evident that bushes and trees are different kinds of things. I would not think this unless I had been taught that it was the case. . . .

Each individual has to learn to construct his own environment in this way. (Leach 1964: 34–5)

Leach's claims in this passage are a vastly overstated introduction to the paper that follows, in which he provides linguistic evidence that sexual and dietary taboos are a matter of degree and should not be understood in terms of simple dichotomies.

4. In a paper first published in 1929, Sapir made the following claims: "The fact of the matter is that the 'real world' is to a large extent unconsciously built up on the language habits of the group. . . . We see and hear and otherwise experience very largely as we do because the language habits of our community predispose certain choices of interpretation" (Sapir 1949: 162).

5. Among American anthropologists, David Schneider provides the clearest statement of the cultural constructionist thesis that I have found:

The world at large, nature, the facts of life, whatever they may be, are always parts of man's perception of them as that perception is formulated through his culture. The world at large is not, indeed, it cannot be, independent of the way in which his culture formulates his vision of what he is seeing. There are only cultural constructions of reality, and these cultural constructions of realities are decisive in what is perceived, what is experienced, what is understood. . . . Meaning is thus not simply attributed to reality. Reality is itself constructed by the beliefs, understandings, and comprehensions entailed in cultural meanings. (Schneider 1976: 204)

A paper about Navajo classification by another American anthropologist, Gary Witherspoon, contains the same sort of overstated introduction as Leach's, mentioned in note 3: "Culture exists on the conceptual level, and consists of a set of concepts, ideas, beliefs and attitudes about the universe of action and being. Cultural concepts do not just (or even necessarily) identify what exists in the objective world; cultural systems, in one sense, create the world. Reality itself is culturally defined, and cultural constructs partition this reality into numerous categories" (Witherspoon 1971: 110). Similarly, Ruth Hubbard begins her paper titled "Have Only Men Evolved?" with the bold claim that "For humans, language plays a major role in generating reality. Without words to objectify and categorize our sensations and place them in relation to one another, we cannot evolve a tradition of what is real in the world" (1979: 225–6). What follows this introduction is simply a review of the gender biases to be found in Darwin and other evolutionary thinkers. These biases are genuine, but it is difficult to see how they constitute evidence that language organizes perceptual reality for us.

6. Durkheim also criticized Spencer and Frazer for having characterized primitive religious thought as confused, absurd, or illogical (1912a: 76–7, 250, t. 1995: 51, 177–8).

7. Bloor (1982) has also tried to revive Durkheim and Mauss's primitive classification hypothesis by offering the explanation that natural classifications

that reflect a society's structure are maintained because they serve certain social interests. But it is not clear why it should be in any group's interest to have its position in society reflected in a system of natural classification. The concept of an interest is notoriously vague. It is just too easy to invent new social, political, or economic interests at will in order to meet objections to interest accounts of systems of classification.

8. Lévy-Bruhl develops this thesis over the course of a half dozen books published in his lifetime and a set of notes that was only posthumously published. See Schmaus (1996).

9. My distinction between concepts and their conceptions reflects my reading of Millikan (2000: 11–12).

10. Collins (1985: 63), Godlove (1989: 44–5), and Parsons (1937: 444–5), each in his own way, have tried to defend Durkheim against this charge by interpreting him as having said that the categories are grounded in timeless social causes. I find little to recommend this interpretation. Parsons, for example, seems to have thought that in locating social life in the mind, Durkheim thereby removed it from the realm of space and time. However, even under the assumption of Cartesian mind–body dualism, which removes the mind from three-dimensional space, the mind nevertheless still exists in time. Kant's views on the mind's relation to space and time will be discussed in the following chapter.

11. In 1995, Neil Gross, then a graduate student in sociology at the University of Wisconsin conducting research at the Sorbonne, discovered a set of notes taken by André Lalande (1867–1962) as a student in Durkheim's course at the Lycée de Sens. Durkheim was transferred to the Lycée de Saint-Quentin in February 1884. For the remainder of the course, Lalande copied the notes taken the previous year by another of Durkheim's students.

12. The system of referring to page numbers in the *Critique of Pure Reason* is explained in Chapter 2, note 2.

13. Exceptions include Susan Stedman Jones (2001: 69ff.), Donald Nielsen (1999), John Brooks (1998: 215), and Terry Godlove (1996), who regard Durkheim's theory of the categories as having been informed by his reading of Charles Renouvier and Octave Hamelin. Brooks (1998, passim) and Jones (2001: 32, 62–3) see Durkheim as having emerged from the eclectic spiritualist tradition, but do not discuss his theory of the categories in this context. Most other commentators on Durkheim's sociology of knowledge have treated it as simply a response to Kant's theory of the categories. These include E. Benoît-Smullyan (1948: 518 n. 67), Steven Collins (1985: 46ff.), Mary Douglas (1975: xv), Anthony Giddens (1978: 111), Robert Alun Jones (1984: 74), Steven Lukes (1973: 447), Stjepan Mestrovic (1989a: 260), William S. F. Pickering (1993: 53), and W. Paul Vogt (Jones and Vogt 1984: 54).

14. That is, during the July Monarchy and the Third Republic. During the first decade of the Second Empire, the only part of philosophy that was allowed to be taught was logic (Janet 1885: 312).

15. For details on Cousin's public administrative career, see Brooks (1998: 36ff.) and Janet (1885: 267ff.).

16. In the appendix of his book, Brooks (1998: 248ff.) provides translations of the official philosophy syllabi of nineteenth-century France, including the syllabus of 1880. See also Brooks (1996).

17. For Janet, see Chapter 4. The other members of Durkheim's doctoral committee were Émile Boutroux, Henri Marion, Charles Waddington, Gabriel Séailles, and Victor Brochard (Lukes 1973: 296–7; Muhlfeld 1893).

18. These are Janet's (1883) text mentioned earlier and Rabier (1884). Durkheim cited both Rabier (Durkheim 1902b: 217, t. 1984: 199 n. 5) and Janet (Durkheim 1893b: 5, t. 1933b: 411) in his dissertation, *The Division of Labor in Society*, which he began while teaching as a lycée professor. He cited Janet again in his lectures on the family (1888c: 276, t. 1978: 222) and Rabier in "Individual and Collective Representations" (1898b: 18, t. 1953b: 5).

19. My functionalist approach to interpreting the meaning of cultural or collective representations has nothing to do with the functionalism of Bronislaw Malinowski or Talcott Parsons, nor does it entail any hypotheses about the functional unity of a society or culture. For Malinowski, a society constitutes a functional unity to which every element of its culture makes some indispensable contribution. Malinowski included among the "axioms" of functionalism the claim that a culture is "a system of objects, activities, and attitudes in which every part exists as a means to an end" (1939: 150).

Notes to Chapter 2

1. Adolf Trendelenburg (1846) traced the history of theories of the categories back to the Pre-socratics, and proceeded through Aristotle, the Scholastics, the Renaissance, and the Enlightenment to Kant and his successors. I would like to thank Nicholas Rescher for bringing this work to my attention.

2. In referring to passages in the *Critique of Pure Reason*, I am following the standard reference system of providing page numbers in the original first edition of 1781, prefixed with the letter *A*, followed by page numbers in the second edition of 1787, prefixed with the letter *B*. Passages that appear in only one edition are indicated accordingly. For quotations from the *Critique*, I have relied mostly on Kemp Smith's translation (Kant 1965), but also consulted Müller's (Kant 1966), Pluhar's (Kant 1996), and Guyer and Wood's (Kant 1998) translations. I have also offered my own translations of passages when these translators do not adequately express my understanding of the original German.

3. I am relying on J. L. Ackrill's translation, Aristotle (1963). All quotations are from this translation. I am following the standard scholarly practice of referring to passages in Aristotle according to the page, column, and line number of the nineteenth-century Berlin Academy edition of his works.

4. I owe this suggestion to James G. Lennox.

5. Kant read Aristotle this way as well, in fact complaining that Aristotle had no guiding principle and simply picked up his categories as he went along (A81/B107).

6. For Leach's categories, see note 3 of Chapter 1.

7. For Gluckman's shapes and colors, also, see note 3 of Chapter 1.

8. For quotations from the *Prolegomena*, I am relying on Hatfield's translation (Kant 1997). I am also following the standard reference system of providing the volume and page number of the German *Akademie* edition of Kant's works (Kant 1902), except for the *Critique of Pure Reason* (see note 2).

9. Hatfield (1992) and Kitcher (1990) defend this interpretation of Kant.

10. Here I follow most scholars in translating *Vorstellung* as "representation." Kant himself provided the Latin *repraesentatio* as a synonym. However, Pluhar argues for "presentation" on the grounds that the German word does not have the sense of standing for something else that the word "representation" has (Kant 1996: 22 n. 73). Indeed, the latter term, with its suggestion of something being present *again* in mental states, appears to presuppose a philosophy of mind quite different from Kant's. Nevertheless, because my purpose here is to draw historical connections with subsequent French philosophers who used the term "*représentation*," I will use the term "representation."

11. That is, that every body remains in a state of rest or motion unless acted upon by an external cause, and that for every action there is an equal and opposite reaction. For the system of referring to Kant's works, see note 8.

12. Janet (1885: 52); Veitch (1910: 330). Although Cousin kept a careful diary of his first trip to Germany in 1817, in which he met Hegel, Goethe, Fries, Schlegel, J. Ancillon, and many other thinkers, he unfortunately did not do so for his second trip in 1818 (Janet 1885: 31–52). Hence, one can only speculate about the exact influence of Jacobi on Cousin, based on similarities in their arguments and terminology.

13. Kant introduced the term "metaphysical deduction" in the second edition at B159 to refer back to the section at A65/B90ff. in which he laid out the tables of judgments and categories and argued for the relation between them.

14. I have been much helped in my interpretation of this passage generally and Kant's concept of a "function" in particular by a discussion that took place in April 1997 on the History of Philosophy of Science listserv HOPOS-L. I found the suggestions of R. Lanier Anderson, Gary Hatfield, and Michael Kremer especially helpful. Of course, the ultimate responsibility for the interpretation is my own. The HOPOS-L listserv is currently maintained by Don Howard on a server at the University of Notre Dame. I would like to thank the participants in this discussion as well as Don Howard for maintaining this list.

15. To return to my example, in "All whales are mammals," "whales" and "mammals" are categorematic and "all" and "are" are syncategorematic terms.

16. As Kant explained in a footnote in *The Metaphysical Foundations of Natural Science* (1786 4: 474), these criticisms were raised by Johann August Heinrich Ulrich (1746–1813) in his *Institutiones Logicae et Metaphysicae* (1785) and in a sympathetic anonymous review of Ulrich's work, which Kant knew to have been written by his friend Johann Schultz. According to Beiser (1987: 205–8), Schultz found the transcendental deduction to be the most important and yet the most difficult and obscure part of the first *Critique*. Schultz, reading the transcendental deduction as attempting to show that synthetic a priori concepts are needed for experience, presented Kant with a dilemma: if

experience includes judgments of perception, Kant's conclusion is false. A judgment of perception such as "When the sun shines the stone is warm" does not commit us to a universal and necessary connection between the sun shining and the warming of the rock. On the other hand, if experience includes only judgments of experience, his conclusion is merely a tautology. It is obvious that a judgment of experience such as "The sun causes the rock to grow warm" requires such concepts.

17. The terms "objective deduction" and "subjective deduction" are also used by Kant scholars to refer to similar arguments in the B deduction.

18. The principles of understanding are given in the chapters on the axioms of intuition (A162/B202ff.), anticipations of perception (A166/B207ff.), analogies of experience (A176/B218ff.), and postulates of empirical thought (A218/B265ff.).

19. I would like to thank an anonymous reviewer for pointing this out to me.

20. I deliberately choose to say a "psychological" as opposed to a "psychologistic" reading of the *Critique*, as the latter term implies the fallacy of attempting to reduce normative rules to the merely descriptive principles of psychology. As Anderson suggests (2001: 288), drawing on the work of Hatfield (1990, 1997), it would be anachronistic to raise the charge of psychologism against Kant's earliest critics, as it assumes the purely naturalistic concept of mind we hold today. During the early modern period, philosophers held a very different concept of mind as something that held intrinsically normative powers of knowing. Epistemology was not distinguished from the philosophy of mind, since the attainment of truth was a question of the right use of these intrinsic powers of the mind. The concept of epistemology as concerned solely with the relations between claims to knowledge and their supporting evidence develops later in the nineteenth century.

21. There was an exchange on the listserv HOPOS-L on just this topic on August 17–19, 2002, initiated by myself (see note 14). None of the other participants, including Michael Kremer, John Ongley, Richard Smyth, and Peter Apostoli, as well as Lanier Anderson, could think of a philosopher prior to Cohen who challenged the psychological reading of Kant.

22. Beiser (1987: 123). See also pp. 4, 46, 81. According to Beiser, Jacobi first uses the term "nihilism" in his 1799 *Brief on Fichte* (ibid., 340 n. 108). More recently, Beiser (1999: 521–2) reports an earlier use of the term among Kant's critics J. H. Obereit and Daniel Jenisch. See also Kuehn (1987: 158–62).

23. Lévy-Bruhl (1894: 187); Beiser (1987: 124).

24. Kuehn (1987: 229), quoting from Jacobi's *Werke,* Vol. 2, 299–304.

25. On Jacobi's debt to Reid, see also Di Giovanni (1997, 1998a, 1998b).

Notes to Chapter 3

1. *Catalogue générale des livres imprimés de la Bibliothèque nationale. Auteurs.* Paris: Impr. nationale, 1897–1981. Vol. 80, 560.

2. *Mémoires de l'Académie Royale des Sciences et Belles-Lettres depuis l'avènement de Frédéric Guillaume III au trône, classe de philosophie spéculative* (Berlin). The

Berlin Academy used the French language until the fall of Napoleon I (Echeverria 1963: 11 n. 6). The Ancillons were a family of French refugees (Janet 1885: 40). However, Engel also signed his memoirs with his name translated into French. Hence, Moore's bibliography of works consulted by Maine de Biran lists him as Jean-Jacques Engel (Moore 1970: 172). For the Ancillons, Moore provides both the French (ibid., 169) and the German versions of their names, Ludwig Friedrich and Johann Peter Friedrich (ibid., 216). Vallois always uses the French version for all of these authors' names (1924: 7ff., 355).

3. Translated as *On the Form and Principles of the Sensible and Intelligible World.*

4. Bréhier (1968: 69).

5. The latter series of lectures was first published in 1842 in an edition prepared by his students and corrected by Cousin himself (Cousin 1846: 1–7).

6. Janet (1885: 2–5); Brooks (1998: 36). Royer-Collard lectured on Reid beginning in 1811 at the Sorbonne (Janet 1885: 2; Boas 1967a: 229).

7. See note 12 to Chapter 2.

8. Cousin's lectures on *The True, the Beautiful, and the Good* went through many editions. According to Cousin, the earliest editions, beginning in 1837, were based on student notes taken in his classes during the years 1815–21. He began making additions and corrections with the 1853 edition (Cousin 1860: x–xi). I am citing from the eighth edition. See also Manns and Madden (1990: 575), who cite Cousin's definition of spiritualism from an 1883 translation.

9. Madden (1984: 102). For Reid's Newtonian opposition to hypotheses, see Laudan (1970).

10. Curiously, he regarded Descartes's work as free of hypotheses (*exempte d'hypothèses* [1860: 3]).

11. Reid had argued against the existence of mediating ideas and impressions in both *An Inquiry into the Human Mind on the Principles of Common Sense* (1764) and the *Essays on the Intellectual Powers of Man* (1785) on the grounds that the belief in ideas leads to the absurd idealistic and skeptical consequences of Berkeley and Hume (Reid 1983: 56ff., 165ff.). Cousin summarizes these arguments in lessons seven and eight of his lectures on Scottish philosophy. As he explains in lesson seven, he had also dealt with Reid's rejection of the way of ideas in earlier courses dealing with John Locke (1864a: 276). On Jacobi's debt to Reid, see the last section of Chapter 2.

12. Cousin's *Elements of Psychology* is addressed to the philosophy of Locke.

13. As I explained in the previous chapter, Jacobi was probably the conduit for Hamann's influence on Cousin. Cousin was a little too quick with Kant with regard to the ideas of reason. According to Kant, these ideas, which include God, the soul, and the cosmos, were necessary not so much for experience in general as for our experience of the good (A318/B375).

14. For Jacobi's preference, see Atlas (1967: 236).

15. Cousin's argument thus resembles Selle's position, mentioned earlier, that conscious reflection reveals metaphysical as well as empirical truths. In addition, Cousin's argument that reason can teach us nothing in abstraction from experience can also be found in Hamann's critique of Kant (Beiser 1987: 39).

16. Unless otherwise indicated, all subsequent references to Biran's writings will be to the volume and page numbers of Maine de Biran (1920–49).

17. However, Ampère himself subscribed to a questionable reading of Kant, equating the noumenal realm with the hypothesized or postulated reality by which scientists attempt to explain appearances. He thought that behind the phenomenal realm there was a noumenal realm of space and time with bodies moving in it, a position from which Biran attempted unsuccessfully to dissuade him (Hofmann 1995: 149ff.; Vallois 1924: 240).

18. In this work, Cabanis argued that impressions that have their origin in internal organs as well as external impressions contribute to the formation of our ideas. For example, he contrasted the ideas formed in the heads of a seven- and a fourteen-year-old boy who nevertheless are receiving the same external impressions while looking at the same beautiful woman. Cabanis explained the difference in terms of the internal impressions received by the older boy from his sex organs (Cabanis 1802: 175–7). Biran's concern with Cabanis's philosophical agenda is reflected in the very title of his prize-winning essay for the competition held by the Academy of Copenhagen, the *Mémoire sur les rapports du physique et du moral de l'homme* (1811), a work that in its original form was never published and subsequently was lost (Moore 1970: 151).

19. The Berlin Academy awarded him an honorable mention for his *De l'aperception immédiate*, which he submitted to their essay competition in 1807 (Moore 1970: 150).

20. I find a certain historical irony in the fact that current psychological work in the perception of causality and other categories postulates special "modules" for this work, deriving this concept from Jerry Fodor, who begins *The Modularity of Mind* (1983) with a discussion of Gall's phrenology.

21. This was in his earliest publication, the *Influence de l'habitude sur la faculté de penser* of 1802 (2: 26, 45–6, 54, t. 1929: 58, 68, 72).

22. This was in his *Mémoire sur la décomposition de la pensée* of 1804 (3: 62–3).

23. Cousin had obtained these and other unpublished manuscripts from Biran's feckless literary executor, Joseph-Louis-Joachin Lainé (1767–1835), who had done nothing with them. Cousin reissued the 1834 volume in 1841 as the fourth and last volume of Biran's *Oeuvres philosophiques*. Curiously, and somewhat misleadingly, Biran's *Examen,* along with his replies to Hume, Engel, and Stapfer, were also included in Volume 3 of Cousin's own *Oeuvres* (1840–1).

24. The *Examen,* along with the replies to Hume, Engel, and Stapfer, appears in Volume 11 of Pierre Tisserand's edition of Biran's *Oeuvres complètes* (1920–49), in which it differs little from the version of it that Cousin published in 1841. The *Essai,* which Tisserand adopted wholesale from Naville's 1859 edition, appears in Volume 8 (Moore 1970: 148).

25. Compare also "The self distinguishes itself very clearly from every represented object or object sensed from without; it is a sui generis internal fact, very evident without doubt for every reflective being, but which demands to be apperceived with the aid of its own special sense" (8: 116).

26. Vallois (1924: 95 n. 98) suggests that Biran's notion of apperception as revealing the activity of the will appears to owe less to Kant than to Villers. For Villers, Kant's transcendental apperception is a separate source of "light" that compensates for the limitations of the sensibility and understanding and reveals the noumenal self as a free, spontaneously active being, independent of the laws of nature (1801: 364–6). I would suggest, on the other hand, that Villers, like Biran, got this idea from reading Kant's inaugural dissertation, and that Biran was reinforced in his interpretation of Kant from reading Villers.

Notes to Chapter 4

1. See note 17 to Chapter 1. Professors from the Paris Faculty of Letters (Sorbonne) served on committees that examined students from the École Normale Supérieure for the *agrégation*, which was required for a teaching position in a lycée, and the doctorate, which was required for a university teaching position (Brooks 1998: 33–4). Durkheim cited Janet repeatedly in the introduction to the first edition of *The Division of Labor in Society* (1893b), which was his dissertation. These pages were removed from the second edition of 1902 but have been reprinted in 1975a, Vol. 2, pp. 257–88 and are included in the appendix to the first English translation (1933b: 411–35).
2. *Catalogue générale. Bibliothèque Nationale*, Vol. 76, p. 1206. Paris, 1929.
3. See note 11 to Chapter 1.
4. See note 18 to Chapter 1.
5. Although Janet's *Traité* thus preceded the new syllabus, it appears to have been written in anticipation of it, as it follows the 1880 syllabus more closely than the 1874 syllabus. The 1880 syllabus in some ways was closer to Cousin's original syllabus of 1832, in that it placed the proofs of the existence of God *after* ethics, instead of before, as in the 1874 syllabus. However, the 1880 syllabus and Janet's text lacked the long historical sections of the syllabi of 1832 and 1874 (Brooks 1998: 248–54). Janet issued a new edition of the *Traité* in 1883, which differed little from the first edition other than in the placement of a few of the chapters and the addition of a long appendix consisting of a *résumé analytique* that correlated each topic of the *programme* with the appropriate sections of the *Traité*. Subsequent editions of this work were little more than new printings. Working in both Chicago and Pittsburgh, I have used both the sixth edition of 1889 and an undated ninth edition with exactly the same pagination. Both refer to the 1880 *programme* or syllabus on the title page. The syllabus was revised again in 1902, after Janet had passed away.
6. One is tempted to compare the Janets to another case in which the uncle promoted the academic career of his nephew, that is, Durkheim and Mauss. However, the Janets did not collaborate with each other in their scholarly work in the way that Durkheim and Mauss did.
7. Susan Stedman Jones suggests that Renouvier may be the ultimate source of the concept of a moral fact (2001: 187, 250 n. 7).
8. He replaced another faculty member who was on leave (Brooks 1998: 198).

9. Bernard is also mentioned in some of Durkheim's earliest publications: Durkheim (1885a, 1886a). Hirst's (1975) *Durkheim, Bernard, and Epistemology* makes no mention of Bernard having influenced Durkheim with regard to the use of hypotheses. Of course, this book was written well before the discovery of Lalande's notes from the Sens lectures.

10. Renouvier defends the use of hypotheses in the physical sciences in the second edition of the first book of the *Essais de critique générale*, titled *Traité de logique générale et de logique formelle* (1875, Vol. I, 111–12). The second edition dates from 1875; the 1912 edition that I use is a reprint of the 1875 edition.

11. See Laudan (1971) for an account of the method of hypothesis in Comte.

12. Tyndall first delivered this paper before the meeting of the British Association at Liverpool on September 16, 1870. He continued to revise, present, and publish different versions of this essay (Beer 1991: 133).

13. Antoine Arnauld made this distinction in the "Port-Royal Logic." See Arnauld (1662, Part I, chap. 6, 51).

14. According to Durkheim (1884a: 399), this was Taine's view.

15. Perhaps it was his reading of Renouvier that led Janet to consider the associationists as having proposed an alternative to Kant's theory of the categories. In Renouvier's account of the categories, in addition to Aristotle and Kant, he also considered the views of British empiricist philosophers such as William Hamilton, John Stuart Mill, Alexander Bain, and Herbert Spencer (1875, Vol. I, 144ff.).

16. Janet's source for this theory may have been Théodule Ribot. In 1870, Ribot published *La psychologie anglaise contemporaine* (*English Psychology*), which included chapters on each of these three figures, among others. Three years later, Ribot defended a dissertation titled "*L'Hérédité psychologique,*" in which he supported Spencer's theory that the categories resulted from the collective experience of the species, as an alternative to both rationalism and empiricism. Janet was a member of Ribot's dissertation committee. Ribot dropped the chapter on Robert Murphy in later editions of *La psychologie anglaise.* (Brooks 1998: 71–8, 89–90, and notes on p. 267.)

17. 1912a: 20; cf. t. 1995: 14. I first mentioned this argument in Chapter 1.

18. Jouffroy was a student of Cousin (Janet 1885: 17).

19. Nineteenth-century thinkers were fascinated with the phenomenon that is now known as "multiple personality." As Ian Hacking explains, Paul Janet's nephew Pierre Janet built his early career in psychiatry around the study of multiples (Hacking 1995: 44, 131–6).

20. Janet quoted the following passages from Biran's *Oeuvres inédites*, edited by Naville in 1859: "The idea of cause has its primitive and unique type in the sensation of the self identified with that of effort" (Vol. I, 258). And "We find deeply imprinted in us the notion of cause or force; but before the notion is the immediate sensation of force, and this sensation is nothing other than that of our very existence, from which that of activity is inseparable" (ibid., 47). Janet then concluded, "it is thus in the consciousness of force deployed by us on our organs that we find in us the type of *active power* and of *efficacious cause*" (1883: 200).

21. Janet provided a fairly detailed and accurate account of the first four arguments Biran drew from Hume and his replies to them. He drew on the version of these arguments Cousin published in Volume 4 of Biran's *Oeuvres philosophiques*, that is, the version in the appendix to Biran's *Examen* of 1817. Rabier (1884) also found Biran's replies to Hume acceptable.

Notes to Chapter 5

1. Durkheim had hoped to base morality on a scientific study of the causes of moral rules in a work to be titled *La Morale*. At the time of his death in 1917, however, he had completed only the introduction to this work (1920a).
2. Brooks reports that records at the library of the École Normale Supérieure show that Durkheim checked out books by Kant in German, but he does not tell us which ones (1998: 214, 294 n. 103).
3. Unless otherwise indicated, all subsequent references in this chapter are to the page numbers in André Lalande's original manuscript notes, taken in Durkheim's class at the Lycée de Sens in the academic year 1883–4.
4. For example, in 1912a: 23, t. 1995: 15; 1913b: 64, 73, which was translated by R. A. Jones and W. P. Vogt in *Knowledge and Society* 5 (1984): 1–44; and 1914a, which has been translated in 1960c: 325–40 and 1973: 149–63.
5. In 1885a: 92, t. 1978: 103; 1897a: 361, t. 1951a: 319; and in a letter to Céléstin Bouglé, dated December 1896 by V. Karady (1975a: Vol. 2, 393) and April 1897 by P. Besnard (1983: 44).
6. Such views have been attributed to Durkheim by Alexander (1982: 211), Catlin (1938: xiv), J. Douglas (1967: 153), Giddens (1976: 132; 1977: 38), Hirst (1975: 97), Mestrovic (1989b), Nye and Ashworth (1971), and Taylor (1982: 34, 203 n. 26, 204 n. 27). For a criticism of this interpretation of Durkheim's methodology, see Schmaus (1994: 85ff.).
7. Lalande's notes contain an apparent error at this point, as he listed the "precision of new facts" as a condition on hypotheses, apparently having run together "precision" and "prediction of new facts" (1884a: 368).
8. The appeal to divination is ambiguous. The French word *deviner* can be translated as "divine," "foretell," "predict," "guess," "conjecture," and so on. Hence, this passage could mean that predictions, hypotheses, or both are needed for the knowledge of concrete reality. His use of this term may reflect his reading of Tyndall's paper "The Scientific Use of the Imagination," which in Battier's French translation speaks of the imagination as a "faculté de divination" (Tyndall 1871: 15). As I mentioned in note 12 to Chapter 4, Tyndall first delivered this paper on September 16, 1870, and went on to present and publish different versions of it. I was unable to find any English equivalent of the term "divination" in the corresponding paragraph of the second edition, which was published in November of that year (Tyndall 1870: 19–20). It is not clear what version Battier consulted or even whether it was through his translation that Durkheim knew of Tyndall's argument. For instance, Durkheim's discussion of Newton's gravitational hypothesis and Kepler's laws, discussed earlier in the text, resembles Tyndall's account of this example in a version that he delivered at the meeting of the British Association at Nottingham

and published in 1871 (cited by Eve and Creasey 1945: 145ff.). However, Kepler's laws are not mentioned at all in the corresponding paragraphs of the November 1870 version (1870: 16) or Battier's translation (1871: 14).

9. Janet was probably more sympathetic to the use of hypotheses than was Rabier. Rabier defended the *méthode psychologique* against the method of hypothesis, regarding the former as an empirical, inductive method with its roots in Descartes (1884: 15–20).

10. See, for example, Cosmides and Tooby (1992), Pinker (1994, 1997), and Tooby and Cosmides (1995), as well as many of the papers in Hirschfeld and Gelman, eds. (1994), and Sperber, Premack, and Premack, eds. (1995). Their concept of a mental module derives from *The Modularity of Mind* (1983) by Jerry Fodor, who in turn drew on the work of Noam Chomsky and David Marr. More recently, Fodor repudiated the evolutionary psychologists' use of this concept in *The Mind Doesn't Work That Way* (2000). Kuhn (2000: 94, 104, 229) also invokes the notion of a mental module, specifically a taxonomic module that is responsible for our concepts of natural, artifactual, social, and other sorts of kinds, but does not explicitly link his notion of a module to Fodor's.

11. Rabier drew the same distinction between conscious psychological and unconscious physiological states (Brooks 1998: 147).

12. Durkheim obviously did not mean that all phenomena are modifications of one and the same substance. After all, this account of Durkheim's thinking is taken from student notes.

13. For instance, as it appears in Lalande's student notes, Durkheim's argument regarding time is that "the mind, if it did not already have the idea of time, would not be able to represent the states of consciousness as situated one after the other" (1884a: 136).

14. Elsewhere in these lectures, Durkheim also argued that Darwin's and Spencer's theory that instincts are inherited habits cannot account for the instincts of neuter insects. In addition, he raised objections to evolutionary theory in general, including the lack of evidence of the formation of new species and the sterility of interspecies hybrids (240–2).

Notes to Chapter 6

1. See note 19 to Chapter 1.

2. Works questioning the empirical basis of Durkheim's sociology of religion and sociology of knowledge have been in the literature for quite some time. See, for example, Cazeneuve (1958), Lukes (1973: 446), Needham (1963: xi–xxix), and Worsley (1956).

3. As I explain in Schmaus (1995), I learned from Willie Watts Miller that there is no evidence that Durkheim had any direct knowledge of Hume. There does not seem to be any explicit reference to Hume anywhere in Durkheim. Furthermore, Miller argued, there are no library records at the École Normale Supérieur showing that Durkheim had ever borrowed any of Hume's works. In this 1995 essay, I gave the mistaken impression that Rabier's

text was Durkheim's sole source for his knowledge of Hume. I would like to correct that and affirm that Janet's text was at least one more source.

4. Durkheim probably had Spencer's evolutionary account in mind, which, as I mentioned in Chapters 1 and 5, he included among empiricist theories of the categories in the introduction (1912a: 18 n. 1, t. 1995: 12 n. 15).

Notes to Chapter 7

1. Parts of these passages have been quoted by Tooby and Cosmides (1992: 24–5), Pinker (2002: 23–4), Wright (1994: 5), and Richards (2000: 63). These authors all quote from the first English translation of *The Rules* (Durkheim 1938b: 104, 105–6).

2. I would like to thank Steven Lukes for directing me to this passage in *Moral Education*.

3. I am referring to the passage at Kant (1783 4: 304) that I discussed in Chapter 2.

4. Millikan (1993: 42–4), citing Pinker and Bloom (1990: 708–12, 766–7; partially reprinted in Barkow, Cosmides, and Tooby, eds., 1992: 453–93).

5. For an excellent introduction to this literature, see Hauser (2000).

6. Leslie also calls ToBy the "Michotte module." In an earlier paper, he calls ToMM simply ToM, for "Theory of Mind" (Leslie 1991). Leslie (1994: 121) attributes to Susan Carey (1985) the idea that intentional and mechanical causality are separate cognitive domains. See note 10 to Chapter 5 for more on mental modules.

7. See, for example, Leslie (1988, 1994, 1995), Baillargeon (1995), Baillargeon, Kotovsky, and Needham (1995), Spelke, Phillips, and Woodward (1995), and Spelke, Vishton, and von Hofsten (1995). Although Michotte's *La Perception de la causalité* dates from 1946, he says that it represents his thinking on this subject from as early as 1929 ([1946] 1963: 15).

8. Fodor (1983: 67ff.) makes the imperviousness of a perceptual process to knowledge and reason a criterion for its being under the control of a mental module.

9. Similarly, Dan Sperber (1995: xvi) distinguishes a philosophical from a psychological sense of perception. In the latter sense, illusions and misperceptions count as perceptions. So, in this psychological sense, people may "perceive" causal relations, while in the philosopher's sense, they perceive an illusion.

10. Both Leslie (1991: 711) and Premack (1988: 164) give four as the age at which children will pass this test. There are many different versions of this experiment, such as replacing the candy with pencils and acting out the whole scenario with dolls.

Bibliography

Works by Émile Durkheim

For references to Durkheim's writings, I follow the numbering system invented by Steven Lukes (1973), which has been updated by Durkheim scholars as new Durkheim texts have been discovered and new collections published. The most recent bibliography of Durkheim's works that uses this system of numbering has been published by Robert Alun Jones on the World Wide Web: http://www.relst.uiuc.edu/durkheim/Bibliography/Bibo1.html.

Because I follow this system of referring to Durkheim's works, the numbering in my bibliography will not always be consecutive, as I do not cite everything he published in every given year. There is no standard set of collected works of Durkheim in either French or English. Instead, there are various collections in which most of his published shorter writings can be found. At the end of the entries for these writings, I indicate in which of these collections these essays and reviews may be found. I have also indicated where English translations of these pieces can be found.

1884a. "Cours de philosophie fait au Lycée de Sens." Bibliothèque de la Sorbonne, manuscript number 2351. Also available from the University of Wisconsin-Madison, Microforms Center, film number 9307, and on the World Wide Web: http://www.relst.uiuc.edu/durkheim/Texts/1884a/oo.html.

1885a. Review of "Schaeffle, A., *Bau und Leben des sozialen Körpers: Erster Band.*" *Revue philosophique* 19: 84–101. Reprinted in 1975a, Vol. 1, pp. 355–77. Translated in 1978, pp. 93–114.

1886a. Les Études de science sociale. *Revue philosophique* 22: 61–80. Reprinted in 1970a, pp. 184–214. Pages 61–9 translated in *Sociological Inquiry* 44 (1974): 205–14; 1975b, pp. 13–23. Pages 78–9 translated in 1972, pp. 55–7.

1887a. La Philosophie dans les universités allemandes. *Revue internationale de l'enseignement* 13: 313–38, 423–40. Reprinted in 1975a, Vol. 3, pp. 437–86.

1888c. Introduction à la sociologie de la famille. *Annales de la faculté des lettres de Bordeaux* 10: 257–81. Reprinted in 1975a, Vol. 3, pp. 9–34. Translated in 1978, pp. 205–28.

1893b. *De la division du travail social: étude sur l'organisation des sociétés supérieures.* Paris: Alcan. Translated 1933b, 1984. The pages from the introduction to the first edition that were removed in subsequent editions have been reprinted in 1975a, Vol. 2, pp. 257–88, and translated in 1933b, pp. 411–35.

1895a. *Les Règles de la méthode sociologique.* Paris: Alcan. Translated 1938b, 1982.

1897a. *Le Suicide: étude de sociologie.* Paris: Alcan. Translated 1951a.

1897f. Contribution to "Enquête sur l'oeuvre de H. Taine." *Revue Blanche* 13: 287–91. Reprinted in 1975a, Vol. 1, pp. 171–7.

1898a(ii). La Prohibition de l'inceste et ses origines. *L'Année sociologique* 1: 1–70. Reprinted in 1969c, pp. 37–100. Translated in 1963a.

1898b. Représentations individuelles et représentations collectives. *Revue de métaphysique et de morale* 6: 273–302. Reprinted in 1924a, pp. 13–50. Translated in 1953b, pp. 1–34.

1899a(ii). De la définition des phénomènes religieux. *L'Année sociologique* 2: 1–28. Reprinted in 1969c, pp. 140–65. Translated in 1975b, pp. 74–99.

1902a(i). Sur le totemisme. *L'Année sociologique* 5: 82–121. Reprinted in 1969c, pp. 315–52.

1902b. *De la division du travail social,* 2nd ed. Paris: Alcan. Translated 1933b, 1984.

1903a(i). With Marcel Mauss. De quelque formes primitives de classification: contribution à l'étude des représentations collectives. *L'Année sociologique* 6: 1–72. Reprinted in Durkheim 1969c, pp. 395–461. Translated 1963b.

1909d. Sociologie religieuse et théorie de la connaissance. *Revue de métaphysique et de morale* 17: 733–58, all of which except pp. 754–8 was incorporated into the "Introduction" to 1912a. These missing pages are reprinted in 1975a, Vol. 1, pp. 185–8, and translated in 1982, pp. 236–40.

1912a. *Les Formes élémentaires de la vie religieuse.* Paris: Alcan. Translated 1995.

1913a(ii) 6&7. Combined review of "Lévy-Bruhl, L., *Les Fonctions mentales dans les sociétés inférieures*," and "Durkheim, Emile, *Les Formes élémentaires de la vie religieuse.*" *L'Année sociologique* 12: 33–7. Reprinted in 1975a, Vol. 1, pp. 405–7. Translated in 1975b, pp. 169–73; 1978, pp. 145–9.

1913b. Contribution to discussion of "Le Problème religieux et la dualité de la nature humaine." *Bulletin de la société française de philosophie* 13: 63–75, 80–7, 90–100, 108–11. Reprinted in 1975a, Vol. 2, pp. 23–64. Translated by R. A. Jones and P. Vogt in *Knowledge and Society* 5 (1984): 1–44.

1914a. Le Dualisme de la nature humaine et ses conditions sociales. *Scientia* 15: 206–21. Reprinted in 1970a, pp. 314–32. Translated in 1960c, pp. 325–40; 1973, pp. 149–63.

1920a. Introduction à la morale. *Revue philosophique* 89: 79–87. Reprinted in 1975a, Vol. 2, pp. 313–31. Translated in 1978, pp. 191–202; 1979, pp. 77–96.

[1924a] 1951, 1974. *Sociologie et philosophie.* Paris: PUF. Translated 1953b.

[1925a] 1961. *Moral Education.* Translated by Everett K. Wilson and Herman Schnurer. New York: Free Press.

1933b. *The Division of Labor in Society.* Translation of 1893b/1902b by George Simpson. New York: Macmillan.

1938b. *The Rules of Sociological Method.* Translation of Durkheim 1895a by Sarah A. Solovay and John H. Mueller, ed. by George E. G. Catlin. New York: Free Press.

1951a. *Suicide: A Study in Sociology.* Translation of 1897a by J. A. Spaulding and G. Simpson. New York: Free Press.

[1953b] 1974. *Sociology and Philosophy.* Translation of 1924a by D. F. Pocock. New York: Free Press/Macmillan.

1955a. *Pragmatisme et Sociologie.* Paris: Vrin. Translated 1983.

1960c. *Emile Durkheim, 1858–1917: A Collection of Essays, with Translations and a Bibliography.* Edited by Kurt H. Wolff. Columbus, OH: Ohio State University Press. Reprinted in 1964 as *Essays on Sociology and Philosophy.* New York: Harper & Row.

1963a. *Incest: The Nature and Origin of the Taboo.* Translation of 1898a(ii) with an Introduction by Edward Sagarin. New York: Lyle Stuart.

1963b. With Marcel Mauss. *Primitive Classification.* Translation of 1903a(i) by Rodney Needham. Chicago: University of Chicago Press.

1969c. *Journal sociologique.* Edited by Jean Duvignaud. Paris: PUF.

1970a. *La Science sociale et l'action.* Edited by J.-C. Filloux. Paris: PUF.

1972. *Emile Durkheim: Selected Writings.* Edited by Anthony Giddens. Cambridge: Cambridge University Press.

1973. *Emile Durkheim on Morality and Society.* Edited by Robert Bellah. Chicago: University of Chicago Press.

1975a. *Textes.* Edited by Victor Karady. Paris: Les Éditions de Minuit.

1975b. *Durkheim on Religion.* Edited by W. S. F. Pickering; translated by J. Redding and W. S. F. Pickering. London: Routledge & Kegan Paul.

1978. *Emile Durkheim on Institutional Analysis.* Edited and translated by Mark Traugott. Chicago: University of Chicago Press.

1979. *Durkheim: Essays on Morals and Education.* Edited by W. S. F. Pickering. London: Routledge & Kegan Paul.

1982. *The Rules of Sociological Method and Selected Texts on Sociology and its Method.* Translation of 1895a by W. D. Halls. New York: Free Press.

1983. *Pragmatism and Sociology.* Translation of 1955a by J. C. Whitehouse. Cambridge: Cambridge University Press.

1984. *The Division of Labor in Society.* Translation of 1893b/1902b by W. D. Halls. New York: Free Press.

1995. *The Elementary Forms of Religious Life.* Translation of 1912a by Karen Fields. New York: Free Press.

Other References

Alexander, Jeffrey. 1982. *Theoretical Logic in Sociology.* Berkeley: University of California Press.

Anderson, R. Lanier. 2001. Synthesis, Cognitive Normativity, and the Meaning of Kant's Question, 'How are synthetic cognitions a priori possible?' *European Journal of Philosophy* 9(3): 275–305.

Aristotle. 1963. *Categories and De Interpretatione*. Trans. J. L. Ackrill. Oxford: Clarendon Press.

Arnauld, Antoine. [1662] 1964. *The Art of Thinking*. Trans. J. Dickoff and P. James. Indianapolis: Bobbs-Merrill.

Atlas, Samuel. 1967. "Jacobi, Friedrich Heinrich." In P. Edwards, ed. *The Encyclopedia of Philosophy*, Vol. 4, pp. 235–8. New York: Macmillan and the Free Press.

Atran, Scott. 1987. "Folkbiological Universals as Common Sense." In S. Modgil and C. Modgil, eds. *Noam Chomsky: Consensus and Controversy*, pp. 247–58. New York: Falmer Press.

1990. *Cognitive Foundations of Natural History*. Cambridge: Cambridge University Press.

1994. "Core domains versus scientific theories: Evidence from systematics and Itza-Maya folkbiology." In L. A. Hirschfeld and S. A. Gelman, eds. *Mapping the Mind: Domain Specificity in Cognition and Culture*, pp. 316–40. Cambridge: Cambridge University Press.

1995. "Causal constraints on categories and categorical constraints on biological reasoning across cultures." In D. Sperber, D. Premack, and A. Premack, eds. *Causal Cognition: A Multidisciplinary Debate*, pp. 205–33. Oxford: Clarendon Press.

Baillargeon, Renée. 1995. "Physical reasoning in infancy." In M. S. Gazzaniga, ed. *The Cognitive Neurosciences*, pp. 181–204. Cambridge, MA: MIT Press.

Baillargeon, Renée, Laura Kotovsky, and Amy Needham. 1995. "The acquisition of physical knowledge in infancy." In D. Sperber et al., eds. *Causal Cognition: A Multidisciplinary Debate*, pp. 79–116. Oxford: Clarendon Press.

Barkow, Jerome H., Leda Cosmides, and John Tooby, eds. 1992. *The Adapted Mind: Evolutionary Psychology and the Generation of Culture*. New York: Oxford University Press.

Beer, Gillian. 1991. Helmholtz, Tyndall, Gerard Manley Hopkins: Leaps of the Prepared Imagination. *Comparative Criticism* 13: 117–45.

Beiser, Frederick C. 1987. *The Fate of Reason: German Philosophy from Kant to Fichte*. Cambridge, MA: Harvard University Press.

1999. "Early sceptical, religious, and literary responses to Kantian Philosophy." In Richard H. Popkin, ed. *The Columbia History of Western Philosophy*, pp. 518–24. New York: Columbia University Press.

Benoît-Smullyan, Emile. 1948. "The sociologism of Emile Durkheim and his school." In Harry Elmer Barnes, ed. *An Introduction to the History of Sociology*, pp. 499–537. Chicago: University of Chicago Press.

Berger, Peter L., and Thomas Luckmann. 1967. *The Social Construction of Reality*. Garden City, NY: Anchor.

Berkeley, George. [1710] 1982. *A Treatise Concerning the Principles of Human Knowledge*. Indianapolis: Hackett.

Berlin, Brent. 1992. *Ethnobiological Classification*. Princeton, NJ: Princeton University Press.

Berlin, Brent, Dennis E. Breedlove, and Peter H. Raven. 1973. General Principles of Classification and Nomenclature in Folk Biology. *American Anthropologist* 75: 214–42.

Berlin, Brent, and Paul Kay. 1969. *Basic Color Terms: Their Universality and Evolution.* Berkeley: University of California Press.

Besnard, Philippe, ed. 1983. *The Sociological Domain: The Durkheimians and the Founding of French Sociology.* Cambridge: Cambridge University Press.

Bijker, Wiebe E. 1995. *Of Bicycles, Bakelites, and Bulbs: Toward a Theory of Sociotechnical Change.* Cambridge, MA: MIT Press.

Bloch, Maurice. 1977. The Past and the Present in the Future. *Man* 12 (ns): 278–92.

Bloor, David. 1982. Durkheim and Mauss Revisited: Classification and the Sociology of Knowledge. *Studies in History and Philosophy of Science* 13: 267–97.

1991. *Knowledge and Social Imagery,* 2nd ed. Chicago: University of Chicago Press.

Boas, George. 1925. *French Philosophies of the Romantic Period.* Baltimore: Johns Hopkins University Press.

1967a. "Royer-Collard, Pierre Paul." In P. Edwards, ed. *The Encyclopedia of Philosophy,* Vol. 7, p. 229. New York: Macmillan and the Free Press.

Bouglé, Célestin. 1908. *Essai sur le régime des castes.* Paris: Alcan.

Boutroux, Émile. 1912. *Historical Studies in Philosophy.* Trans. Fred Rothwell. Port Washington, NY, and London: Kennikat Press.

1965. *La philosophie de Kant. Cours de M. Émile Boutroux professé à la Sorbonne en 1896–97.* Paris: Vrin.

Boyer, Pascal. 1994a. *The Naturalness of Religious Ideas.* Berkeley: University of California Press.

1994b. "Cognitive constraints on cultural representations: Natural ontologies and religious ideas." In L. A. Hirschfeld and S. A. Gelman, eds. *Mapping the Mind: Domain Specificity in Cognition and Culture,* pp. 391–411. Cambridge: Cambridge University Press.

Bréhier, Émile. 1968. *The Nineteenth Century: Period of Systems, 1800–1850 (The History of Philosophy,* Vol. 6). Trans. Wade Baskin. Chicago: University of Chicago Press.

Brooks, John I., III. 1993. Philosophy and Psychology at the Sorbonne, 1885–1913. *Journal of the History of the Behavioral Sciences* 29: 123–45.

1996. The Definition of Sociology and the Sociology of Definition: Durkheim's *Rules of Sociological Method* and High School Philosophy in France. *Journal of the History of the Behavioral Sciences* 32 (4): 379–407.

1998. *The Eclectic Legacy.* Newark: University of Delaware Press.

Brothers, Leslie. 1995. "Neurophysiology of the perception of intentions by primates." In M. S. Gazzaniga, ed. *The Cognitive Neurosciences,* pp. 1107–15. Cambridge, MA: MIT Press.

Brown, Roger. 1958. *Words and Things.* New York: Free Press.

Cabanis, Pierre-Jean Georges. [1802] 1956. *Rapports du physique et du moral de l'homme.* In Claude Lehec and Jean Cazeneuve, eds. *Oeuvres Philosophiques,* Vol. 1, pp. 105–631. Paris: Presses Universitaires de France.

Carey, Susan. 1985. *Conceptual Change in Childhood.* Cambridge, MA: Bradford/MIT Press.

Catlin, George E. G. 1938. "Introduction to the translation." In Durkheim, Émile, *The Rules of Sociological Method*, pp. xi–xxxvi. New York: Free Press.

Cazeneuve, Jean. 1958. Les Zuñis dans l'oeuvre de Durkheim et de Mauss. *Revue philosophique* 83: 452–61.

Clark, Terry N. 1972. "Emile Durkheim and the French University." In Anthony Oberschall, ed. *The Establishment of Empirical Sociology*, pp. 152–86. New York: Harper & Row.

Cole, Michael, and Sylvia Scribner. 1974. *Culture and Thought*. New York: Wiley.

Collins, Steven. 1985. "Categories, concepts, or predicaments? Remarks on Mauss's use of philosophical terminology." In M. Carrithers, S. Collins, and S. Lukes, eds. *The Category of the Person: Anthropology, Philosophy, History*, pp. 46–82. Cambridge: Cambridge University Press.

Cosmides, Leda, and John Tooby. 1992. "Cognitive adaptations for social exchange." In J. H. Barkow, L. Cosmides, and J. Tooby, eds. *The Adapted Mind: Evolutionary Psychology and the Generation of Culture*, pp. 163–228. New York: Oxford University Press.

1994. "Origins of domain specificity: The evolution of functional organization." In L. A. Hirschfeld and S. A. Gelman, eds. *Mapping the Mind: Domain Specificity in Cognition and Culture*, pp. 85–116. Cambridge: Cambridge University Press.

Cousin, Victor. 1840–1. *Oeuvres*. Brussells: Hauman.

1846. *Cours de l'histoire de la philosophie moderne. Histoire de la philosophie au XVIIIe siècle. École de Kant*. New ed., first ser., Vol. 5. Paris: Ladrange, Éditeur, and Librairie de Didier.

1860. *Du Vrai, de beau et du bien*. Paris: Didier et Cie, Libraires-Editeurs.

1864a. *Philosophie écossaise*, 4th ed. Paris: Michel Lévy Frères, Libraires Éditeurs.

1864b. *Elements of Psychology*, 4th ed. Trans. C. S. Henry. New York: Ivison, Phinney, Blakeman.

Darwin, Charles. [1859] 1972. *On the Origin of Species*. New York: Atheneum.

Davidson, Donald. [1974] 1984. "On the very idea of a conceptual scheme." In *Inquiries into Truth and Interpretation*, pp. 183–98. Oxford: Clarendon Press.

Dennes, William Ray. 1924. The Methods and Presuppositions of Group Psychology. *University of California Publications in Philosophy* 6, no. 1, pp. 1–182. Berkeley: University of California Press.

Devitt, Michael, and Kim Sterelny. 1987. *Language and Reality*. Cambridge, MA: Bradford/MIT Press.

Di Giovanni, George. 1997. The Early Fichte as Disciple of Jacobi. *Fichte-Studien* 9: 257–73.

1998a. The Jacobi–Fichte–Reinhold Dialogue and Analytical Philosophy. *Fichte-Studien* 14: 63–86.

1998b. Hume, Jacobi, and Common Sense: An Episode in the Reception of Hume in Germany at the Time of Kant. *Kant-Studien* 89: 44–58.

Douglas, Jack. 1967. *The Social Meanings of Suicide*. Princeton, NJ: Princeton University Press.

Douglas, Mary. 1970. *Natural Symbols: Explorations in Cosmology*. New York: Pantheon Books.

1975. *Implicit Meanings*. London: Routledge & Kegan Paul.

Echeverria, José. 1963. Introduction to Maine de Biran, François-Pierre-Gonthier. *De l'aperception immédiate.* Paris: Vrin.

Evans-Pritchard, Edward Evan. 1937. *Witchcraft, Oracles, and Magic among the Azande.* Oxford: Clarendon Press.

Eve, Arthur Stewart, and C. H. Creasey. 1945. *Life and Work of John Tyndall.* London: Macmillan.

Fodor, Jerry A. 1983. *The Modularity of Mind.* Cambridge, MA: Bradford/MIT Press.

2000. *The Mind Doesn't Work That Way.* Cambridge, MA: MIT Press.

Foucault, Michel. 1966. *The Order of Things.* New York: Vintage Books.

Frege, Gottlob. [1892] 1952. "On sense and reference." In P. Geach and M. Black, eds. *Translations from the Philosophical Writings of Gottlob Frege,* pp. 56–78. Oxford: Basil Blackwell.

Friedman, Michael. 1992. "Causal laws and the foundations of natural science." In P. Guyer, ed. *The Cambridge Companion to Kant,* pp. 161–99. Cambridge: Cambridge University Press.

Gehlke, Charles Elmer. [1915] 1969. *Emile Durkheim's Contribution to Sociological Theory.* New York: AMS Press.

Giddens, Anthony. 1976. *New Rules of Sociological Method.* New York: Basic Books.

1977. "Positivism and its critics." In *Studies in Social and Political Theory,* pp. 29–89. New York: Basic Books.

1978. *Emile Durkheim.* New York: Viking.

Gilbert, Margaret. 1989. *On Social Facts.* Princeton, NJ: Princeton University Press.

Gluckman, Max. 1949–50. Social Beliefs and Individual Thinking in Primitive Society. *Memoirs and Proceedings of the Manchester Literary and Philosophical Society* 91: 73–98.

1963. *Order and Rebellion in Tribal Africa: Collected Essays with an Autobiographical Introduction.* New York: Free Press.

Godlove, Terry F., Jr. 1986. Epistemology in Durkheim's *Elementary Forms of the Religious Life. Journal of the History of Philosophy* 24: 385–401.

1989. *Religion, Interpretation, and Diversity of Belief: The Framework Model from Kant to Durkheim and Davidson.* New York: Cambridge University Press.

1996. Is "Space" a Concept? Kant, Durkheim, and French Neo-Kantianism. *Journal of the History of the Behavioral Sciences* 32(4): 441–55.

Granet, Marcel. 1934. *La pensée chinoise.* Paris: Alcan.

Guyer, Paul. 1992. "The transcendental deduction of the categories." In P. Guyer, ed. *The Cambridge Companion to Kant,* pp. 123–60. Cambridge: Cambridge University Press.

Guyer, Paul, and Allen Wood. 1988. "Introduction to the *Critique of Pure Reason.*" In Kant, Immanuel, *Critique of Pure Reason.* Trans. 1781/1787 by Paul Guyer and Allen W. Wood. Cambridge: Cambridge University Press.

Hacking, Ian. 1995. *Rewriting the Soul: Multiple Personality and the Sciences of Memory.* Princeton, NJ: Princeton University Press.

1999. *The Social Construction of What?* Cambridge, MA: Harvard University Press.

Halbwachs, Maurice. [1950] 1980. *The Collective Memory.* New York: Harper & Row.

Hallpike, Christopher Robert. 1979. *The Foundations of Primitive Thought*. Oxford: Clarendon Press.

Hart, H. L. A., and A. Honoré. 1985. *Causation in the Law*, 2nd ed. Oxford: Clarendon Press.

Hatfield, Gary. 1990. *The Natural and the Normative: Theories of Spatial Perception from Kant to Helmholtz*. Cambridge, MA: MIT Press.

——— 1992. "Empirical, rational, and transcendental psychology: Psychology as science and as philosophy." In P. Guyer, ed. *The Cambridge Companion to Kant*, pp. 200–27. Cambridge: Cambridge University Press.

——— 1995. "Remaking the science of mind: Psychology as natural science." In C. Fox, R. Porter, and R. Wokler, eds. *Inventing Human Science: Eighteenth Century Domains*, pp. 184–231. Berkeley: University of California Press.

——— 1997. "The workings of the intellect: Mind and psychology." In Patricia Easton, ed. *Logic and the Workings of the Mind: The Logic of Ideas and Faculty Psychology in Early Modern Philosophy*. North American Kant Society Studies in Philosophy 5, pp. 21–45. Atascadero, CA: Ridgeview.

Hauser, Marc D. 2000. *Wild Minds*. New York: Henry Holt.

Hertz, Robert. [1909] 1960. *Death and the Right Hand*. New York: Free Press.

Hirschfeld, Lawrence A., and Susan A. Gelman, eds. 1994. *Mapping the Mind: Domain Specificity in Cognition and Culture*. Cambridge: Cambridge University Press.

Hirst, Paul Q. 1975. *Durkheim, Bernard, and Epistemology*. London: Routledge & Kegan Paul.

Hofmann, James R. 1995. *André-Marie Ampère*. Oxford: Blackwell.

Holy, Ladislav, and Milan Stuchlik. 1983. *Actions, Norms, and Representations*. Cambridge: Cambridge University Press.

Horkheimer, Max, and Theodor W. Adorno. 1997. *Dialectic of Enlightenment*. New York: Continuum.

Horstmann, Rolf P. 1981. The Metaphysical Deduction in Kant's *Critique of Pure Reason*. *Philosophical Forum* 13: 32–47.

Hubbard, Ruth. 1979. "Have only men evolved?" In R. Hubbard, M. S. Henifen, and F. Fried, eds. *Women Look at Biology Looking at Women*, pp. 7–36. Cambridge, MA: Schenkman. Reprinted in Kourany, J., ed., 1998, *Scientific Knowledge*, 2nd ed., pp. 225–42. Belmont, CA: Wadsworth.

Hubert, Henri. 1905. *Étude sommaire de la représentation du temps dans la religion et la magie*. Paris: Imprimérie Nationale. Trans. 1999.

——— 1999. *Essay on time: A brief study of the representation of time in religion and magic*. Translation of 1905 by Robert Parkin and Jacqueline Redding. Oxford: Durkheim Press.

Hume, David. [1739] 1975. *A Treatise of Human Nature*. Oxford: Clarendon Press.

——— [1748] 1966. *Enquiries Concerning the Human Understanding and Concerning the Principles of Morals*. Oxford: Clarendon Press.

Hutchins, Edwin. 1980. *Culture and Inference*. Cambridge, MA: Harvard University Press.

Irzik, Gürol, and Teo Grünberg. 1998. Whorfian Variations on Kantian Themes: Kuhn's Linguistic Turn. *Studies in History and Philosophy of Science* 29: 207–21.

Jahoda, Gustav. 1982. *Psychology and Anthropology: A Psychological Perspective.* London: Academic.

Janet, Paul. 1883. *Traité élémentaire de philosophie à l'usage des classes.* Paris: Librairie Ch. Delagrave.

1885. *Victor Cousin et son oeuvre.* Paris: Calmann Lévy Éditeur.

Jones, Robert Alun. 1984. Demythologizing Durkheim: A Reply to Gerstein. *Knowledge and Society: Studies in the Sociology of Culture Past and Present* 5: 63–83.

Jones, Robert Alun, and W. Paul Vogt. 1984. Durkheim's Defense of *Les Formes élémentaires de la vie religieuse.* *Knowledge and Society: Studies in the Sociology of Culture Past and Present* 5: 45–62.

Jones, Susan Stedman. 2001. *Durkheim Reconsidered.* Cambridge: Polity Press.

Kant, Immanuel. [1770] 1968. *De mundi sensibilis atque intelligibilis forma et principiis.* Trans. G. B. Kerford and D. E. Walford as *On the Form and Principles of the Sensible and Intelligible World.* In *Kant: Selected Pre-Critical Writings and Correspondence with Beck.* Manchester, UK: Manchester University Press, and New York: Barnes & Noble.

1781/1787. *Kritik der Reinen Vernunft.* Riga: Hartknoch. Reprinted in Kant (1902), Vols. 3 and 4, pp. 1–252. Trans. 1965, 1966, 1996, 1998.

1783. *Prolegomena zu einer jeden künftigen Metaphysik, die als Wissenschaft wird auftreten können.* Riga: Hartknoch. Reprinted in Kant (1902), Vol. 4. Trans. 1977, 1997.

1786. *Metaphysiche Anfangsgründe der Naturwissenschaft.* Riga: Hartknoch. Reprinted in Kant (1902), Vol. 4. Trans. 1970.

1902. *Kants Gesammelte Schriften.* Berlin: Georg Reimer; subsequently Walter de Gruyter.

1965. *Critique of Pure Reason.* Trans. 1781/1787 by Max Müller. Garden City, NY: Anchor.

1966. *Critique of Pure Reason.* Trans. 1781/1787 by Norman Kemp Smith. New York: St. Martin's Press.

1970. *Metaphysical Foundations of Natural Science.* Trans. 1786 by James W. Ellington. Indianapolis: Bobbs-Merrill.

1977. *Prolegomena to Any Future Metaphysics.* Trans. 1783 by Paul Carus; rev. by James W. Ellington. Indianapolis: Hackett.

1996. *Critique of Pure Reason.* Trans. 1781/1787 by Werner S. Pluhar. Indianapolis: Hackett.

1997. *Prolegomena to Any Future Metaphysics.* Trans. 1783 by Gary Hatfield. Cambridge: Cambridge University Press.

1998. *Critique of Pure Reason.* Trans. 1781/1787 by Paul Guyer and Allen W. Wood. Cambridge: Cambridge University Press.

Käsler, Dirk. 1991. *Sociological Adventures: Earle Edward Eubank's Visits with European Sociologists.* New Brunswick, NJ: Transaction Publishers.

Kennedy, Emmet. 1978. *A Philosophe in the Age of Revolution: Destutt de Tracy and the Origins of "Ideology."* Philadelphia: American Philosophical Society.

Kitcher, Patricia. 1990. *Kant's Transcendental Psychology.* New York: Oxford University Press.

Kitcher, Philip. 2001. *Science, Truth, and Democracy.* New York: Oxford University Press.

Kuehn, Manfred. 1987. *Scottish Common Sense in Germany, 1768–1800: A Contribution to the History of Critical Philosophy*. Kingston and Montreal: McGill-Queen's University Press.

Kuhn, Thomas S. 1970. *The Structure of Scientific Revolutions*, 2nd ed. Chicago: University of Chicago Press.

1991. "The Road Since *Structure*." In A. Fine, M. Forbes, and L. Wessels, eds. *PSA 1990*, Vol. 2, pp. 3–13. East Lansing, MI: Philosophy of Science Association. Reprinted in Kuhn 2000, pp. 90–104.

1993. "Afterwords." In P. Horwich, ed. *World Changes*, pp. 311–41. Cambridge, MA: MIT Press. Reprinted in Kuhn 2000, pp. 224–52.

2000. *The Road Since Structure*. Ed. James Conant and John Haugeland. Chicago: University of Chicago Press.

Latour, Bruno. 1987. *Science in Action*. Cambridge, MA: Harvard University Press.

Latour, Bruno, and Steve Woolgar. 1986. *Laboratory Life: The Construction of Scientific Facts*, 2nd ed. Princeton, NJ: Princeton University Press.

Laudan, Larry. 1970. "Thomas Reid and the Newtonian turn of British methodological thought." In R. Butts and Davis, eds. *The Methodological Heritage of Newton*. Toronto: University of Toronto Press. Reprinted in Laudan, 1981, *Science and Hypothesis*, pp. 86–110. Dordrecht, the Netherlands: D. Reidel.

1971. Towards a Reassessment of Comte's "Méthode Positive." *Philosophy of Science* 38: 35–53. Reprinted in Laudan, 1981, *Science and Hypothesis*, pp. 141–62. Dordrecht, the Netherlands: D. Reidel.

Leach, Edmund R. 1964. "Anthropological aspects of language: Animal categories and verbal abuse." In Eric H. Lenneberg, ed. *New Directions in the Study of Language*, pp. 23–63. Cambridge, MA: MIT Press.

Lenneberg, Eric H. 1953. Cognition in Ethnolinguistics. *Language* 29: 463–71.

Leslie, Alan M. 1982. The perception of causality in infants. *Perception* 11: 173–86.

1988. "The necessity of illusion." In L. Weiskrantz, ed. *Thought without Language*, pp. 185–210. New York: Oxford University Press.

1991. "The theory of mind impairment in autism: Evidence for a modular mechanism of development?" In Andrew Whiten, ed. *Natural Theories of Mind: Evolution, Development, and Simulation of Everyday Mindreading*, pp. 63–78. Oxford: Basil Blackwell.

1994. "ToMM, ToBy, and agency: Core architecture and domain specificity." In L. A. Hirschfeld and S. A. Gelman, eds. *Mapping the Mind: Domain Specificity in Cognition and Culture*, pp. 119–48. Cambridge: Cambridge University Press.

1995. "A theory of agency." In D. Sperber et al., eds. *Causal Cognition: A Multidisciplinary Debate*, pp. 121–49. Oxford: Clarendon Press.

Leslie, Alan M., and Stephanie Keeble. 1987. Do six-month-old infants perceive causality? *Cognition* 25: 265–88.

Lévi-Strauss, Claude. 1945. "French sociology." In G. Gurvitch and W. E. Moore, eds. *Twentieth Century Sociology*, pp. 503–36. New York: Philosophical Library.

1950. *Introduction to the Work of Marcel Mauss*. Trans. Felicity Baker. London: Routledge & Kegan Paul.

[1964] 1966. Overture to *Le Cru et le cuit*. *Yale French Studies* nos. 36–7: 41–65.

1966. *The Savage Mind*. Chicago: University of Chicago Press.

Lévy-Bruhl, Lucien. 1894. *La philosophie de Jacobi.* Paris: Alcan.
1900. *La philosophie d'Auguste Comte.* Paris: Alcan.
1903. *The Philosophy of Auguste Comte.* Authorized trans. of Lévy-Bruhl 1900. New York: G. P. Putnam's Sons.
1910. *Les fonctions mentales dans les sociétés inférieures.* Paris: Alcan. Trans. 1926 by Lilian A. Clare.
1922. *La mentalité primitive.* Paris: Alcan. Trans. 1923.
[1923] 1978. *Primitive Mentality.* Authorized trans. by Lilian A. Clare of Lévy-Bruhl 1922. New York: Macmillan.
[1926] 1985. *How Natives Think.* Authorized trans. by Lilian A. Clare of Lévy-Bruhl 1910. Princeton, NJ: Princeton University Press.
[1927] 1963. *L'Âme primitive.* Paris: PUF. Trans. 1928 by Lilian A. Clare.
1928. *The Soul of the Primitive.* Authorized trans. by Lilian A. Clare of Lévy-Bruhl 1927. New York: MacMillan.
[1931] 1963. *Le surnaturel et la nature dans la mentalité primitive.* Paris: PUF. Trans. 1935 by Lilian A. Clare.
1935. *La mythologie primitive: le monde mythique des Australiens et des Papous.* Paris: Alcan. Trans. 1983 by Brian Elliot.
[1935] 1973. *Primitives and the Supernatural.* Authorized trans. by Lilian A. Clare of Lévy-Bruhl 1931. New York: Haskell House.
1938. *L'Expérience mystique et les symboles chez les primitifs.* Paris: Alcan.
1949. *Les Carnets de Lucien Lévy-Bruhl.* Paris: PUF. Trans. 1975 by Peter Rivière.
1975. *The Notebooks on Primitive Mentality.* Trans. of 1949 by Peter Rivière. New York: Harper & Row.
1983. *Primitive Mythology: The Mythic World of the Australian and Papuan Natives.* Translation of 1935 by Brian Elliot. St. Lucia, Australia: University of Queensland Press.
Lilla, Mark. 1998. The Politics of Jacques Derrida. *The New York Review of Books* 45, no. 11 (June 25): 36–41.
Littleton, C. Scott. 1985. "Lucien Lévy-Bruhl and the concept of cognitive relativity." Introduction to Lévy-Bruhl [1926] 1985. *How Natives Think,* pp. v–lviii. Princeton, NJ: Princeton University Press.
Locke, John. [1690] 1995. *An Essay Concerning Human Understanding.* Amherst, New York: Prometheus Books.
Luginbühl, Rodolphe. 1888. *Philippe-Albert Stapfer, ancien ministre des arts et des sciences et ministre plénipotentiaire de la République helvétique 1766–1840.* Paris: Librairie Fischbacher.
Lukes, Steven. 1973. *Emile Durkheim: His Life and Work.* New York: Penguin Books.
Madden, Edward H. 1984. Victor Cousin and the Commonsense Tradition. *History of Philosophy Quarterly* 1: 93–109.
Maine de Biran, François-Pierre-Gonthier. 1841. *Oeuvres philosophiques de Maine de Biran.* 4 vols. Ed. Victor Cousin. Paris: Ladrange.
1920–49. *Oeuvres complètes.* 14 vols. Ed. Pierre Tisserand and Henri Gouhier. Paris: Alcan. Reprinted 1982 in Geneva and Paris: Slatkine.
[1929] 1970. *The Influence of Habit on the Faculty of Thinking.* Trans. Margaret Donaldson Boehm. Westport, CT: Greenwood Press.
1963. *De l'aperception immédiate.* Ed. José Echeverria. Paris: Vrin.

Malinowski, Bronislaw. [1939] 1944. "The functional theory." In *A Scientific Theory of Culture and Other Essays*, pp. 145–76. Chapel Hill, NC: University of North Carolina Press.

Manns, James W., and Edward H. Madden. 1990. Victor Cousin: Commonsense and the Absolute. *Review of Metaphysics* 43: 569–89.

Mauss, Marcel. 1924. Rapports réels et pratiques de la psychologie et de la sociologie. *Journal de psychologie normale et pathologique* 21: 892–922. Reprinted in Mauss 1950, pp. 281–310. Trans. in Mauss 1979.

   1938. Une catégorie de l'esprit humaine: la notion de personne, celle de 'moi.' *Journal of the Royal Anthropological Institute* 68: 263–81. Trans. by B. Brewster in Mauss 1979 and by W. D. Halls in M. Carrithers et al., eds., 1985, *The Category of the Person: Anthropology, Philosophy, History*, pp. 1–25. Cambridge: Cambridge University Press.

   1950. *Sociologie et anthropologie*. Paris: PUF.

   1979. *Sociology and Psychology*. Trans. Ben Brewster. London: Routledge & Kegan Paul.

Mauss, Marcel, and Henri Beuchat. 1906. Essai sur les variations saisonnières des sociétés eskimos. Étude de morphologie sociale. *L'Année sociologique* 9: 26–132. Reprinted in the 1966 second edition and the 1973 third edition of Mauss 1950.

May, Todd. 1997. "Introduction." In *Twentieth Century Continental Philosophy*, pp. 1–37. Upper Saddle River, NJ: Prentice-Hall.

McGinn, Colin. 2002. An Ardent Fallibilist (review of *Invariances: The Structure of the Objective World*, by Robert Nozick). *The New York Review of Books* 49, no. 11 (June 27): 39–41.

Meerbote, Ralf. 1990. "Kant's functionalism." In J. C. Smith, ed. *Historical Foundations of Cognitive Science*, pp. 161–87. Dordrecht, the Netherlands: D. Reidel.

Merllié, Dominique. 1989a. Présentation: Le Cas Lévy-Bruhl. *Revue philosophique de la France et de l'étranger* 114: 419–48.

   1989b. Lévy-Bruhl et Durkheim. Notes biographiques en marge d'une correspondence. *Revue philosophique de la France et de l'étranger* 114: 493–514.

Mestrovic, Stjepan G. 1989a. Reappraising Durkheim's *Elementary Forms of the Religious Life* in the Context of Schopenhauer's Philosophy. *Journal for the Scientific Study of Religion* 28(3): 255–72.

   1989b. Searching for the starting points of scientific inquiry: Durkheim's rules of sociological method and Schopenhauer's philosophy. *Sociological Inquiry* 59: 267–86.

Michotte, Albert Edouard. [1946] 1963. *The Perception of Causality*. Trans. T. R. and Elaine Miles. New York: Basic Books.

Millikan, Ruth G. 1993. *White Queen Psychology and Other Essays for Alice*. Cambridge, MA: Bradford/MIT Press.

   2000. *On Clear and Confused Ideas*. New York: Cambridge University Press.

Moore, Francis Charles Timothy. 1970. *The Psychology of Maine de Biran*. Oxford: Clarendon Press.

Muhlfeld, L. 1893. Débat sur les types de solidarité et la division social du travail (report on Durkheim's oral thesis defense). *Revue universitaire* 2(1): 440–3. Reprinted in Durkheim 1975a, Vol. 2, pp. 288–91.

Nandan, Yash. 1977. *The Durkheimian School: A Systematic and Comprehensive Bibliography*. Westport, CT: Greenwood Press.

Needham, Rodney. 1963. "Introduction." In Durkheim, Émile, and Marcel Mauss, *Primitive Classification*, pp. vii–xlviii. Chicago: University of Chicago Press.

Nielsen, Donald A. 1999. *Three Faces of God: Society, Religion, and the Categories of Totality in the Philosophy of Émile Durkheim*. Albany: State University of New York Press.

Nye, D. A., and C. E. Ashworth. 1971. Emile Durkheim: Was he a nominalist or a realist? *British Journal of Sociology* 22: 133–48.

Parsons, Charles. 1992. "The transcendental aesthetic." In P. Guyer, ed. *The Cambridge Companion to Kant*, pp. 62–100. Cambridge: Cambridge University Press.

Parsons, Talcott. 1937. *The Structure of Social Action*. New York: Free Press, 1968.

Pickering, Andrew. 1984. *Constructing Quarks: A Sociological History of Particle Physics*. Chicago: University of Chicago Press.

Pickering, William S. F. 1993. "The origins of conceptual thinking in Durkheim: Social or religious?" In Stephen P. Turner, ed. *Emile Durkheim: Sociologist and Moralist*, pp. 52–70. New York: Routledge.

Pinker, Steven. 1994. *The Language Instinct*. New York: William Morrow.

1997. *How the Mind Works*. New York: W. W. Norton.

2002. *The Blank Slate: The Modern Denial of Human Nature*. New York: Viking.

Pinker, Steven, Paul Bloom, and commentators. 1990. Natural language and natural selection. *Behavioral and Brain Sciences* 13: 707–84. Partially reprinted in J. H. Barkow et al., eds., 1992, *The Adapted Mind: Evolutionary Psychology and the Generation of Culture*, pp. 451–93. New York: Oxford University Press.

Premack, David. 1988. " 'Does the chimpanzee have a theory of mind?' Revisited." In R. W. Byrne and A. Whiten, eds. *Machiavellian Intelligence: Social Expertise and the Evolution of Intellect in Monkeys, Apes, and Humans*, pp. 160–79. Oxford: Clarendon Press.

Premack, David, and Guy Woodruff. 1978. Does the chimpanzee have a theory of mind? *The Behavioral and Brain Sciences* 1 (4): 515–26, 616–29.

Rabier, Élie. [1884] 1893. *Leçons de Philosophie. I. Psychologie*, 4th ed. Paris: Librairie Hachette et Cie.

Rawls, Anne Warfield. 1996. Durkheim's epistemology: The neglected argument. *American Journal of Sociology* 102 (2): 430–82.

Reid, Thomas. 1983. *Thomas Reid's Inquiry and Essays*. Ed. Ronald E. Beanblossom and Keith Lehrer. Indianapolis: Hackett.

Renouvier, Charles. [1875] 1912. *Essais de critique générale. Premier Essai: Traité de logique générale et de logique formelle*. Paris: Librairie Armand Colin.

Richards, Janet Radcliffe Richards. 2000. *Human Nature after Darwin*. London and New York: Routledge.

Sapir, Edward. 1949. "The status of linguistics as a science." In D. G. Mandelbaum, ed. *Selected Writings of Edward Sapir*, pp. 160–6. Berkeley: University of California Press.

Schaub, Edward L. 1920. A sociological theory of knowledge. *Philosophical Review* 29: 319–39.

Schmaus, Warren. 1994. *Durkheim's Philosophy of Science and the Sociology of Knowledge: Creating an Intellectual Niche.* Chicago: University of Chicago Press.

1995. Rabier as Durkheim's Source for Hume's Arguments. *Durkheimian Studies/Études durkheimiennes* 1 (ns): 17–23.

1996. Lévy-Bruhl, Durkheim, and the positivist roots of the sociology of knowledge. *Journal of the History of the Behavioral Sciences* 32 (4): 424–40.

Schneider, David M. 1976. "Notes toward a theory of culture." In Keith H. Basso and Henry A. Selby, eds. *Meaning in Anthropology*, pp. 197–220. Albuquerque: University of New Mexico Press.

Schneider, Ulrich. 1998. Eclecticism Rediscovered. *Journal of the History of Ideas* 59 (1): 173–82.

Sellars, Wilfrid. 1974. "This I or He or It (the thing) which thinks . . ." In *Essays in Philosophy and Its History*. Dordrecht, the Netherlands: D. Reidel.

Slobin, Dan I. 1971. *Psycholinguistics.* Glenview, IL: Scott, Foresman.

Spelke, Elizabeth S., Ann Phillips, and Amanda L. Woodward. 1995. "Infants' knowledge of object motion and human action." In D. Sperber et al., eds. *Causal Cognition: A Multidisciplinary Debate*, pp. 44–78. Oxford: Clarendon Press.

Spelke, Elizabeth S., Peter Vishton, and Claes von Hofsten. 1995. "Object perception, object-directed action, and physical knowledge in infancy." In M. S. Gazzaniga, ed. *The Cognitive Neurosciences*, pp. 165–79. Cambridge, MA: MIT.

Sperber, Dan. 1995. "Introduction." In D. Sperber et al., eds. *Causal Cognition: A Multidisciplinary Debate*, pp. xv ff. Oxford: Clarendon Press.

1996. *Explaining Culture: A Naturalistic Approach.* Oxford: Basil Blackwell.

Sperber, Dan, David Premack, and Ann Premack, eds. 1995. *Causal Cognition: A Multidisciplinary Debate.* Oxford: Clarendon Press.

Sterelny, Kim. 1995. The Adapted Mind. *Biology and Philosophy* 10: 365–80.

Symons, Donald. 1989. A Critique of Darwinian Anthropology. *Ethology and Sociobiology* 10: 1313–44.

1990. Adaptiveness and adaptation. *Ethology and Sociobiology* 11: 427–44.

1992. "On the use and misuse of Darwinism in the study of human behavior." In J. H. Barkow et al., eds., *The Adapted Mind: Evolutionary Psychology and the Generation of Culture*, pp. 137–59. New York: Oxford University Press.

Tardieu, Maurice, ed. 1903. Comte et la métaphysique. *Bulletin de la Société française de Philosophie* 3: 1–24.

Taylor, Steve. 1982. *Durkheim and the Study of Suicide.* New York: St. Martin's Press.

Tooby, John, and Leda Cosmides. 1989. Evolutionary psychology and the generation of culture, Part I: Theoretical considerations. *Ethology and Sociobiology* 10: 29–49.

1992. The psychological foundations of culture. In J. H. Barkow et al., eds. *The Adapted Mind: Evolutionary Psychology and the Generation of Culture*, pp. 19–136. New York: Oxford University Press.

1995. "Mapping the evolved functional organization of mind and brain." In M. S. Gazzaniga, ed. *The Cognitive Neurosciences*, pp. 1185–97. Cambridge, MA: MIT Press.

Trendelenburg, Adolf. [1846] 1963. *Geschichte der Kategorienlehre.* Hildesheim, Germany: Georg Olms Verlagsbuchhandlung.

Tyndall, John. 1870. *Essays on the Use and Limit of the Imagination in Science.* London: Longmans, Green.

1871. Rôle de l'imagination dans les sciences. *La Revue scientifique de la France et de l'étranger. Revue des cours scientifiques* second ser., 1 (1): 13–24.

Vallois, Maximilien. 1924. *La Formation de l'influence Kantienne en France.* Paris: Alcan.

Veitch, John. 1910. "Cousin, Victor (1792–1867)." In *The Encyclopedia Britannica,* 11th ed., Vol. 7, pp. 330–5. Cambridge: Cambridge University Press.

Villers, Charles. 1801. *Philosophie de Kant.* Metz: Collignon.

Wilkerson, T. E. 1976. *Kant's Critique of Pure Reason.* Oxford: Clarendon Press.

Witherspoon, Gary J. 1971. Navajo categories of objects at rest. *American Anthropologist* 73: 110–27.

Woolgar, Steve. [1988] 1993. *Science: The Very Idea.* Chichester, UK: Ellis Horwood Limited, and London and New York: Tavistock. Reprinted in London and New York: Routledge.

Worsley, Peter M. 1956. Emile Durkheim's theory of knowledge. *Sociological Review* 4 (ns): 47–62.

Wright, Robert. 1994. *The Moral Animal.* New York: Vintage Books.

Index

Abelard, Peter 82, 121
  Cousin's edition of 82, 87
  see also conceptualism
absolute, category of 83, 84, 87, 89,
    91, 94, 113
action, category of 28, 29
adaptation 143–5, 148–9
  see also evolution
Adorno, Theodor, and Max
    Horkheimer 8
Alexander, Jeffrey 128, 163
Ampère, André-Marie 59, 68, 137,
    160
analogy 105
Ancillon, Jean-Pierre-Fréderic 57, 58,
    68, 157, 159
  Mélanges de literature et de
    philosophie 58
Ancillon, Louis-Fréderic 57, 58,
    159
  Essai ontologique sur l'âme 58
  Mémoire sur les fondements de la
    métaphysique 58
Anderson, R. Lanier 53, 157, 158
animism and the animistic theory of
    the origin of religion 124–5,
    127, 146
Année sociologique 3
anthropology, social and cultural 7,
    22, 123, 145

apperception
  Cousin on 65–7
  empirical 48, 51, 52, 65–6, 67, 69,
    70, 137
  limitations of 73
  Maine de Biran on 69–71, 72, 128,
    161
  transcendental 24, 48, 50–2, 53,
    58, 65–6, 67, 69, 70, 99, 137,
    161
  see also Descartes, cogito;
    introspection; Kant, unity of
    consciousness
a priori philosophy or rationalism
    12–15, 18, 78, 84, 95, 98,
    120
  see also Descartes; Kant
Aristotle 1, 4, 6, 24, 27–30, 38, 42,
    44, 62, 82, 84, 91, 114, 156,
    162
  Categories 28
  On Interpretation 29
  Metaphysics 29
  Posterior Analytics 29
Arnauld, Antoine 162
  Port-Royal Logic 162
Ashworth, C. E., and D. A. Nye
    163
association of ideas 36, 86, 88, 116,
    129

associationism 84, 86, 162
  see also Bain; empiricism; Hamilton;
    Hume; Mill; Spencer
Atlas, Samuel 56
Atran, Scott 146
Australian indigenes 99, 123, 130,
  142
autism, childhood 149
Azande 8

Baillargeon, Renée 147
Bain, Alexander 104, 162
being-acted-upon, category of 28,
  29
Beiser, Frederick 39, 57
Benoît-Smullyan, Émile 155
Berger, Peter, and Thomas
    Luckmann 7–8
Bergson, Henri 91–2, 93–4, 98, 114,
  162
Berkeley, George 18, 55, 58, 81, 101,
    103, 159
  idealism 81
  nominalism 81
Berlin Academy 57
Bernard, Claude 162
Beuchat, Henri
  and Marcel Mauss 3
biological taxa 10, 153
Bloch, Maurice 10
Bloom, Paul 144
Bloor, David 8, 154
  interests and 96, 155
Bordeaux, University of 95, 99
Bouglé, Célestin 3, 163
Boutroux, Émile 79, 95, 98, 156
Boyer, Pascal 10
Brooks, John x, 155, 163
Brothers, Leslie 148
Brown, Roger 10
Brown, Thomas 85

Cabanis, Pierre-Jean-George 68–9,
  160
  *Rapports du physique et du moral de
    l'homme* 68
Carey, Susan 165

Cartesian, *see* Descartes
categories
  and biological function 143
  and collective representations 2, 4,
    14, 15, 22, 23, 121–2, 135, 136,
    137, 138, 139
  and cognitive abilities, capacities,
    or mechanisms 143–4, 145,
    146, 147, 148, 149, 150, 151, 152
  and cultural representations
    146–7, 151, 152
  divine source of 14, 19, 20, 25, 74,
    84, 114
  Durkheim's early views on 112–17
  eliminative arguments or
    arguments to the best
    explanation regarding 12, 62,
    78, 84, 120
  empirical deduction of 25, 46, 52,
    71
  Maine de Biran on 69, 70–1, 82,
    91, 113
  morality and 62
  social causes and origins of 1, 3, 7,
    12, 14, 17, 18, 22, 23, 25, 73, 78,
    95, 99, 100, 114, 121, 123, 125,
    127, 128, 129, 130, 131, 132,
    134, 137, 155
  social functions of 2, 4, 17, 22, 121,
    122, 123, 129, 131, 132, 134,
    135, 137, 138, 139, 145, 151
  transcendental deduction of 25,
    41, 45–8, 50, 52–4, 71, 90, 99,
    137, 157
  universal and necessary character
    of 2, 5, 12–17, 22, 50, 62–3, 74,
    78, 83, 85, 88, 97, 112, 114, 120,
    121, 129, 137
  variability of 6–7, 12–16, 22, 78, 97,
    120, 121, 138
  see also absolute; action;
    being-acted-upon; causality;
    Chinese categories; class or
    genus; Cousin; Durkheim;
    existence; final causality;
    interaction; Paul Janet; Kant;
    person, personality, or personal

identity; position or posture;
quality; quantity or number;
relation; space or place;
Spencer; state or condition;
substance; time
Catlin, George 163
causality
category, idea, or concept of 1, 2,
3, 4, 5, 15, 16, 18, 23, 24, 25, 29,
36, 49, 52, 53, 60, 62, 66, 69, 71,
77, 83, 85–7, 88, 89, 90, 91,
93–4, 100, 108, 113, 117, 120,
121, 122–36, 142, 143, 146–51,
162
causal illusion 147–8, 150, 165
and explanation 20, 107, 109
Hume's analysis of 33–6
idea of power or force 121, 123–8,
131, 132, 135
idea of power, force, or necessary
connection 18, 71, 73, 94, 100,
124, 126, 147, 148
idea of necessary connection 123,
128, 129–35, 150–1
intentional or animate 133, 146,
147, 148, 165
see also Theory of Mind, ToMM
invariable sequence 74, 85, 86,
133, 147, 148
physical or mechanical 136, 146,
147, 165
see also ToBy
principle of 37, 62, 73–4, 85–6, 90,
113, 116, 129–30, 136
see also Durkheim, ideas of power
and necessary connection;
force; Hart and Honoré; Maine
de Biran, causality and; power
Chinese categories 5, 23, 24, 78
Chomsky, Noam 127, 129, 164
class or genus, category of 1, 3, 4, 5,
12, 29, 143, 151
cognitive abilities, capacities, or
mechanisms 143–4, 145, 146,
147, 148, 149, 150, 151, 152
see also modularity of mind
cognitive ethology 123, 145

cognitive neurosciences 22, 142–3,
145, 151, 152
cognitive science 147
Cohen, Hermann 53, 158
Cole, Michael, and Sylvia Scribner 10
collective effervescence 14, 127
collective representations 2, 4, 12, 14,
16, 17, 18, 22, 25, 26, 77, 82, 97,
100, 102, 104, 110, 111, 113, 117,
120–2, 131, 136, 138, 139–40,
141, 142, 153, 156
and categories 2, 4, 14, 15, 22, 23,
121–2, 135, 136, 137, 138, 139
cultural distinguished from
collective representations 140
see also cultural representations
collective or social consciousness 102,
104, 111
collective or social forces 3, 18, 21, 25,
73, 77, 97, 100, 121, 125–6,
127
Collins, Steven 155
color terms and categories 8, 10, 30,
153, 157
common-sense philosophy 24, 25, 56,
59, 64, 118
direct perception and 64–5, 128,
129, 138, 139
see also Cousin; eclectic
spiritualism; Jacobi; Reid
Comte, Auguste 79, 97, 98, 141, 162
Course de philosophie positive 79, 98
conceptualism 82, 102, 110, 111, 121
Condillac, Étienne Bonnot de 61, 67,
69, 84, 103
construction, cultural and social 1, 2,
7–12, 153–4
Cosmides, Leda, and John Tooby 10,
164, 165
Cousin, Victor x, 1, 18, 19–20, 24, 25,
39, 50, 58, 59–68, 69, 73, 74–5,
76, 77, 78, 79, 81, 82, 83, 84, 90,
94, 96, 97, 100, 108, 110, 114,
118, 119, 120, 128, 132, 139,
157, 159, 160, 161, 162,
163
and Peter Abelard 82, 87

Cousin, Victor (*cont.*)
    administrative positions 19, 61,
        155
    denies distinction between Kant's
        empirical and transcendental
        deduction 65–7
    direct perception 64–5, 128, 129,
        138, 139
    divine source of categories 14, 19,
        20, 25, 74, 84, 114
    Elements of Psychology 64, 159
    influence on philosophical
        curriculum in France 20, 61,
        76, 98, 101, 156, 161
    lectures on Kant 59, 159
    Méthode psychologique 33, 59, 61, 96,
        107
    Oeuvres 160
    opposition to hypotheses 61, 66,
        82, 96
    opposition to Kant 39, 60, 157
    preference for first edition of
        Kant's *Critique of Pure Reason* 66
    and Thomas Reid 60, 61, 64, 159
    rejects distinction between forms
        of intuition and categories 39,
        83, 113
    *The True, the Beautiful, and the
        Good* 60, 159
    universal and necessary principles
        of the mind 61–3
    visit to Jacobi and Schelling 39, 60,
        157
    will, freedom of 67
    see also Durkheim; Paul Janet
cultural development 146, 151
    convergent 144–5, 151
cultural representations 7, 142, 145,
        151
    categories and 146–7, 151,
        152
    see also collective representations
Cuvier, Frédéric 59
Cuvier, Georges 59

Darwin, Charles 79, 154
    On the Origin of Species 145
    see also evolution

Davidson, Donald 9
Degérando, Joseph-Marie 59, 68
    *Histoire comparée des systèmes de
        philosophie* 59
Dennes, William Ray 17
Derrida, Jacques 7
Descartes, René 50, 52, 60, 61, 66, 71,
        84, 87, 91, 98, 139, 159, 164
    Cartesian foundations 20, 52, 70,
        107
    Cartesian philosophy and
        science 2, 20, 52, 78, 101, 155
    cogito or Cartesian introspection
        24, 50, 52, 55, 63, 92, 99, 107,
        158
    Meditations 87
Destutt de Tracy, Antoine-Louis-
        Claude 68–9
    "De la métaphysique de Kant" 68
direct or unmediated perception
        64–5, 128, 129, 138, 139
divine reason as source or foundation
        of categories 14, 19, 20, 25, 74,
        84, 114
Douglas, Jack 163
Douglas, Mary 7, 153, 155
Down syndrome 149
Durkheim, Émile ix, x, 1–5, 6, 8,
        12–23, 25, 27–30, 39, 54, 56,
        60, 64, 76, 77–8, 79, 82, 83, 84,
        87, 90, 94–5, 96–119, 120–36,
        137–42, 143, 150, 151, 153, 154,
        155, 156, 161, 163, 164
    categories in the Sens lectures
        112–17
    circularity objection and 16–18,
        115, 120
    Cousin, criticism of 108, 114,
        116–17
    Division of Labor in Society
        (1893) 78, 102, 112, 156, 161
    duality of human nature 102
    Durkheim–Mauss Thesis 3, 8, 10,
        154
    Elementary Forms of Religious Life
        (1912) ix, 3–4, 5, 12–16, 27, 78,
        95, 97, 98, 100, 102, 114, 115,
        120, 121, 122–31, 141, 145, 152

explanation in the sciences 107, 109

fellowship trip to Germany 101, 111

and Hume 126, 164

idea of causal power 121, 123–8, 131, 132, 135

idea of necessary connection 123, 128, 129–35, 150–1

ideas of power and necessary connection 73

"Individual and Collective Representations" (1898) 156

and Kant 117–18, 123

La Morale (1920) 18, 163

Maine de Biran, criticism of 106, 108, 113, 116

and Mauss 1, 2–3, 14, 27, 99, 112, 153, 161

methodology 25, 79, 96, 100, 104–12, 163

Moral Education (1925) 141, 165

moral, social, and historical sciences 111

philosophy, as a teacher of 19, 20, 25, 60, 78, 99, 101, 155

philosophy as a science 107–11

Pragmatism and Sociology (1955) 5, 121

Primitive Classification (1903) 2–3, 14, 99, 153

psychological capacities and characteristics and 5, 143

psychology, method of 107–10

rejects distinction between forms of intuition and categories 113

Rules of Sociological Method (1895) 22, 107, 119, 140, 141, 165

sacred and profane 99

Sens lectures (1884) 20, 25, 79, 82, 96–7, 98, 100–19, 121, 155, 162, 163, 164

social or cultural determinist interpretation of 140–1

sociological explanation 119

sociology distinguished from psychology 14, 138, 140, 141

sociology of knowledge and sociological theory of the categories 2, 7, 12, 14, 26, 97, 99, 115, 120–36, 137, 138, 139, 145

sociology of religion (*see also* animism, totemism) 99, 123, 145

spiritualist realism 101, 123

Suicide (1897) 126, 141

"surprising prerogative" of the mind to impose its categories on experience 14, 39, 90

theory of meaning 16, 25, 77, 82, 100, 102–104, 111, 121–2, 138

two senses of category 116–17

unconscious, on the 109–10

will and 118, 119, 124–7

see also categories; collective effervescence; collective or social consciousness; collective representations; social causes and origins; social facts; social functions; social or collective forces; social structure

eclectic spiritualism x, 1, 18, 19–21, 25, 26, 39, 56, 61, 73, 75, 76, 77, 78, 82, 95, 96, 97, 98, 99, 100, 101–104, 107, 108, 112, 113, 117, 118, 119, 120, 123, 124, 126, 127, 137, 138

see also Cousin; Paul Janet; Maine de Biran

École Normale Supérieure 20, 77, 79, 95, 98, 161, 163, 164

merger with Faculty of Letters, Paris 98

École Polytechnique 79

empiricism 12–15, 18, 62, 66, 84, 85–8, 89, 95, 98, 100, 113, 114, 115, 120, 129–30

see also associationism; Bain; Berkeley; Brown, Thomas; Condillac; Hamilton; Hume; Locke; Mill; Spencer

Engel, Johann Jakob 57, 69, 159, 160

Epicurus 84
epistemology or theory of
    knowledge 21, 53, 97, 99, 101,
    117, 158
ethics, morality, or moral
    philosophy 20, 21, 59, 61, 62,
    76, 84, 97, 101, 108, 109, 161,
    163
Evans-Pritchard, Edward Evan 8
evolution
    Darwinian 10, 79, 88, 96, 142,
        143–6, 149, 150, 151, 152, 154,
        164
    Lamarckian 87–8
    Spencer and 87, 91, 116, 117, 130,
        164, 165
    see also adaptation
evolutionary psychology 164
    see also Cosmides and Tooby;
        Pinker
existence, category of 52, 66, 71,
    83

Faculty of Letters, Paris
    (Sorbonne) 59, 76, 77, 95, 98,
    155, 159, 161
    merger with École Normale
        Supérieure 98
Feder, J. G. 55, 58
final causality, or end, goal, or
    purpose, category of 62, 83,
    113
Fodor, Jerry 160, 164, 165
    Modularity of Mind (1983) 160,
        164
    The Mind Doesn't Work That Way
        (2000) 59
folk psychology 149, 150
force, idea of
    distinguished from idea of
        power 128, 136
    primitive notion of 148
    see also causality; Durkheim;
        Hume; social or collective
        forces
Foucault, Michel 6
Frazer, James 154

Frege, Gottlob 80
Friedman, Michael 37, 90
functionalism
    in psychology 109
    in social sciences 156

Galileo Galilei 106, 108, 113, 116
Gall, Francis Joseph 69, 160
    see also phrenology
Garve, Christian 55, 58
Gassendi, Pierre 84
Gehlke, Charles Elmer 17
gender 11, 154
genus or class, category of 1, 3, 4, 5,
    12, 29, 143, 151
Giddens, Anthony 155, 163
Gilbert, Margaret 130, 164
Gluckman, Max 7, 30, 153, 157
Godlove, Terry 15, 17, 155
Granet, Marcel 5
Gross, Neil x, 155
Grünberg, Teo, and Gürol Irzik 9
Guizot, François 59
Guyer, Paul 45, 52, 53, 70
    and Allen Wood 70

Hacking, Ian 11, 162
Halbwachs, Maurice 5
Hallpike, Christopher 10
Hamann, Johann Georg 39, 55, 65,
    90, 159
    critiques Kant's distinction
        between forms of intuition
        and categories of the
        understanding 39, 83
    *Metakritik über den Purismum der
        Reinen Vernunft* 39, 65
Hamelin, Octave 155
Hamilton, William 162
    see also Mill
Hart, H. L. A., and Anthony
    Honoré 133
Hartmann, Eduard von 110
Hatfield, Gary 157, 158
Helmholtz, Hermann Ludwig
    Ferdinand von 86
Hertz, Robert 3, 29

Hirst, Paul Q 162, 163
  Durkheim, Bernard, and Epistemology
    (1975) 162
Holy, Ladislav, and Milan Stuchlik 10
Honoré, Anthony, and H. L. A.
  Hart 133
Hopi 10
Horkheimer, Max, and Theodor
  Adorno 8
Hubbard, Ruth 154
Hubert, Henri 3
Hume, David 18, 21, 24, 33–8, 69, 71,
    73, 81, 85, 94, 103, 124, 126,
    127, 129, 130, 133, 146, 148,
    159, 160, 163
  analysis of causation 33–6
  and Durkheim 126, 164
  *Enquiry Concerning Human
    Understanding* 18, 71
  idea of power, force, energy, or
    necessary connection 18, 71, 73,
    94, 100, 124, 126, 147, 148
  and Rabier 126
  Treatise of Human Nature 71
  hypothesis, method of, or
    hypothetico-deductive
    method 25, 77, 78–9, 96, 97,
    104–11
  creative imagination and 105–107
  see also Durkheim; Paul Janet;
    Tyndall

ideas
  abstract 80–1, 102–103
  mistakes and 65, 72
  representative 2, 64, 72, 77, 78, 79,
    80–2, 96, 100, 102–104, 139
  see also collective representations;
    intentional states; Kant,
    representations, mental; mental
    states; perception
idéologues 59, 68–9
  see also Cabanis; Destutt de Tracy;
    Maine de Biran
incommensurability 9, 23, 26, 59, 122,
    138, 140
India, caste system in 3, 7–8

induction 104
intentionality 133, 146, 147, 148, 165
  see also causality, intentional;
    intentional states
intentional states 133, 135, 149, 150
  see also ideas
interaction, category of 53, 83
introspection or internal reflection 2,
    20, 25, 51, 52, 60, 61, 67, 69, 72,
    73, 79, 95, 96, 100, 127, 128,
    141, 142
  see also apperception; Descartes;
    Maine de Biran; psychology,
    philosophical
Inuit or Eskimo conceptions of
  time 3
Iroquois notion of causal power 16
  see also Native Americans; *orenda*
Irzik, Gürol, and Teo Grünberg 9

Jacobi, Friedrich 39, 55–6, 60, 63, 64,
    66, 90, 100, 139, 157, 158, 159
  common-sense philosophy of 56,
    158
  "nihilism" in Kant 24, 50, 52, 55,
    63, 92, 99, 107, 158
  rejects distinction between forms
    of intuition and categories 39,
    83
Janet, Paul 2, 20, 22, 25, 50, 64, 69,
    75, 76–95, 96, 97, 98, 100, 102,
    104, 107, 113, 114, 116, 126,
    128, 139, 156, 161, 162, 164
  categories and 82–94
  and Cousin 76, 83
  and Kant 83, 84, 87, 89–91
  and Maine de Biran 91–2, 93–4,
    98, 114, 162
  meaning and 77, 78, 80–2, 138,
    139
  rejects distinction between forms
    of intuition and categories 83
  *Traité élémentaire de philosophie à
    l'usage des classes* 20, 25, 76, 77,
    78, 99, 107, 156, 161
Janet, Pierre 22, 77, 94, 161, 162
Jones, Robert Alun 155

Jones, Susan Stedman 155, 161
Jouffroy, Théodor 91–2, 93–4, 98,
    114, 162

Kant, Immanuel 1–2, 4, 6, 9, 17, 18,
    20, 21, 24, 27–34, 36–56, 57–60,
    61, 62–4, 65–7, 68–71, 74, 82,
    83, 84, 85, 87–8, 89–91, 94, 96,
    99–100, 109, 117–19, 132, 137,
    138, 139, 142, 143, 155, 156,
    157, 159, 160, 161, 162
  antinomies of pure reason 67,
    118
  chemistry as a science 37–8
  Critique of Judgment 57
  Critique of Practical Reason 57
  Critique of Pure Reason 31, 33, 37,
    46, 53, 54, 55, 56, 57, 58, 66, 68,
    70, 74, 153, 155, 156, 157, 158
  Durkheim's lectures on 117–18,
    123
  empirical apperception 48, 51, 52,
    65–6, 67, 69, 70, 137
  forms of judgment 42–5
  freedom of the will 42, 118, 119
  functions 42–5, 49, 157
  idealist or subjectivist
    interpretation of 55, 63, 90, 137
  intuition, forms of 38–41
  metaphysical deduction 41, 42–5,
    52, 123, 157
  *Metaphysical Foundations of Natural
    Science* 37, 45, 157
  noumena 51, 70, 90, 118
  object: concept, experience,
    intuition, or knowledge of 29,
    31, 33, 37, 40, 41, 42, 43, 44,
    45–9, 51, 52, 53–4, 55, 56, 63,
    117, 118, 138, 142
  *On the Form and Principles of the
    Sensible and Intelligible World*
    (Latin inaugural dissertation)
    58, 68, 69, 72
  paralogisms of pure reason 66, 100
  *Prolegomena to Any Future
    Metaphysics* 33, 53, 54, 55, 57,
    142, 157
  psychological reading or
    interpretation of 4, 13, 17, 20,
    24, 28, 43, 49–53, 56, 58, 59,
    60, 89, 91, 99, 158
  representations, mental 31–2
  schematism of the categories and
    principles of the
    understanding 45, 47, 48–9, 52
  synthetic a priori knowledge 37,
    157
  transcendental aesthetic 34, 40–1,
    54, 87
  transcendental analytic 33
  transcendental apperception 24,
    48, 50–2, 53, 58, 65–6, 67, 69,
    70, 99, 137, 161
  transcendental deduction 25, 41,
    45–8, 50, 52–4, 71, 90, 99, 137,
    157
  transcendental dialectic 33, 59, 61,
    96, 107
  transcendental idealism 54, 55,
    91
  transcendental logic 29, 32–3, 50,
    66
  translations of 57, 60
  understanding, on the 29, 31–3,
    36, 38, 39, 41, 49
  unity of consciousness 45–8, 51,
    52, 99, 100, 137, 138
  see also Cousin; Durkheim; Feder;
    Garve; Hamann; Jacobi; Kinker;
    Maine de Biran; Schultz;
    Villers
Kepler, Johannes 106, 163
Kinker, Johannes 59
  *Essai d'une exposition succincte
    de la Critique de la Raison Pure*
    59
Kitcher, Patricia 33, 50, 157
Kitcher, Philip 139
Kremer, Michael 157
Kuhn, Thomas S.
  Post-Darwinian Kantianism 9
  *The Structure of Scientific
    Revolutions* 9
  see also incommensurability

Lachelier, Jules 101
Lalande, André x, 20, 77, 96, 155, 162, 163
  see also Durkheim, Sens lectures
language 1, 7, 9, 10, 60, 64, 74, 81, 82, 102–104, 129, 149, 150, 153–4
Laromiguière, Pierre 60
Latour, Bruno 8, 11
law
  common law 135, 147
  legal obligation 133
  legal reasoning 10
  see also Hart and Honoré
Leach, Edmund 7, 29, 153, 154, 156
Leibniz, Gottfried Wilhelm 33, 71, 84, 85, 88, 91, 94, 98, 101, 114
Lenneberg, Eric 10
Leslie, Alan 147–8, 149, 165
  childhood autism and 149
  ToBy 147, 148, 150, 165
  ToMM 147, 148, 149–50
Lévi-Strauss, Claude 6, 30
Lévy-Bruhl, Lucien 3, 5, 8, 19, 98, 135, 155
  and Comte 98
  La Philosophie d'Auguste Comte 98
  La Philosophie de Jacobi 98
  participation and 60, 136
Lewes, George Henry 87
Locke, John 18, 61, 71, 84, 87, 90, 94, 139, 159
  An Essay Concerning Human Understanding 71
logic 8–9, 12, 13, 20, 32–3, 50, 61, 76, 96, 97, 101, 105, 106, 108, 109, 155
  legal reasoning 10
  see also Kant, transcendental logic
Luckmann, Thomas, and Peter Berger 7–8
Lukes, Steven 17, 153, 155, 165, 167
Lycée de Saint-Quentin 77, 155

Lycée de Sens x, 20, 25, 76, 96, 101, 155, 163
Lyotard, Jean-François 6

Madden, Edward 64
Maine de Biran, Pierre x, 1, 18, 21, 24, 52, 58, 59, 60, 61, 67–75, 77, 82, 84, 86, 91–2, 93–4, 100, 108, 113, 119, 126, 128, 129, 130, 138, 160–1, 162–3
  apperception and 69–71, 72, 128, 161
  categories and 69, 70–1, 82, 91, 113
  causality and 71, 86
  De l'aperception immédiate 160
  "double personality" argument 72, 92
  Essai sur les fondements de la psychologie et sur ses rapports avec l'étude de la nature 69, 160
  Examen des leçons de Laromiguière 67, 69, 160, 161, 163
  and Hume 71–2
  ideology and 59, 68–9
  Influence de l'habitude sur la faculté de penser 160
  internal sense 69, 94
  and Kant 68
  Mémoire sur la décomposition de la pensée 160
  Mémoire sur les rapports du physique et du moral de l'homme 160
  "Observations sur les divisions du cerveau" 68
  Oeuvres inédites 69, 160, 162
  Oeuvres philosophiques 67, 160, 163
  psychological induction 74
  will and willed effort 21, 52, 60, 67, 69, 70–2, 73–4, 83, 91, 93, 94, 119, 123, 124, 128, 161
  see also Durkheim; Paul Janet
Malebranche, Nicolas 84
Malinowski, Bronislaw 156
mana, Melanesian notion of 16, 125
Marr, David 130, 164

Mauss, Marcel 1, 2–3, 5, 6, 12, 19, 27, 28, 29, 99, 161
  and Beuchat 3
  and Durkheim 1, 2–3, 14, 27, 99, 112, 153, 161
  Primitive Classification (1903) 2–3, 14, 99, 153
  primitive classification thesis 3, 8, 10, 154
meaning
  comprehension and 80, 81, 102, 122
  extension and 80, 81, 102, 122
  see also conceptualism; Durkheim; Paul Janet; nominalism; realism
Melanesia 16
  see also mana; Pacific Islanders
mental or intentional states 133, 135, 149, 150
  see also collective representations; ideas; intentionality
Mestrovic, Stjepan 155, 163
metaphysics 21, 33, 36, 37, 38, 58, 61, 76, 84, 97, 101, 108, 109
Michotte, Albert Edouard 147
  La Perception de la causalité 165
  see also Leslie; ToBy
Mill, John Stuart 84, 85, 87, 98, 113, 115, 162
  An Examination of Sir William Hamilton's Philosophy 82, 87
Millikan, Ruth Garrett 144
modularity of mind 109, 164, 165
  see also Fodor; Leslie; ToMM
monism 101, 102
moon illusion 148
moral fact 77, 161
morality or moral philosophy 20, 21, 59, 61, 62, 76, 84, 97, 101, 108, 109, 161, 163
moral obligation 3, 15, 131, 132, 133, 134–5, 137, 150, 151
  religious rites and 130, 134
moral responsibility or accountability 134–6, 151
  see also intentional states

Murphy, Robert 87, 162

Napoleon's suppression of philosophy 60
Native Americans 123, 145
  see also Inuit; Iroquois; Navajo; Sioux; Zuñi
natural selection, *see* evolution, Darwinian
Navajo 154
Naville, Ernest 69, 162
necessary connection, idea of 123, 128, 129–35, 150–1
  ambiguity of 131–2
Needham, Rodney 10
Newton, Isaac 61, 106, 163
Nielsen, Donald 155
nihilism 24, 50, 52, 55, 63, 92, 99, 107, 158
nominalism 82, 102, 122
  see also Berkeley
number or quantity, category of 3, 4, 17, 28, 29, 30, 49, 84
Nye, D. A., and C. E. Ashworth 163

orenda, Iroquois notion of 16, 125

Pacific Islanders 7, 22, 123, 145
  see also Melanesia
Parsons, Talcott 155, 156
participation, witchcraft and 60, 136
Pascal, Blaise 105
perception, direct or unmediated 64–5, 128, 129, 138, 139
person, personality, or personal identity, category of 3, 4, 5, 30, 62
phenomenology 3, 7–8
philosophical curricula and syllabi in France 20, 61, 76, 98, 101, 156, 161
phrenology 69, 160
Pickering, William S. F. 153, 155
Pinker, Steven 10, 144, 146, 164, 165
Plato 88

Pluhar, Werner 157
position or posture, category of
    28
positivism 12, 97, 98, 102
    see also Comte; Lévy-Bruhl; Taine
poststructuralism and
    structuralism 7, 12
power, idea of, distinguished from
    idea of force 128, 136
    see also causality; Durkheim; Hume;
    Maine de Biran
Premack, David 149, 165
    and Guy Woodruff, "Does the
    Chimpanzee Have a Theory of
    Mind?" 149
primates, nonhuman 149–50
primitives
    primitive classification: see
    Durkheim; Mauss
    primitive mentality: see Azande;
    Evans-Pritchard; Lévy-Bruhl
    primitive societies 122
psychology
    empirical 22, 25, 26, 30, 50, 67, 77,
    96, 98, 137, 140, 142, 151
    evolutionary 164
    folk 149, 150
    functionalism and 109
    philosophical 1, 2, 7–12, 153–4
    see also Baillargeon; cognitive
    neuroscience; cognitive science;
    Cousin, méthode psychologique;
    Durkheim, psychology, method
    of; Fodor; Leslie; Michotte;
    Spelke

quality, category of 28, 29, 49
quantity or number, category of 3, 4,
    17, 28, 29, 30, 49, 84

Rabier, Élie 69, 76, 79, 107, 124, 156,
    163, 164
    and Hume 126
    Leçons de Philosophie 76, 77, 79, 126,
    156, 164
Radcliffe-Brown, Alfred Reginald 22,
    77, 94, 161, 162

rationalism or a priori
    philosophy 12–15, 18, 78, 84,
    95, 98, 120
    see also Descartes; Kant
Ravaisson-Mollien, Félix 101
Rawls, Anne 127, 129, 164
realism 82, 102, 122
Reid, Thomas 2, 24, 56, 59, 60, 61,
    64, 79, 81, 103, 139
    An Inquiry into the Human Mind on
    the Principles of Common Sense 59,
    159
    Essays on the Intellectual Powers of
    Man 81, 159
    opposition to hypotheses 61, 159
    opposition to representative
    ideas 64, 159
    see also common-sense philosophy;
    Cousin; Jacobi; Newton;
    Royer-Collard
relation, category of 28, 30, 97
relativism 8, 138
religious rites, moral obligation
    and 130, 134
Renouvier, Charles 30, 79, 94, 155,
    161, 162
    Essais de Critique Générale 162
representative ideas 2, 64, 72, 77, 78,
    79, 80–2, 96, 100, 102–104,
    139
Revue philosophique 19, 98, 141
Ribot, Théodule 162
    L'Hérédité psychologique 162
    La psychologie anglaise
    contemporaine 162
Rousseau, Jean-Jacques 131
Royer-Collard, Pierre Paul 59, 60, 64,
    79, 85, 159

Sapir, Edward 7, 154
Schaub, Edward L. 17
Schelling, Friedrich Heinrich 39, 60,
    113
Schneider, David 154
Schneider, Ulrich 20
Schultz, Johann, critique of Kant's
    transcendental deduction 157

Scottish philosophy
  see common-sense philosophy;
    Reid
Scribner, Sylvia, and Michael Cole 10
Sellars, Wilfrid 51
Selle, Christian Gottlieb 57–8, 159
  *De la réalité et de l'idéalité des objets de
    nos connaissances* 58
Sioux 16
  see also Native Americans; *wakan*
Slobin, Dan 10
social causes and origins 8, 17, 22, 78,
    95, 99, 100, 114, 122, 155
  categories and 1, 3, 7, 12, 14, 17,
    18, 22, 23, 25, 73, 78, 95, 99,
    100, 114, 121, 123, 125, 127, 128,
    129, 130, 131, 132, 134, 137,
    155
social facts 77, 107
social or collective forces 3, 18, 21, 25,
    73, 77, 97, 100, 121, 125–6,
    127
social functions 2, 4, 5, 23, 24, 26, 122
  categories and 2, 4, 17, 22, 121,
    122, 123, 129, 131, 132, 134,
    135, 137, 138, 139, 145, 151
social structure 6, 10, 65, 99, 155
Société française de philosophie 98
sociology
  as an academic discipline 19, 22,
    26
  sociology of knowledge 22, 140,
    142, 145, 146, 151
  see also Durkheim
Socrates 61
Sorbonne (Faculty of Letters,
    Paris) 59, 76, 77, 95, 98, 155,
    159, 161
  merger with École Normale
    Supérieure 98
space or place
  category of 1, 2, 3, 4, 5, 6, 7, 12, 15,
    16, 18, 24, 28, 29, 62, 63, 83, 84,
    87, 88, 89, 91, 94, 108, 112, 113,
    115, 120, 143, 146, 151
  form of intuition of 29, 39–41, 64,
    65, 91, 94, 142

Spelke, Elizabeth 147
Spencer, Herbert 17, 18, 19, 84, 113,
    115, 141, 154, 162
  evolution and 87, 91, 116, 117, 130,
    164, 165
Sperber, Dan 144, 165
Spinoza, Benedict 119
spiritualist realism 101, 123
Staël, Madame de 59
  De l'Allemagne 59
Stapfer, Philippe-Albert 59, 68, 69,
    73, 160
state or condition, category of 28
Sterelny, Kim 150
structuralism and post-
    structuralism 7, 12
Stuchlik, Milan, and Ladislav Holy
    10
substance
  category of 3, 4, 6, 16, 24, 28, 29,
    36, 49, 51, 52, 53, 62, 66, 71, 83,
    84, 85, 86, 87, 88, 89, 91, 93–4,
    113, 117
  primary and secondary
    substances 29–30
Symons, Donald 144

Taine, Hippolyte 102, 103, 108, 162
Taylor, Steve 163
Theory of Mind 147, 148, 149–50
  see also Leslie; Premack and
    Woodruff; ToMM
time
  category of 1, 2, 3, 4, 5, 6, 7, 12, 15,
    16, 18, 24, 28, 62, 63, 83, 87, 88,
    89, 91, 94, 108, 112, 113, 115,
    120, 143, 146, 151
  form of intuition of 29, 39, 41, 64,
    65, 91, 94, 142
ToBy or Theory of Body 147, 148,
    150, 165
  see also Leslie
ToMM or Theory of Mental
    Mechanism 147, 148, 149–50
  see also Leslie
Tooby, John, and Leda Cosmides 10,
    164, 165

totemism, totemic principles, and the totemistic theory of the origin of religion 123, 124, 125, 134
transcendental arguments 14
  see also Kant, transcendental deduction
Tyndall, John 162, 163
  "The Scientific Use of the Imagination" 163–4

utilitarianism 109

Villers, Charles 59, 68, 161
  Philosophie de Kant 59, 60
Vogt, W. Paul 155

wakan, Sioux notion of 16, 125
Watts Miller, Willie 164

Whorf, Benjamin Lee 7, 9, 10
will
  Durkheim and 118, 119, 124–7
  Maine de Biran and willed effort 21, 52, 60, 67, 69, 70–2, 73–4, 83, 91, 93, 94, 119, 123, 124, 128, 161
  see also Cousin; Kant
witchcraft, participation and 60, 136
Witherspoon, Gary 154
Wood, Allen, and Paul Guyer 70
Woodruff, Guy 149
  and David Premack, "Does the Chimpanzee Have a Theory of Mind?" 149
Woolgar, Steve 11
Wundt, Wilhelm 112

Zuñi conceptions of space 3, 16, 24

D1453692